Essential classification

Vanda Broughton

facet publishing

© Vanda Broughton 2004

Published by
Facet Publishing
7 Ridgmount Street
London WC1E 7AE
www.facetpublishing.co.uk

Facet Publishing is wholly owned by CILIP: the Chartered Institute of
Library and Information Professionals.

Vanda Broughton has asserted her right under the Copyright, Designs
and Patents Act, 1988, to be identified as author of this work.

Except as otherwise permitted under the Copyright, Designs and Patents
Act 1988 this publication may only be reproduced, stored or transmitted
in any form or by any means, with the prior permission of the publisher,
or, in the case of reprographic reproduction, in accordance with the
terms of a licence issued by The Copyright Licensing Agency. Enquiries
concerning reproduction outside those terms should be sent to Facet
Publishing, 7 Ridgmount Street, London WC1E 7AE.

First published 2004
Reprinted 2008 (three times)
Reprinted digitally from 2009

British Library Cataloguing in Publication Data
A catalogue record for this book is available from the British Library.

ISBN 978-1-85604-514-8

Typeset in 11/14pt Aldine 721 and Humanist by Facet Publishing.

Contents

Acknowledgements

I should like to thank my colleague John Bowman who originally proposed to Facet Publishing that I should write this book. He also read all the drafts, and made many pertinent and helpful comments and suggestions. I did not always act on this good advice, so the errors and shortcomings of the book are entirely my own.

I must also acknowledge the part played by the students of the School of Library, Archive and Information Studies, University College London; their journeys through the difficult terrain of classification have highlighted the rocks and the hard places, and taught me where beginners most need help and guidance.

My thanks to the editors and rights holders of the general schemes of classification for their assistance and permission to use excerpts from those schemes: to Ia McIlwaine, Editor-in-chief, and Alan Stevens, Chair of the UDC Consortium, for the Universal Decimal Classification, to Joan Mitchell and OCLC for the Dewey Decimal Classification, to Cheryl Cook and the Library of Congress for *Classweb*, and to the Bliss Classification Association for the Bliss Bibliographic Classification Second Edition. Special thanks are owed to Jack Mills, Editor of BC2, my colleague, teacher and mentor for the last thirty-two years.

Excerpts from the Dewey Decimal Classification are taken from the *Dewey Decimal Classification and Relative Index, Edition 22* which is Copyright 2003 OCLC Online Computer Library Center, Inc. DDC, Dewey, Dewey Decimal Classification and WebDewey are registered trademarks of OCLC Online Computer Library Center, Inc.

I would also thank the following publishers for permission to reproduce title pages and other elements from their books:

Figure 8.1 *Birds of coast and sea*, by Bruce Campbell, illustrations by Raymond Watson (reproduced by permission of Oxford University Press).
Figure 8.2 *Hoping for a hoopoe* by John Updike (reproduced by permission

of Victor Gollancz, a division of The Orion Publishing Group).

Figure 8.5 *Saints: the chosen few* by Manuela Dunn-Mascetti (reproduced by permission of Macmillan Publishing).

Figure 8.6 *Bird behaviour* by Louise Dawson and Mike Langman (reproduced by permission of Hamlyn).

Figure 8.7 *The British Museum book of cats: ancient and modern* by Juliet Clutton Brock (reproduced by permission of the British Museum Company Ltd).

Figure 8.8 *Railway architecture of Greater London* by Rodney Symes and David Cole (reproduced by permission of Osprey Publishing Ltd).

Figure 8.10 *First aid for dogs: what to do when emergencies happen* by Bruce Fogle (reproduced by permission of the Penguin Group (UK)).

Figure 9.2 *Bee hives of the ancient world*, by Eva Crane and A. J. Graham (reproduced by permission of the International Bee Research Association (www.ibra.org.uk)).

Figure 19.1 *Domus Anguli Puensis* ((Latin for *The House at Pooh Corner*) ©1980 Egmont Books Ltd, London and used with permission).

Every effort has been made to trace the holders of copyright in the title pages reproduced. If there are any queries please contact Facet Publishing.

1 Introduction

Classification is everywhere. We classify birds and animals, languages and ethnic groups, stars, volcanoes, minerals and clouds, wine and blood, and colours and roses. We classify diseases, occupations and social status; the size of notepaper (grand eagle, elephant and pott); the dimensions of icebergs (small, bergy bits and growlers); and brandy (mellow, pale and superior).

It is natural to the human mind to classify, and essential if we want to make sense of the world, which is full of unique creatures and objects. Each day we encounter hundreds of these which we might never have seen before, but the process of classification allows us to recognize a street lamp, a dog, a magazine, a train, sandwiches for lunch, bananas, music on the radio, and make sense of those things. We don't need to investigate and learn about every new event in our lives because most of them conform to other objects and phenomena in our personal experience; we know what to expect of a dog or a banana, since they are similar to dogs and bananas we already know.

Everybody can and does classify, and if we spend so much time and energy classifying the world about us, it is natural to attempt to organize our stores of information about the world. It's necessary, too, to have systems for managing stored information in a way that allow us to find it again – systems that use our human classificatory skills to organize, to match, to predict and to interpret.

This is a book about some of the systems which people have created for organizing information. It also examines the problems we face in sorting out the relationships between subjects, and imposing order on chaos. It's about the nature of knowledge as it is found in books and other information-carrying media. It is also first and foremost a book about *how* to classify. The emphasis throughout is on the activity of classification rather than the theory, the practical problems of the organization of collections, and the needs of users.

You don't need any knowledge or experience of classification to use this book. It's intended for beginners, for students, and for people working in libraries who have never had any formal education or training in classification or subject cataloguing. It is based very largely on the cataloguing and classification module of the MA in Library and Information Studies taught at the School of Library, Archive and Information Studies, University College London, although most of the practical exercises are new.

We'll proceed step by step through the basics of organizing a collection, the problems of linear arrangement, and the difficulties posed by complicated subjects and their interrelationships. We'll look at how to decide on the subject of a document, and how the needs of different groups of users can affect that decision. We shall learn how to apply those systems that are frequently encountered in libraries – the Dewey Decimal Classification (DDC), the Universal Decimal Classification (UDC) and the Library of Congress Classification (LCC), as well as Library of Congress Subject Headings (LCSH).

A major difficulty in writing a textbook about classification is that the book to be classified should always be to hand, and clearly the reader can't be expected to have access to every title mentioned. For the most part, therefore, the works chosen have titles that indicate plainly their content. The chapters on content analysis deal with less straightforward situations and provide a strategy for coping with these.

This book is principally distinguished from other current books about classification by the very large number of practical exercises and activities, but nobody learned to classify documents by any means other than doing it, and certainly not by reading about the philosophic principles of X or Y classification. If you work through all the exercises you should acquire a knowledge of the basic workings of the different schemes covered. No preference for any particular scheme is intended, but I hope readers will gain a sense of the characteristics of these classifications and of the different situations where each would be an appropriate choice as a subject access tool.

All of the titles included are real books, or occasionally journal articles or conference papers. They have been taken from the catalogue of the Library of Congress, and COPAC, the merged catalogue of 24 large UK academic and research libraries, including the British Library. The occasional article has been selected from Zetoc, the British Library's electronic table of contents. With a very few exceptions the titles are all recent publications.

The great majority of the examples are books, but there is no reason why the techniques learned cannot be applied to non-book materials, notably electronic resources. There is no difference in the analysis of subject content of different media, since the only thing under consideration is the 'aboutness' of the resource. On the same basis there is usually no reason why classification schemes can't be used to organize resources in any format, print and electronic, text and image, sound and vision and multimedia, objects and data, and representations or surrogates of all of these. Throughout the text I've used the term book or document or item when referring to the things to be classified, but any sort of information carrier is always implicit in those terms.

Although the main stress is on things practical, it's impossible to understand the rationale behind classifications without some introduction to the theory, and the early chapters provide an outline of the principles of bibliographic classification. This, and the practical application of schemes, uses a technical vocabulary which you need to be familiar with. Technical terms are explained in the text, but for convenience they are also gathered together in a glossary. Terms included in the glossary are in **bold** typeface in the text, at least on the first few occasions of their appearance.

After reading the book and trying the exercises, you should have all you need to carry out basic classification, but I've included a brief bibliography, should you become interested and want to find out more, as I did as a student over thirty years ago. I still find it the most intellectually stimulating part of the professional curriculum, and also the most intriguing and the most entertaining. I hope you will be stimulated and intrigued, and at least a little entertained by it.

2 The need for classification

When you go into a library you usually have one of two purposes in mind. In some cases you may be looking for a particular book or journal, report or recording. You know that you want the latest Jeffrey Archer novel, an article about global warming in last week's *New Scientist*, or the film version of *Romeo and Juliet* directed by Zeffirelli. Generally you have enough information about the author, title or source of the item for the library staff to help you locate it. Even if you are lacking some details, you know that you don't want the latest Barbara Cartland novel, a piece on global warming in last week's *Woman's Weekly*, or the film version of *Romeo and Juliet* directed by Luhrmann. Finding what you want in this case is called **known item retrieval**, because you already know about the specific work that will meet your needs. Normally the item can be traced using the author's name or the title of the work, or some combination of elements from these.

In many other cases you don't want any particular item, but you do want *some* information about global warming, or 17th-century drama, or how to grow petunias. You're not bothered who wrote the book or article, what it is called, or who published it, as long as it contains relevant information. The library may have lots of material that will meet your information needs, but none of it can be retrieved using an author, title or publisher, because these are not known.

In order for anyone to find material about a given topic it is essential that the individual books and other items in the collection have had their subject content identified and recorded. Looking for information based on the content of documents is known as **subject retrieval, subject searching**, or **subject access**. In the majority of libraries and information services this formal identification of the subject content, and subsequent searching, is done by using a **classification scheme** and/or a system of **subject headings**.

In this book we shall be looking at some of the problems that arise when we try to organize documents by their subjects, and how classification schemes and subject headings are applied to the items in a collection in order for readers (and library staff) to find what they want in the most effective way.

Until the last quarter of the 19th century libraries did not use classification schemes in the way that we do today. Certain sections of the library (or certain bookcases or shelves) might be assigned to particular subjects, but this was usually in a fairly broad system of subject arrangement, and the notations, if any, that were applied to books related to their position on the shelf rather than to their subject content. At that time it was more common for libraries to operate on the basis of **closed access**: that is to say readers were not permitted to browse among the stock, but had books fetched for them by library staff. Identifying books on a particular subject would have depended on the librarian's knowledge of the book stock, and there was usually no systematic means of searching for a book by subject.

Around the end of the 19th century libraries increasingly moved towards systems of **open access**, where users were able to go to the shelves and select books for themselves. It then became necessary to have ways of organizing the collections that were clear and understandable to users. Librarians at the time decided that the most helpful way to arrange their books was by subject, and this has remained the basis on which almost every library is managed to this day.

At about the same time, librarians became increasingly interested in the theoretical problems of the organization of knowledge and in the development of standards for cataloguing and classification. Within a period of about 40 years from the first publication of Melvil Dewey's Decimal Classification in 1876, all the general schemes of classification that are widely used today, as well as the major system of subject headings, came into being. Nowadays the majority of libraries use one of the major schemes of classification (or a subject specialist scheme in the case of special libraries) to organize the materials physically in the collection: in other words, the classification is the means by which we arrange books on shelves. The classification scheme may also be used to organize the results of searches on the library catalogue, to arrange printed bibliographies or lists of new books, or even to structure the content of library intranets and online directories. Classification is a fundamental tool in the process of organizing a collection and in the complementary process of searching for and retrieving information.

3 First principles of classification

Two ideas are fundamental to any system of classification: grouping and ordering. Grouping is the primary act of classification and one that is inherent in human thinking, as we saw in the introduction. We can all classify in this sense quite instinctively.

Grouping

Exercise 3.1

Consider the following sets of concepts, and identify the odd one out in each.

1	banana	sausage	aubergine	cauliflower
2	spade	rake	trowel	frying pan
3	karate	kung-fu	knitting	kick-boxing
4	Paris	Rome	Idaho	Cairo

I hope your answers will be:

1 sausage (because the others are fruits and vegetables)
2 frying pan (because the others are garden implements)
3 knitting (because it is not a martial art)
4 Idaho (because it is not a capital city)

This may seem to be a trivial exercise, but it serves to illustrate the essence of classification – the act of putting like with like and separating unlike – and it shows that at the broad level it is quite easy to do. Hopefully you were able not only to group the concepts, but also to identify the principles by which you did this, so that there was a logical and philosophical basis to your classification. The principle used to create a group is sometimes called the **principle of division** or **characteristic of division**: this is the technical term for the property or attribute that all the members of a group have in common.

Ordering

This process of grouping together related terms or concepts is central to a classification scheme, and it forms the first stage in constructing a classification. The second stage is to decide on the relationships *between* groups, since this determines the order in which the groups will be arranged.

Let's start by making some groups within the general area of vegetables. By putting like with like, we could organize the carrots, parsnips and turnips to make a class of root vegetables. Now we need to consider what will be placed next. We might want to position other groups of vegetables (leafy vegetables, and pulses) near to the roots, and then locate the whole class of vegetables near to other crops, such as fruits and cereals. The next problem will be to decide what follows on from the crops: will it be other plants that are not crops (such as wild flowers or woodlands), or should it be animal 'crops' (pigs, cattle, chickens), or perhaps the end products of the plant crops (bread, processed vegetables, fruit drinks)?

There is obviously more than one potential answer here, and it's impossible to say that there is a correct order, or that one arrangement is better than another in any absolute sense. The difficulty arises because we're trying to put all of these subjects (and potentially the whole of knowledge) into a straight line: the single sequence, or linear order, can't take account of the variety of relationships that exist between subjects. This problem isn't limited to arranging books on shelves: it also occurs in other situations where goods need to be displayed – shops are an obvious example. The parallels between the library collection and the supermarket are numerous and we shall return to this useful analogy later.

The fact of this complexity of relationships, and how they are sorted out in practice, will determine how effective a classification is for a particular subject, or in a particular context: our example of plants, animals, crops and products would have different optimum orders for a biologist, a farmer, a food technologist or an economist, and this variability is multiplied a thousandfold across the whole of knowledge. This gives us the first fundamental law of classification – there are lots of possible right ways to do things. There is usually not a single 'correct' order of subjects, but only an appropriate or helpful order, which changes according to the situation, and the needs and interests of the users.

Some general theoretical principles of ordering are used in classification schemes: chronological order is an obvious one, and proximity is used as the basis of ordering geographical places. Developmental orders and orders based on complexity can be used in classifying the natural world, and the idea of dependency is also often employed: for example, life forms are dependent on their chemical constituents and therefore biochemistry must precede botany and zoology. Nevertheless, much ordering in classifications is done on a pragmatic and arbitrary basis. Who can say whether motorways should precede or follow metal fatigue, or how ice-skating is related to infinitesimal calculus?

Compound subjects

Let's go back to the odd-one-out game.

Exercise 3.2
Consider the following groups of terms and identify the misfit in each:

1 Brahms   Schumann   Bizet   Goethe
2 hamster   chicken   sheep   pig
3 chimney   window frame   door   table
4 whooping cough   chickenpox   asthma   tuberculosis

Now we begin to see the 'no-right-answer' syndrome in action. Is the answer to number 1 Bizet (the Frenchman among Germans) or Goethe (the poet among musicians)? Number 2 could be the chicken (the odd bird out) or the hamster (which isn't on the menu for Sunday lunch), and number 3 might be the table (which isn't part of a house) or the chimney (which is unlikely to be made of wood). Number 4 is slightly trickier to sort out but here are either three infectious diseases and one with environmental causes (asthma), or three diseases of the respiratory system and a more general systemic condition, chickenpox.

What is happening here is a demonstration of the fact that concepts usually have more than one characteristic or attribute. While in the first game the principles for grouping were clear, in this case two properties have equal claim as the basis for arrangement.

If we consider the problems of storage and retrieval at the supermarket we see that the same difficulty occurs. If I want to buy some frozen peas I need to know whether they will be found with other types of peas (fresh, tinned and dried), or with other frozen goods (sweetcorn, beans and broccoli). From the customer's point of view it doesn't matter very much which way round the shop does this as long as it's clear what the arrangement is. If the organization is predictable then I can retrieve what I want efficiently, since I can go straight to the correct location. The same is true of documents: if I want a book on deficiency diseases of the bones, I need to know whether all books on deficiency diseases are kept together (divided by parts of the body affected) or whether books on specific parts of the body are grouped (divided by types of disease). Then I can make an informed decision about where the documents I want will be located. Subjects of this kind, with more than one aspect or component, are called **compound subjects**.

The question of where to put the frozen peas may have only two possible answers, but the subjects of books can be a great deal more complicated. When Dewey first published his Decimal Classification, in 1876, the subjects of books were usually less complex than they are today. Although there will always be books with subjects such as mathematics or cookery or cricket, the majority of modern publications are much more complicated. Consider the following:

Example

        Nineteenth-century French poetry / Michael Bishop . -
        New York : Twayne, 1993

The subject in this example clearly has three parts: language (French), form (poetry) and period (19th century). Imagine that your library has been given a large collection of literature books of this type, all having subjects which contain a language, a literary form and a period. Some typical titles might be 'Twentieth-century Russian fiction', 'Mediaeval French poetry', 'Swedish drama in the 19th century', 'Plays of the Italian cinquecento' and 'The novel in 17th-century England'. Your task is to sort them out.

Perhaps you're in a library in a college where foreign literature is taught alongside foreign languages, and it occurs to you that the most useful arrangement of the books would be to group them into sets dealing with each separate language: a French collection, a Swedish collection, an Italian collection and so on. You could of course sort them into groups of the different periods, or into different literary forms, but let's go with the first option.

After you've done this you should have several heaps of books, each of which contains only books about a particular language. Select one of these heaps – let's say the Italian books. There's still a degree of disorder here because some of them are about 16th-century Italian poetry, and some are about mediaeval Italian drama, or 20th-century Italian novels, and so on. Now you can do one of two things – you can sort the Italian books into piles of each different period, or you can sort them into piles of the different forms of literature. Let's take the second option this time, and create some sets of Italian poetry, Italian novels, Italian essays, etc., etc. The only thing left to do now is to take each of these groups and divide them up by period, so that Italian poetry is sorted into mediaeval Italian poetry, 16th-century Italian poetry, 17th-century Italian poetry and so on.

Now turn to the other heaps of languages and repeat the process: it would be sensible to sort these out on the same basis as the Italian books, sorting first into groups of the different literary forms, and then subdividing these by period. Finally you can arrange all the books on shelves, keeping your separate sections together in their logical order.

At this point if a library user comes along and asks you how the collection is organized you can say that everything is arranged firstly by *language* and then by *form* and then finally by *period*. You have used three principles of division – language, form and period – and you have applied the principles of division in the order: 1. Language; 2. Form; 3. Period. This order is called the **citation order** for the classification of literature books you've created.

Citation order

Whether it has been logically arrived at or not, some sort of citation order exists in any collection of compound subjects. In supermarkets the citation order is 'form of preservation' followed by 'type of food', as shown in Figure 3.1. When we apply a citation order we're bringing the two classificatory principles of grouping and ordering together, in order to create a logical and predictable sequence. Citation order is consequently a very important principle in classification, and we shall be returning to it frequently.

F R E S H	Beans	T I N N E D	Beans	F R O Z E N	Beans
	Peas		Peas		Peas
	Sweetcorn		Sweetcorn		Sweetcorn
	Carrots		Carrots		Carrots

Figure 3.1 Supermarket citation order

An inescapable outcome of bringing together objects on the basis of one attribute is that other attributes are scattered. At the shop, all the frozen foods are kept together, but the carrots are in different places according to whether they are in tins, freezer bags or loose; these different sets of carrots are known as **distributed relatives**. When we have to produce a linear order, as on the library (or supermarket) shelf, or in a screen display or a printed list, this scattering is inevitable, and we must decide which aspects of things are more important for grouping, and which are secondary and can be distributed. The citation order can be varied for different groups of users, although only one citation order should be used in a particular collection: if citation orders are muddled searchers won't be able to predict locations, and retrieval will be much more difficult to achieve.

Summary
- The first act in classification is that of grouping objects or concepts.
- Grouping brings together like concepts, according to their properties or attributes.
- Ordering is the next process, to determine the sequence of groups.
- Problems occur when objects have more than one attribute and we have to decide which is most important for grouping.
- The order of importance of attributes is called citation order.
- Properties which are scattered by the citation order are called distributed relatives.

4 The variety of classification: systems and structures

So far we've looked at fairly informal examples of sorting and arrangement – what might be done on a pragmatic basis and at a local level. One wouldn't expect the supermarket classification, or a rough arrangement of literature books, to be written down or distributed for others to use. The world is full of examples of this sort of local or personal classification; office filing systems are a typical example, as is any arrangement of the content of your kitchen cupboards or your wardrobe.

At a more public level there are a vast number of formal, published classifications of an immense variety of entities and phenomena. A search for 'classification of' using *Google* will return you in excess of two million sites. Among these are classifications for proteins, reptiles, disabilities, wetlands, daffodils, scorpions, depression, learning skills, theories of divine action, caviar, parachutes, subtle changes in facial expression, portable fire extinguishers, Bible commands, angles, thunderstorms, millionaires, chickens and tea.

Scientific classifications and taxonomies

For the most part these are classifications of different sorts of physical and biological entities, and they're constructed using the fundamental principles of grouping and ordering, which we discussed in Chapter 3, in a more extended, rigorous and systematic manner. The methodology they employ goes back to the Greek philosopher Aristotle, who, in the *Organon*, laid down the rules for creating categories of objects in the natural world. Aristotle produced the first classification for natural history, and the methods he used endure to the present day. He grouped natural phenomena (plants, birds, animals, people) into sets based on attributes or properties relating to their external appearance and behaviour, and he ordered these groups on the basis of their comparative similarity (or dissimilarity).

A classification of this kind is referred to as a **taxonomy** (from the Greek *taxis* meaning arrangement or order, and *nomos*, meaning law or rule).

Although information managers often use the term taxonomy today to mean any vaguely structured set of terms in a subject area, taxonomy is a major scientific discipline with a highly developed, exact and complex methodology, usually supported by computational techniques.

Aristotle's methods were taken up by scientists of the Renaissance and the Enlightenment, such as the Swedish naturalist Linnaeus. He used the same techniques to produce a classification of living things that is still, with some modifications, widely used today. Linnaeus's classification is based on the anatomical structure or morphology of living things, and it contains some odd associations: hydrangeas and gooseberries are in the same family, and elm trees and stinging nettles are also close relations. Nevertheless, the principles underlying the classification are clear and its long persistence demonstrates its value.

Linnaeus's classification is typical of a taxonomy in that the relationships between living things are depicted by means of a **hierarchical** structure. This is a structure in which successive steps in division create smaller and more specific classes. It is usually represented visually as a **tree** structure, with the tree branching at each new level. This sort of structure is probably what is ordinarily thought of as a system of classification.

Linnaeus attached labels to each level of his hierarchy, as shown in Figure 4.2, but these apply only to the classification of living things, and a hierarchy for other objects could be created without this specific structure.

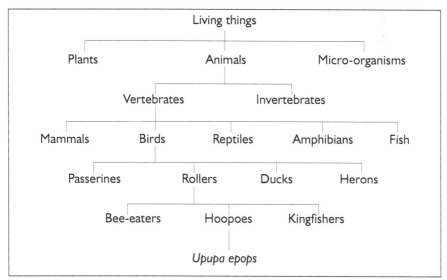

Figure 4.1   Classificatory tree structure

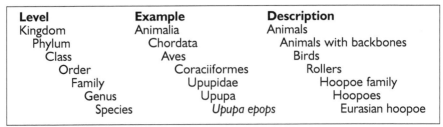

Level	Example	Description
Kingdom	Animalia	Animals
Phylum	Chordata	Animals with backbones
Class	Aves	Birds
Order	Coraciiformes	Rollers
Family	Upupidae	Hoopoe family
Genus	Upupa	Hoopoes
Species	*Upupa epops*	Eurasian hoopoe

Figure 4.2 Linnaean classification of *Upupa epops*

Taxonomic classifications of this sort are highly structured, predictable and logical creations, but they're not necessarily true in any objective or permanent sense. In 1993 Dr Charles Sibley and his associates developed a new classification for birds (the Sibley/Ahlquist/Monroe or SAM classification) which was based on properties of the DNA of birds, rather than their anatomy. This changed some of the traditional groupings of birds and caused heated debate in ornithological circles. During the late 1990s similar work in the field of botany produced a series of new classifications for plants. These new findings mean not that the old Linnaean classification was completely wrong, simply that the groups based on genetic principles are different to the groups based on morphology. In reality the Linnaean classification is probably more useful to amateur ornithologists and bird-watchers than the DNA classification, which is primarily of interest to zoologists, geneticists and, of course, taxonomists.

Figure 4.3 shows another typical scientific classification based on Aristotle's principles. It is Mendeleev's classification of the elements, which are arranged according to the number of electrons in the molecule. These affect the physical properties of an element, and the way it reacts with other elements, and Mendeleev's structure shows a very compact and coherent pattern. The periodic table is also interesting because it demonstrates the predictive function of classification: it enabled Mendeleev to forecast the existence of several chemical elements that hadn't been discovered at the time that he devised the table. He was able to do this because each entity in the classification has a unique place based on its attributes, and the potential occupants of any empty places can be described on the basis of their expected properties.

This predictability can be said to be a general feature of taxonomies, but of course, if the taxonomy has not been accurately constructed, putting one's faith in it may lead to error and disappointment. When Marco Polo travelled to Java he encountered a one-horned quadruped, which, on the basis

Periodic Table of the Elements

Period	Group**																	
	1 IA 1A																	18 VIIIA 8A
1	1 H 1.008	2 IIA 2A											13 IIIA 3A	14 IVA 4A	15 VA 5A	16 VIA 6A	17 VIIA 7A	2 He 4.003
2	3 Li 6.941	4 Be 9.012											5 B 10.81	6 C 12.01	7 N 14.01	8 O 16.00	9 F 19.00	10 Ne 20.18
3	11 Na 22.99	12 Mg 24.31	3 IIIB 3B	4 IVB 4B	5 VB 5B	6 VIB 6B	7 VIIB 7B	8	9	10	11 IB 1B	12 IIB 2B	13 Al 26.98	14 Si 28.09	15 P 30.97	16 S 32.07	17 Cl 35.45	18 Ar 39.95
								------- VIII ----- -- ------- 8 -------										
4	19 K 39.10	20 Ca 40.08	21 Sc 44.96	22 Ti 47.88	23 V 50.94	24 Cr 52.00	25 Mn 54.94	26 Fe 55.85	27 Co 58.47	28 Ni 58.69	29 Cu 63.55	30 Zn 65.39	31 Ga 69.72	32 Ge 72.59	33 As 74.92	34 Se 78.96	35 Br 79.90	36 Kr 83.80
5	37 Rb 85.47	38 Sr 87.62	39 Y 88.91	40 Zr 91.22	41 Nb 92.91	42 Mo 95.94	43 Tc (98)	44 Ru 101.1	45 Rh 102.9	46 Pd 106.4	47 Ag 107.9	48 Cd 112.4	49 In 114.8	50 Sn 118.7	51 Sb 121.8	52 Te 127.6	53 I 126.9	54 Xe 131.3
6	55 Cs 132.9	56 Ba 137.3	57 La* 138.9	72 Hf 178.5	73 Ta 180.9	74 W 183.9	75 Re 186.2	76 Os 190.2	77 Ir 190.2	78 Pt 195.1	79 Au 197.0	80 Hg 200.5	81 Tl 204.4	82 Pb 207.2	83 Bi 209.0	84 Po (210)	85 At (210)	86 Rn (222)
7	87 Fr (223)	88 Ra (226)	89 Ac~ (227)	104 Rf (257)	105 Db (260)	106 Sg (263)	107 Bh (262)	108 Hs (265)	109 Mt (266)	110 --- ()	111 --- ()	112 --- ()		114 --- ()		116 --- ()		118 --- ()
Lanthanide Series*			58 Ce 140.1	59 Pr 140.9	60 Nd 144.2	61 Pm (147)	62 Sm 150.4	63 Eu 152.0	64 Gd 157.3	65 Tb 158.9	66 Dy 162.5	67 Ho 164.9	68 Er 167.3	69 Tm 168.9	70 Yb 173.0	71 Lu 175.0		
Actinide Series~			90 Th 232.0	91 Pa (231)	92 U (238)	93 Np (237)	94 Pu (242)	95 Am (243)	96 Cm (247)	97 Bk (247)	98 Cf (249)	99 Es (254)	100 Fm (253)	101 Md (256)	102 No (254)	103 Lr (257)		

Los Alamos National Laboratory's Chemistry Division
http://pearl1.lanl.gov/periodic/downloads/main.html

Figure 4.3 Mendeleev's classification of the elements

of the zoological classifications of the time, he assumed to be a unicorn despite its failure to exhibit other unicorn-ly characteristics, such as slenderness, whiteness and willingness to lie in the laps of virgins: it was in fact a black rhinoceros. Similar profound puzzlement was felt in 1797 by the first Europeans to observe the duck-billed platypus, which couldn't be accommodated anywhere in the existing zoological classifications. It was considered variously to be related to the mole, the beaver and the turtle, and to be a bird, amphibian, reptile or mammal. The first platypuses to arrive in Britain (either stuffed or as skins) were regarded as fakes, after the fashion of the 'mermaids' that were imported from the Far East, and which were constructed from parts of monkeys and fish. The platypus continued to surprise: it wasn't until 1864 that it was observed laying eggs, and eventually the taxonomies had to be reconstructed to accommodate it. In fact the platypus occupies its own unique taxonomic niche (it's a monotreme) and has no relations at all except the echidna.

Folk classifications

The classifications described above depend on the principles of Greek scientific thought for their construction. In the Western world our patterns of thinking are derived from Greek philosophy and science, but this is not necessarily true of other cultures.

Anthropologists have for a long time been aware of other classifications of the natural world common among pre-literate societies, whose methods of grouping or categorization produce taxonomies that look quite different from the Linnaean model. Folk classifications can appear odd to Western eyes because the categories are based on characteristics of animals that are not very significant to the scientist, although they may be of vital importance to the community that produces them.

Folk taxonomies tend to emphasize function rather than form as the basis of classification; plants are grouped according to their habit of growth – trees, shrubs, grasses, herbaceous plants and climbers. Animals may be divided into egg-layers and milk-makers, grass-eaters and flesh-eaters, flyers and runners, or climbers and burrowers. These divisions cut quite across 'scientific' divisions of birds, mammals, fish or reptiles, since the main concern is how to utilize, or possibly catch, the animal in question. Folk classifications tend to focus on genera – dogs, oaks, snakes or ducks – and have only three or four levels of hierarchy. Such taxonomies are mirrored in our society by alternative, non-scientific classifications of animals and plants for farmers, whose concern is not with the theoretical relationships between living things, but with their husbandry, harvesting and marketing. A modern agricultural classification is only a folk taxonomy for the developed world.

Sometimes the basis of a folk classification completely escapes the scientific mind, as in the case of this classification belonging to the

Dyirbal people of Australia. It combines a folk taxonomy with a linguistic classification, as is common in primitive cultures, and provides a spectacular example of an alternative view of the world. The classification contains four classes:

1 men, kangaroos, possums, bats, most snakes, most fish, some birds, most insects, the moon, storms, rainbows, boomerangs
2 women, bandicoots, dogs, platypuses, echidnas, some snakes, some fish, most birds, fireflies, scorpions, crickets, the hairy mary grub, anything connected with water or fire, the sun and stars
3 all edible fruit and the plants that bear them, ferns, honey, cigarettes, wine, cake
4 parts of the body, meat, bees, wind, yamsticks, some spears, most trees, grass, mud, stones, noises, language.

The first group evidently contains mainly boys' stuff. The second group looks generally rather more dangerous and unreliable than the first (although it is hard to see why 'most birds' are here), and group three consists of all good things. What the members of group four have in common is a mystery. But our inability to see the logic in this classification doesn't invalidate it; the principles on which it's based are just not known to us.

Linnaeus's classification of living things and the SAM classification of birds, although quite different, are both valid classifications; a classification of animals for farmers will also differ from Linnaeus's, for different reasons, as will a folk taxonomy devised by hunters and gatherers. The use of different criteria for grouping and ordering generate different classifications relevant to the needs of different users. There is no one true correct classification of the world, but a variety of classifications from different viewpoints and for different purposes.

So far we've been looking at different kinds of classifications, but they have all been classifications of *things* of various sorts. A classification which deals with things is called an **entity classification** or **phenomenon classification**. Scientific classifications such as those of Aristotle, Linnaeus, Mendeleev and Sibley, as well as folk taxonomies, are all phenomenon or entity classifications. Their general properties can be summarized as follows.

Summary

Entity or phenomenon classifications usually:

- deal with objects or entities, rather than events or activities
- can be arranged in a tree or hierarchical structure
- have a single place for each item.

While these phenomenon classifications are different from documentary or bibliographic classifications, they are often used within documentary classification schemes (in the biology classes, for example), since there is no need for bibliographic classificationists to reinvent classifications for phenomena where authoritative systems already exist.

In the century before Linnaeus built his biological taxonomy, the English philosopher, essayist and statesman Francis Bacon was engaged in creating a plan of the order of the universe, which he called the *Novum Organum* or *New Organon* after Aristotle's original work. The structure that Bacon used for his classification was fundamentally different from Aristotle's in that it was a classification of *knowledge* rather than a classification of *things*. It was an **aspect classification**, and modern library classifications are all built on this classificatory model.

Aspect classifications

Exercise 4.1
Imagine a rabbit. Try to think of all the ways in which people use rabbits. Don't be overly sensitive about the rabbit, but try not to stray into the realms of fantasy. A list of possible answers is on p. 20.

You have probably come up with several suggestions which include at least: keeping it as a pet, farming it and eating it. The rabbit has a role to play in pet husbandry, in farming, in zoology, in medical research, in cookery, in conjuring, and so on. There's a literature on all these different interests and activities relating to rabbits, and the library classification scheme has to accommodate it. The classification schemes in current use do this, not by focusing on the rabbit as a collecting point, but by assigning the various aspects of rabbits to an appropriate **discipline**, such as zoology, agriculture or cookery. The library classification consists of a series of these *disciplines* or fields of study, rather than an arrangement of *things*, and books about rabbits may be located in several different places in the scheme.

Like the tinned carrots and the frozen peas at the supermarket, the rabbit is a distributed relative in the bibliographic world. It doesn't have a unique place in the classification, but occurs wherever it's of interest in a particular field of study or activity. A classification which treats rabbits, and other entities, from the point of view of those observing, exploiting or otherwise engaged with them is called an **aspect classification**.

Bacon's classification of knowledge divided it up into areas such as memory, reason and poesy, which were further subdivided into subjects such as history, mathematics, logic and literature. The classification was based on the way in which universities of that period organized their teaching, and since the time of Bacon knowledge classifications have tended to follow this sort of structure, with new disciplines being added as they occur over time. The famous Paris bookseller's classification was based on the Baconian model, as was the classification used by the compilers of the first encyclopaedias in 18th-century France. Today bookshops still arrange their stock according to areas of study, and large encyclopaedias may have such a systematic arrangement implicit in their structure (as in the Propaedia of the *Encyclopaedia Britannica*).

This knowledge-based model of classification was also foremost in the minds of those who designed the big 19th- and 20th-century library classifications. The major areas of knowledge, fields of study or disciplines make a very good starting point for a classification intended for books or other carriers of recorded knowledge, since the disciplines themselves are the basis of study, of research and of much publishing activity.

The bibliographic classification also differs from the taxonomy in that it needs to accommodate large numbers of concepts that are not *things* or *entities*. Classifying the thing itself is not the same as classifying literature about it. The literature will contain lots of concepts that relate to activities, events, places and periods, as well as things, and a bibliographic classification has to take account of all of them.

Summary

Aspect classifications usually:

- deal with disciplines or fields of study rather than things
- locate entities in several different places
- contain classes for actions and events as well as entities.

All of this goes to show that a classification is not in itself true or false, but is appropriate only for a particular situation. Classification is essentially a *methodology* for creating a arrangement, using a particular set of criteria for grouping and ordering; provided these criteria are applied logically, and the location of any item can be reasonably predicted, we can ask no more of it than that. When we created the classification for literature books in Chapter 3, we made certain decisions about the citation order, and about the priorities for arrangement; other decisions would have resulted in a different classification – not necessarily better or more correct, just different.

You can see that the order and structure of a classification will be affected by such decisions, and that the priorities in one situation will produce a different classification from those of another. It's very difficult indeed for a classification not to reflect something of the culture that has produced it. This is as true of library classifications as it is of scientific classifications. It simply isn't possible to create a classification that is truly objective or neutral and absolutely correct. As we shall see when looking at the major schemes of classification, they all reflect something of the societies that produced them, and the purposes for which they were intended.

Answers to Exercises
Exercise 4.1

Uses for a rabbit: the conventional answers to this usually include keeping it as a pet, farming it, shooting it as a pest, experimenting on it, drawing it (in the artistic sense), using its fur and eating it. More imaginative suggestions include: pulling it out of a hat, using its foot for luck and worshipping it.

5 The classification scheme: internal structure

As we saw in the last chapter, the basis on which a classification can be built may vary, and the structure and order of a classification will differ according to the principles that are used to make the initial grouping. In this chapter we are going to look at some of the ways in which classification schemes arrange subjects in order to support browsing and information retrieval. We have already said that a major purpose of classification is to group, or collocate, subjects that are related in some way, and here we'll explore some of the relationships themselves.

Grouping, categorization, classing

First of all, let's have another look at the business of sorting out concepts into groups. If we have to organize a list of subjects such as those in Figure 5.1 there are various ways in which we can do this.

Apple	Cucumber	Pear
Banana	Gooseberry	Radish
Broccoli	Lemon	Swede
Cabbage	Lettuce	Watercress
Carrot	Marrow	

Figure 5.1 Alphabetical list of terms for grouping

There are several different properties of these items which we could use as the basis of an arrangement, and the resulting groups of objects might be more or less useful in different contexts. Take a few minutes to think about how you might do this. You could imagine you're playing that game where you're secretly given the name of something and you have to describe it to a partner who must guess what it is. What would you say about an apple that would immediately allow someone to identify it correctly? These characteristics of the apple might be ways of sorting out your list into groups.

If you have to describe an apple, you might say, 'it's red, it's round, it grows on a tree, it's a fruit'. The fruit part could give us one way of organizing the terms: we could sort them into a culinary classification, into groups of fruit, vegetables and salads (Figure 5.2):

Fruit	Vegetables	Salads
Apple	Broccoli	Cucumber
Banana	Cabbage	Lettuce
Gooseberry	Carrot	Radish
Lemon	Marrow	Watercress
Pear	Swede	

Figure 5.2   Classification by purpose

We could also group the items by colour, or by shape, although in what context this might be useful isn't perhaps very obvious. It would be more obviously useful to group the items according to the part of the plant that is consumed, as in Figure 5.3. This would create an arrangement appropriate to gardening or farming, since the different parts might require similar cultivation and harvesting methods.

Fruit	Root	Leaf	Flower
Apple	Carrot	Cabbage	Broccoli
Banana	Radish	Lettuce	
Cucumber	Swede	Watercress	
Gooseberry			
Lemon			
Marrow			
Pear			

Figure 5.3   Classification by part

These different classifications are like the taxonomies in Chapter 4. They use different criteria to arrange the items, and they're all valid arrangements for different purposes. The first step in any classification is to sort out the concepts into appropriate groups in this way.

Exercise 5.1

Suggest different ways in which the following topics might be arranged: archery, badminton, boxing, bridge, chess, cricket, croquet, darts, gymnastics, ice-skating, javelin throwing, judo, hockey, ludo, netball, rowing, showjumping, skiing, soccer, tennis, volleyball.

All these groupings are a way of creating linear ordering – we're collocating or bringing together related subjects – but essentially our 'classification' is still in the form of a list. There is no indication of any relationship between the items, other than their membership of the same group.

Relationships between terms: the idea of hierarchy

In a typical classification we can distinguish several sorts of relationships between items; the simplest of these is the relationship between a class and its subdivisions, arranged in what is known as a **hierarchy**. In Chapter 4 we saw an example of a hierarchy in Linnaeus's classification of living things. A hierarchy demonstrates the relationships of **subordination** and **superordination** (Figure 5.4).

> Birds
> Parrots
> Macaws
> Polly

Figure 5.4 A hierarchy showing subordination and superordination

A class is said to be subordinate to its containing class: for example, 'tigers' are subordinate to 'cats' and, conversely, 'cats' are superordinate to 'tigers'.

Hierarchies are the backbone of library classifications, and in the layout of a classification schedule the subdivisions of any class are commonly displayed by indenting them under the containing class. The deeper we go into the hierarchy, and the narrower and more specific the classes become, the further the classes are indented. The visual display corresponds to the conceptual structure, and allows us to move up and down the hierarchy from a broader (or more general) class to a narrower (or more specific) class, and vice versa.

Exercise 5.2
Arrange the following sets of terms to show their hierarchies:

1 Canada, CN Tower, North America, Toronto, Ontario
2 Wind instruments, alto saxophone, musical instruments, saxophones, woodwinds
3 Apples, foods, Golden Delicious, fruit, orchard fruit
4 Houses, bungalows, domestic buildings, buildings.

The relationships in a hierarchy can also be represented as a logical diagram, as in Figure 5.5, which shows graphically the containment of one class by another. Classes get smaller as they become more specific, and the hierarchy is a case of ever-decreasing circles.

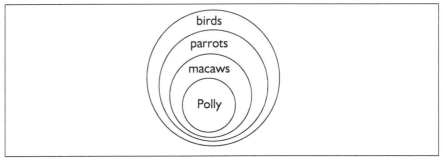

Figure 5.5   Hierarchy shown as a logical diagram

All bibliographic classifications make extensive use of this sort of structure, and it is not confined to hierarchies of objects or entities, as in the case of the parrots above, and the Linnaean taxonomies in Chapter 4. You can also find hierarchies of, for example, places (Figure 5.6), actions (Figure 5.7) or properties (Figure 5.8); in fact almost any category of terms can display hierarchy.

Europe
    United Kingdom
        England
            London
                City of London

Figure 5.6   Hierarchy of places

Cultivation
    Propagation
        Vegetative propagation
            Layering

Figure 5.7   Hierarchy of actions

Optical properties
    Colour
        Primary colours
            Blue
                Cobalt blue

Figure 5.8   Hierarchy of properties

Semantic relationships: hierarchical relationships proper

The hierarchical relationships shown above are the permanent, fixed relationships in a classification (London will always be in England, blue is always a colour). There are three main sorts of these relationships, the two commonest being 'thing–kind' (sometimes called **taxonomic,** or genus–species), and 'whole–part' (sometimes called **partonomic**) relationships.

The thing–kind relationship (Figure 5.9) is that of an entity (or action or property) and its kinds or types. The whole–part relationship (Figure 5.10) is that of an entity and its constituents.

1. Cheese
Camembert
Stilton
Wensleydale
2. Rodents
Gerbils
Mice
Rats
3. Spaniels
Cocker spaniels
Springer spaniels
Water spaniels

Figure 5.9   Thing–kind relationships

1. Europe
England
France
Spain
2. Flowers
Sepals
Petals
Stamens
3. Atoms
Electrons
Neutrons
Protons

Figure 5.10 Whole–part relationships

Relationships of this sort are sometimes called **semantic relationships,** because the meaning of words can be defined by them and the structure they give to a subject. For example, you can define a parrot as 'a kind of bird, a member of the class Psittacidae'.

The third type of semantic relationship is the instantive relationship (Figure 5.11), where the subordinate class is an instance, or specific example, of the broader class. This instance or example will be an individual person, entity or event, and it forms a class with one member. In the hierarchy in Figure 5.5 'Polly' is an example of an instantive relationship with 'macaws'.

Mountains	Artists	Canaries
Mount Everest	Leonarda da Vinci	Tweetie Pie

Figure 5.11 Instantive relationships

You can always tell whether two terms are in a semantic relationship by asking 'is term B a kind or part of term A, or an instance of it?'

Summary
- The hierarchy is the main structure in a classification.
- Relationships in a hierarchy are those of subordination and superordination, or broader and narrower classes.
- The different kinds of hierarchical relationship are: a thing and its kinds; a whole and its parts; and a thing and an instance, or specific example.
- These relationships are known as semantic relationships.

Syntactic relationships: non-hierarchical relationships

There are other sorts of relationships between terms which are not part of the permanent structure of a subject field. You'll find these in compound

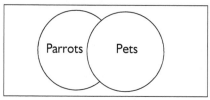

Figure 5.12 'Overlapping' compounds

subjects where they describe the relationship between the parts of the compound. They sometimes happen when a subordinate class arises as the result of two classes combining or overlapping. One example is the case of 'pet parrots' in Figure 5.12.

If the hierarchy is a series of 'nested' sets (Figure 5.5), we can think of a compound class as two intersecting sets. Sometimes the two overlapping or intersecting sets are both groups of *entities*. In this case the class of 'pet parrots' doesn't belong wholly to one class or another, but is shared between them. We call such a relationship a poly-hierarchy (because the pet parrots are in a hierarchical relationship with more than one broader class, namely 'pets' and 'parrots').

Most 'overlapping' subjects are not like the pet parrots in that they're not poly-hierarchical. More usually they're the combination of an *entity* and some other sort of term – an *activity* or a *place* or a *property*. 'Serials management' is a typical example of an overlapping or compound class of this kind. It does not belong to the hierarchy of 'serials', because it is not a kind or a part of a serial; it could be said to be a kind of management, although not in the sense that 'total quality management' is a kind of management. Certainly neither 'serials' nor 'management' can be defined in terms of the other, in the way that 'cats' and 'tigers' or 'molecules' and 'atoms' can. There is no connection at all, in the semantic sense, between 'serials' and 'management'. The relationship only occurs when you bring them together in the compound class 'serials management'. A relationship of this type is called a **syntactic relationship**.

Whereas semantic relationships are always between two terms of the same basic kind (for example, between two entities, or two actions, or two places), syntactic relationships occur between two terms of different sorts (for example, between an entity and an action). This means that there are potentially a very large number of them, and they haven't been categorized in the same way as the semantic relations. Some other examples are 'football boots' (equipment and an activity), 'British birds' (a place and an entity), 'mediaeval art' (a time and an activity), 'timber buildings' (a material and an entity).

Exercise 5.3

Say whether the parts of the following compounds are actions/activities, entities, places, times, equipment, or materials:

heart surgery, nylon carpets, apple picking, Italian opera, foreign cooking, modern art, boat building, swimming pools.

When two concepts joined together in this way are listed in a classification scheme they are said to be 'pre-coordinated'. Pre-coordination of terms is very common in classification schemes, and the way in which it is done tells you whether the scheme is based on logical principles, and how well it has been constructed. Ideally the combination of terms should be based on a **citation order** of the sort we discussed in Chapter 3. For example, if there are numerous terms combining actions and equipment (as you might find in a classification of sport) it is necessary to decide whether the citation order is activity-equipment or equipment-activity (or whether the football boots go with football or with other sorts of boots). If the pre-coordination is consistent and predictable the scheme will be much easier to use, and locating documents will be a much more straightforward task.

Summary

- Relationships often occur between terms that are not in the same hierarchy.
- These are usually compounds of different types of terms, such as entity/action, time/action, place/entity, etc.
- The relationship between such terms is called a syntactic relationship.
- Compound terms of this kind that are listed in a classification are said to be pre-coordinated.

Answers to exercises
Exercise 5.1

Several different possibilities suggest themselves; these are listed below with some members of each group:

- Outdoor games (cross-country running, rowing, skiing), indoor games (badminton, chess, darts), games played either indoor or outdoor (ice-skating, tennis, volleyball).
- Games played with balls (netball, soccer, volleyball), games played with other equipment (archery, darts, skiing, showjumping), games not requiring equipment (cross-country running, judo).
- Team games (cricket, hockey, netball, soccer), games played individually (archery, javelin throwing, judo), games played individually or in pairs (badminton, croquet, tennis), games played individually, in pairs and in groups (rowing).
- Summer games (cricket, croquet), winter games (skiing, soccer), all-year-round games (boxing, gymnastics, showjumping).
- Physical games (hockey, rowing, netball), mental games (bridge, chess).
- Games with opponents (badminton, chess, hockey), games marked by judges (gymnastics, ice-skating).
- Games of chance (ludo), games of skill (all the others!).

Games are very interesting from a classificatory point of view, as there seem to be no properties that all games must have. If you add some more games to the list you can probably think of more ways to divide them up.

Exercise 5.2

1 North America
   Canada
      Ontario
         Toronto
            CN Tower
2 Musical instruments
   Wind instruments
      Woodwinds
         Saxophones
            Alto saxophones
3 Foods
   Fruit
      Orchard fruit
         Apples
            Golden Delicious
4 Buildings
   Domestic buildings
      Houses
         Bungalows

Exercise 5.3

Heart surgery	entity/action
Nylon carpets	entity/material
Apple picking	entity/action
Italian opera	place/activity
Foreign cooking	place/activity
Modern art	time/activity
Boat building	entity/action
Swimming pools	action/equipment.

6 Types of classification scheme

We can use the way in which they deal with compound classes, and the syntactic relationships between terms, to classify classification schemes themselves. It's probably easiest to start with a very simple classification scheme and to look at it in two dimensions.

Tree structures

Tree structures are often used for pictorial representations of classifications, since they can show very clearly the complex relationships between the classes. They're particularly useful in the biological sciences for depicting taxonomies of organisms, or evolutionary development. Figure 6.1 shows a tree structure for a simple partial classification of agriculture which introduces some pre-coordinated classes.

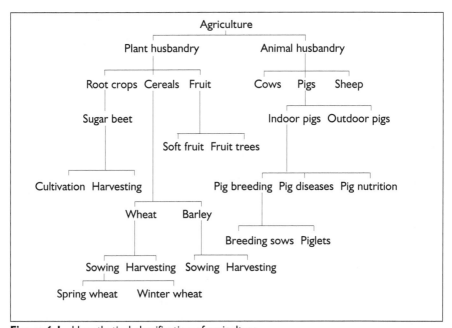

Figure 6.1 Hypothetical classification of agriculture

You can see that at each branching of the tree a new aspect of the subject, or principle of division, has been introduced, so that different crops, activities, environments and times of the year are all included in the tree.

In a bibliographic classification this two-dimensional structure has to be translated into a one-dimensional or linear order, since, in a physical environment such as a library, we need to have one sequence of items on the shelves. This linear order of classes is achieved by travelling down one 'branch' of the tree at a time, as in Figure 6.2. If you turn the schedule sideways you can see the tree structure reflected in the indentation.

Main types of classification structures
Enumerative classifications
A classification whose schedules look like the example below, with a long list of subordinate classes of ever increasing specificity, and lots of pre-coordinated compound classes, is called an **enumerative classification**. An

```
            Agriculture
              Plant husbandry
                Root crops
                  Sugar beet
                      Cultivation
                      Harvesting
                Cereals
                  Wheat
                      Sowing
                          Spring wheat
                          Winter wheat
                      Harvesting
                  Barley
                      Sowing
                      Harvesting
                Fruit
                    Soft fruit
                    Fruit trees
              Animal husbandry
                Cows
                Pigs
                    Indoor pigs
                      Pig breeding
                        Sows
                        Piglets
                      Pig diseases
                      Pig nutrition
                    Outdoor pigs
                Sheep
```

Figure 6.2 Schedule for agriculture derived from a tree structure

enumerative classification lists, or enumerates, all the possible classes in the classification. The rules of such schemes don't allow the classifier to create new classes by building **classmarks,** so you can properly classify a compound subject such as 'the economic history of coal mining in Brazil' only if such a class is 'ready-made' i.e., pre-coordinated, and listed in the schedules.

The earliest bibliographic classifications were of this type. These classifications, such as Dewey, Library of Congress, and Cutter's Expansive Classification (on which the Library of Congress Classification was based), treat knowledge as if it were a unity which can be subdivided into smaller and smaller units. At the top of the tree is the whole universe, which is divided and subdivided to arrive at all the different entities, events and activities represented in the subjects of books. Classifications which start from this position are sometimes also called **top-down classifications**.

This is not to say that the early bibliographic classifications concerned themselves very closely with the precise relationships between subjects, or with any very detailed analysis of the terminology. They were mainly occupied with the problems of broad subject groupings and the creation of notations for ordering the collection. It must also be remembered that at that time (the end of the 19th and the beginning of the 20th century) classification was being used only for monographs, and the subjects of documents were not as complex as they are now.

If you look at examples of enumerative classifications you'll notice that the subordinate classes are sometimes thing–kind relationships, and sometimes they are compounded of two or more concepts from different categories. The hierarchies of semantic relationships are mixed up with hierarchies created from syntactic relationships, and the schedules are sometimes not very logical, nor very consistent, in the way in which the various principles and attributes of division and citation order are applied.

The classic example of an enumerative classification is the Library of Congress Classification. This contains very lengthy listings of compound and complex subjects, many of which don't improve the specificity of the classification very much. If you look through the LCC schedules you will notice that some types of term occur again and again in all subjects. The commonest of these terms are places, periods, and forms.

Analytico-synthetic classifications

It occurred to the makers of some classifications – Paul Otlet and Henri La Fontaine with the Universal Decimal Classification, H. E. Bliss in his

Bibliographic Classification (BC), and James Duff Brown in the Subject Classification – that, rather than repeating them relentlessly within every class, there was a simpler way to express these commonly occurring ideas that would cut down enumeration and allow for briefer schedules. In these schemes the commonly occurring concepts were listed only once, in a set of common schedules, or common auxiliary tables, the notational codes from which could be added to *any* classmark to express the idea of place, or time, or physical form, and so on.

Later on in practical classification, we'll look at how exactly this is achieved in the different schemes, but those of you who are familiar with Dewey might have noticed that DDC always uses 09 on the end of a number to introduce the idea of a place, e.g. education in Great Britain, 370.942, or 03 to mean a dictionary or glossary, e.g. a dictionary of Judaism, 296.03. The notation for Great Britain and for the dictionary is taken from a set of tables at the beginning of the classification; these are used whenever these concepts are required in a classmark.

A scheme which uses distinct notation for separate concepts like this, and links them together when required, rather like building houses out of Lego, is called an **analytico-synthetic classification**. The subject of a document is *analysed* into its constituent parts and the codes for these are *synthesized* or joined together to create the classmark. 'The economic history of coal mining in Brazil' might be dealt with in an analytico-synthetic scheme by joining together the notations for 'Economic history', 'coal mining' and 'Brazil'.

A classification which is analytico-synthetic does not have to provide lots of ready-made compound classes; it lists individual terms or concepts and classifiers can join them together as they need to. Analytico-synthetic schemes usually include pre-coordinated classes, but they don't need to be as numerous as in the enumerative scheme, since there isn't any need to cover every possibility. When compared to an equivalent enumerative scheme, an analytico-synthetic scheme is much shorter in length, but has many more potential classes than are actually listed in the schedules.

The best example of an analytico-synthetic scheme is the Universal Decimal Classification. It has a very large number of systematic tables for commonly occurring concepts, and also allows most other classes to be joined together. The Dewey Decimal Classification now has more ways of building numbers for compound subjects, and can be regarded as an enumerative scheme with analytico-synthetic features.

Faceted classifications

A **faceted classification** takes the idea of analytico-synthesis to its logical conclusion, and 'deconstructs' the vocabulary of the classification into its simplest constituent parts. Facet analysis (as this process is called) was originated by the Indian librarian S. R. Ranganathan in the 1920s and 1930s, and his theory has had the most profound influence on subsequent classification and indexing principles and practice. There is a fuller discussion of the ideas of faceted classification in Chapter 20, so we'll just consider them briefly here.

Ranganathan saw that as well as *space* and *time* (his words for place and period) there were other sorts of terms that occur very frequently in all subjects. Terms relating to *materials* appear regularly, and he also saw that *activities, operations* and *processes* of all sorts are represented in every subject, as well as *objects, entities* and *systems*. He called these groups 'fundamental categories' and he considered that they were five in number: personality, matter, energy, space and time:

P = Personality (strictly speaking the main object of study in a subject, usually entities, objects, systems)
M = Matter (substances, materials, constituents)
E = Energy (actions, activities, processes)
S = Space
T = Time

Ranganathan's system, which was ultimately published as the Colon Classification (CC), is quite complex and demanding to apply because the categories he uses are very broad. During the 1960s and 1970s work on faceted classification carried out by members of the UK Classification Research Group extended the range of fundamental categories that could be used to organize vocabulary. A number of librarians and theorists involved in the development of faceted classification schemes for specific subjects arrived at a standard set of categories for the purpose of analysing concepts (Figure 6.3).

> Thing – kind – part – material – property – process – operation – patient – agent – product – by-product – space – time

Figure 6.3 Standard categories for modern faceted schemes

A faceted classification is constructed by taking terms belonging to the subject, and organizing them into these categories; these are then refined using other ordering techniques into the finished classification. A classification created by this method is known as a **bottom-up classification**, in contrast to the **top-down classification** structure of the early bibliographic schemes. So far no subject has been found which cannot be handled in this way, but in some subjects additional categories are required, notably in the arts, where genre, form and style are important extra categories. Figure 6.4 shows how you might allocate terms from agriculture into the standard categories in a faceted classification.

Things. Entities	Plants
Kinds of plants	Cereals. Root crops. Vegetables. Fruit trees
Parts of plants	Roots. Leaves. Stems. Flowers. Seeds. Stamens. Petals
Materials	Water. Cellulose. Pigments
Properties of plants	Coniferous. Evergreen. Poisonous. Edible. Scented
Processes	Growth. Flowering. Transpiration
Operations	Sowing. Planting. Feeding. Harvesting
Products	Food. Textiles. Drugs
Agents	Spades. Tractors. Hoes. Fertilizer. Scarecrow
Space	Dry places. Seaside. Tropics
Time	Victorian. Mediaeval. Modern. Weekend. Winter. Summer

Figure 6.4   Facet analysis of terms in agriculture

Using these categories the vocabulary of a subject is reduced to a set of groupings of simple terms or concepts, which the classifier can combine when classifying a compound subject. A classification based on a faceted structure like this doesn't have lots of compound subjects in the schedule, but generally consists of simple, often single, terms. In a faceted system our example of 'The economic history of coal mining in Brazil' would be built up from the notational codes for the individual concepts 'economics', 'history', 'coal', 'mining', 'Brazil'.

If we return to our original tree structure for agriculture we can see that a faceted classification would deal with the concepts contained in the tree in a very different manner (Figure 6.5). In this classification there aren't any pre-coordinated compound subjects; classmarks for compound subjects have to be put together by classifiers as and when they need them. The classification schedules are much shorter and simpler than in an enumerative scheme, but the potential number of classes is enormously greater.

```
                    Agriculture

               (Season)
                     Spring
                     Winter

               (Location)
                     Indoor
                     Outdoor

               (Actions)
                     Husbandry
                     Sowing
                     Cultivation
                     Harvesting
                     Breeding
                     Disease control
                     Nutrition

               ('Things' farmed)
                Plants
                     Root crops
                          Sugar beet
                     Cereals
                          Barley
                          Wheat
                     Fruit
                          Soft fruit
                          Top fruit
                Animals
                     Cows
                     Pigs
                          Sows
                          Piglets
                     Sheep
```

Figure 6.5   Faceted classification schedule for agriculture

A more detailed consideration of faceted schemes and their principles and application is given in Chapter 20. Facet analysis has produced only two general schemes of classification – the Colon Classification of Ranganathan and the revised edition of Bliss's Bibliographic Classification which is not yet complete – but it has greatly influenced the other general schemes. Their modern revisions, particularly those of UDC, but also DDC, now show a greater awareness of the need for consistency and logic in structure and flexibility in compounding.

Summary

- There are three basic types of classification structures.
- The enumerative scheme lists all the possible classes in the classification, and has many examples of pre-coordinated compound subjects.
- The analytico-synthetic scheme allows the classifier to build some compound classes, using auxiliary tables and other linking devices.
- The faceted scheme contains only simple classes and the classifier must construct any compound classes required.

7 Order in the classification scheme

Now that we have examined the ways in which the internal structure of a scheme might be organized, we'll consider the broader question of order throughout the scheme.

Main classes

In Chapter 4, we looked at the difference between scientific and bibliographic classifications, and at the fact that the bibliographic scheme is usually an aspect classification. That is to say, the organization of topics is based on areas of study or activity, and the first division of the scheme is into disciplines or subject domains.

This first division of a classification creates what are called main classes. A rough definition of a main class is that it corresponds to a single notational character: for example, in UDC, class 2 is the main class Religion, and in LCC, class N is the main class Fine Arts. You can see from Figure 7.1 that the number of main classes depends on the notation used. Not everybody would agree with this interpretation, and another understanding of main classes is that they equate to the traditional disciplines. In these terms, chemistry would always be a main class, whether it has notational main class status (as in the Bibliographic Classification's class C) or not (as in DDC's class 54).

Whatever the notational status of a main class, it is clear that the classification must treat it as a coherent subject. The different aspects of geography as studied in the UK aren't brought together in DDC, so students of this subject using a DDC classified library will find their books in several different places. It could therefore be said that DDC has no main class 'geography'.

What constitutes a main class varies from one scheme to another, and the provision of main classes for unusual subjects can encourage the adoption of that classification in special libraries. For example, the Bibliographic Classification is the only one to have a main class for social welfare, and

Dewey Decimal Classification	Bibliographic Classification
Generalities	Philosophy
Philosophy	Mathematics
Religion	Physics
Social sciences	Chemistry
Languages	Earth sciences
Pure sciences	Biology
Applied sciences & Technology	Botany
Arts	Zoology
Literature	Medicine
History & Geography	Psychology
	Education
	Sociology
	History
	Religion
	Social welfare
	Politics
	Law
	Economics
	Technology
	Arts
	Language
	Literature
	Bibliography

Figure 7.1   Main classes in DDC and BC

this has led to its adoption by many social service libraries and libraries of charitable organizations. LCC is the only scheme that has main classes for military and naval science.

Cross-disciplinary studies and phenomena classes

Users of the big general classification schemes will have trouble in classifying books about cross-disciplinary studies. A cross-discipline is one in which some particular *phenomenon* is the object of study, and where this phenomenon is considered from the point of view of any number of different disciplines. The terms multi-disciplinary and interdisciplinary are also used to describe this kind of study.

In the academic world, the classic example is women's studies, where 'women' are the focus, and the study is of their place in literature, history, society, art, law and so on. Women's studies was the forerunner of a series of 'person'-based cross-disciplines, such as black studies or refugee studies. These have now been joined by historically and culturally based programmes – mediaeval studies, Victorian studies and Celtic studies all spring to mind. The cross-disciplinary approach has also become popular in school curricula, with a consequent increase in the number of books dealing with cross-disciplinary themes such as water or castles.

Traditional discipline-based classifications don't accommodate such topics very satisfactorily, and some pragmatic solution has to be found. Most classifiers will adopt the principle of the place of unique definition – that is, the class where the object of study is defined in the most fundamental sense. For example, the dandelion is primarily classified as a plant; it might occur in disciplines other than botany, perhaps in pharmacology, cookery or wine-making, as an animal food or in complementary medicine, but it is first and foremost a plant. The place of **unique definition** of the dandelion is therefore in the classification of plants, i.e. in botany.

This principle locates women's studies in the sociology class (because it is here that persons by gender are primarily dealt with) but it can look odd to see other aspects of the cross-discipline sitting here. Other compromise solutions include putting the 'object' at its first occurrence in the schedules (often the same as the place of unique definition), or putting it with that discipline which occupies the major part of the document.

The problem can only be completely solved by the inclusion of 'phenomena' classes – a series of classes preceding the main classification that have no disciplinary basis, but deal instead with entities. Such a classification would be like a scientific classification or taxonomy. To date, no general classification has offered such an approach.

Main class order

The sequence of main classes is also important. In academic departments, some subjects are taught in groups – the physical or biological sciences, or languages and their literatures – and we would expect these subjects to be close together. Most subjects also have what are known as **fringe disciplines** – that is, other subjects that impinge on, or support the main study. For example, students of the Bible will need to know about archaeology, languages and ancient history as well as theology.

The order in which the main classes are listed is often discussed at a theoretical level, and some orders are considered to be better than others. The compilers of the early schemes such as DDC had not given much thought to how one class followed another. Dewey admitted as much. When later schemes, with the benefit of evolving classification theory, exhibited a more logical sequence of main classes this was seen as more scholarly, and hence superior. The order of the main classes in Bliss's Bibliographic

Classification (Figure 7.1) is widely regarded as the best of all the general schemes. Bliss put much thought and effort into his structure, and there is certainly a strong sense of progression of disciplines from the abstract to the material to the living world. Living things are in order of complexity, culminating in mankind and the human sciences; society and social activities come next, followed by the products of society, firstly material and then intellectual. Nevertheless, it is extremely difficult to put all major subjects into a single sequence and take account of all the potential relationships between them. Bliss can be criticized for not collocating philosophy and religion, and for the separation of pure and applied sciences. All one can safely say is that there is no perfect order. As with so many features of classification schemes, a good main class order is related to the needs of the particular collection and its users.

Summary
- The first division of knowledge in a classification creates main classes.
- Main classes are usually equivalent to traditional disciplines.
- What constitutes a main class will vary from one classification to another.
- Cross-disciplinary or interdisciplinary studies are difficult to place in a main class.
- The usual solution is to locate the cross-disciplinary topic at its place of unique definition.
- Phenomena classes would solve the problem but no existing schemes contain them.
- The perfect order of main classes does not exist.
- It's impossible to find a single sequence that accommodates all the potential links between subjects..

Schedule order and filing order

Having decided on the order of main classes, the compiler of a classification scheme has also to determine in which order the sub-classes or topics within each main class will occur. We have seen above that main class order can be arrived at on a very arbitrary basis. Is the order of more specific topics the same, or are there rules to help us?

One of the problems of main class order is that all the main classes are more or less equivalent in terms of their importance. It's very hard to decide an order of priority among them. The concepts within a class can be somewhat easier to deal with because they exhibit relationships with each other which can help to determine order.

Let's go back to the idea of our hierarchical relationships from Chapter 5, and the notion of broader and narrower terms. In a hierarchy involving birds, parrots, macaws and Polly, we began with the broadest term, birds, and worked towards the narrowest, or most specific, term, Polly. Similarly, the hierarchy of place in Figure 5.6 produced an order: Europe, United Kingdom, England, London, City of London. See Figure 7.2.

Birds → Parrots → Macaws → Polly
Europe → UK → England → London → City

Figure 7.2 Broad to narrow order

The order of concepts in both cases moved from the broad to the narrow, from the general to the specific. Do you think it likely that the reverse would be a sensible or helpful order? It appears to be intuitive to most people that general to specific is the most logical and natural order. Bliss called this rule of ordering **general before special**, and it's inherent in all classifications. Ranganathan had a variation of the rule, which he called the rule of **increasing concreteness**. This suggests that more abstract ideas should come first in a sequence, and it is an important rule in deciding on citation order, of which more later.

In addition to the general-before-special rule, there are some pragmatic rules for ordering which are often applied. Common ordering principles such as: chronological order for historical events; west to east (or north to south) order for places; developmental order for processes such as life cycles or manufacturing processes; evolutionary order for living things; orders of magnitude or dimensions for manufactured objects, such as champagne bottles, all have a part to play in sorting out concepts.

Otherwise, when sorting out classes, two important ideas have played a part in the development of the big general classification schemes. These ideas are **literary warrant** and **educational consensus**. The principle of literary warrant proposes that bibliographic classifications should reflect the way in which subjects are represented in books, and that a classification shouldn't be developed purely on a philosophical basis. Modern classification schemes usually do start with the literature *and* have strong underlying philosophical principles, so the two are not necessarily in conflict, but the idea is a sound one. A bibliographic classification shouldn't be a classification of ideas alone. Nobody wants a classification that does not match the subjects of books.

Educational consensus is also important because it involves the grouping of subjects to reflect how they are taught and studied. Any of you who have worked in college libraries will be familiar with the demand to have 'all our books in one place', accompanied by loud complaints about the classification if it separates them. Undoubtedly life is easier for teachers and students if all the books for a particular course are together, and although it shouldn't be taken to extremes, a classification should reflect the general patterns of academic study.

The whole process of bringing together related subjects is called **collocation**. Neighbouring subjects are said to be collocated, and the collocation of topics in a scheme can be considered good or bad.

The resulting order of subjects, or classes, in the classification is known as the **schedule order**. The schedule order is the order of classes in the published classification. **Filing order** is the order in which the notational symbols run (which isn't negotiable when numbers or letters are employed) and hence the order in which documents are arranged. It is sometimes called the shelf order. In a sequence of classified documents some scheduled classes may be missing (because there are no documents corresponding to those classes) but there may be additional, built, numbers not represented in the schedule. Clearly the filing order of classmarks is parallel, if not equivalent, to the schedule order.

Summary
- The rule of general before special is used to order topics within main classes.
- The rule of increasing concreteness is a different way of saying the same thing.
- A scheme based on the subjects of books is said to have literary warrant.
- A scheme that mirrors the way subjects are studied is said to reflect educational consensus.
- The bringing together of subjects is called collocation.
- Schedule order and filing order are parallel.

Notation

Although the order of topics in a classification may be logical, it has no natural filing order like alphabetical order or numerical order. If the user is to know where parrots fit into the sequence, or whether philosophy comes before or after physics, each class must have a code that indicates its position relative to other classes.

Dewey introduced this idea of **relative location**, and it's a fundamental feature of the modern library classification. The alternative is a system of **fixed location** where the codes refer to a physical position in the library (such as bookcase A, shelf 2, book number 37). Dewey brought in the idea that the code would represent the subject of the book and its position in the overall sequence. With this system, when books are added or withdrawn, or the whole collection needs to be moved, the relative positions of the books are unchanged, and no renumbering is necessary.

The main purpose of the notation, then, is to maintain the order of classes, since without a notation there is no way of establishing the correct sequence. Notation is therefore an essential feature of a classification scheme. Most end-users are far more aware of the notation than they are of the structure of the scheme, and many users regard it as the classification scheme. If you ask a non-librarian friend which classification is used in a library they know, they will probably not tell you that it separates physics and engineering, or has a main class for military science. They certainly will tell you if it uses numbers and letters, or has very long classmarks with odd symbols.

Notational symbols

A variety of different symbols are commonly used in notation:

- Arabic numerals
- letters
- punctuation marks and other symbols.

A system that uses only one set of characters is known as a 'pure' notation, whereas one that combines letters and numbers is known as a 'mixed' notation. The complete set of characters used in any classification is called the notational base. The more characters that are available, the shorter the classmarks will be, since compilers have more choices open to them. For example, the number of possible combinations of three numerals is 1000 (from 000 to 999), but the number of possible three-letter combinations (from AAA to ZZZ) is 17,576. A classification with three-letter classmarks can thus have much more detail than a corresponding numerical one. The potential of a mixed notation is even greater.

Arabic numerals are often regarded as being the most 'user friendly' notation; they have a clear filing order, they are understood internationally, and their use is intuitive for the majority of users. But because there are only ten numerals, classmarks using numbers tend to be longer than those using letters.

Letter (or literal) notations have shorter classmarks, and can make use of mnemonics (see below), but people in different countries may not be familiar with them. All the general schemes that use letters (LCC, BC, CC) use the Roman alphabet, which is not the normal alphabet in Eastern Europe and Asia. Moreover, even where Roman letters are the norm, and alphabetical order is a common method of arrangement, many people appear to have difficulty filing and retrieving letter codes as opposed to 'real' words.

Mixed notations, with their substantial notational base, can have very short classmarks for quite specific topics. The change from letters to numbers (or vice versa) can also help to make classmarks more memorable to the user.

Filing order of notation

Both numbers and letters have a natural filing order. Notations using other symbols are usually more difficult for users, particularly if more than a few symbols are used. Punctuation marks, such as commas, colons and oblique strokes, are commonly used, particularly in special classifications, but they have no natural filing order. This can leave users (and library staff) unclear about the order and location of items; the filing order, which is arbitrary, must be learnt. On the other hand, symbols can help to show the structure of synthesized or faceted classmarks, and make a more complicated notation clearer to the user.

The filing order of letters should present no special problems for the user. Nevertheless, many people seem to find letter codes much more difficult to deal with than real words when it comes to alphabetical order. There is nothing to be done about this, except that library staff should take great care in filing and shelving.

Numbers can cause minor difficulties as they can file in two ways: ordinal and decimal. Ordinal filing places the numbers in order of their numerical value, starting at 1 and rising. Decimal filing treats the numbers

Decimal filing	Ordinal filing
125	2
13	3
135	4
136	13
2	27
27	28
28	37
293	125
3	135
37	136
375	293
4	375

Figure 7.3   Decimal and ordinal filing

as decimal fractions, that is, as if they had an invisible decimal point at the beginning. Examples of ordinal and decimal sequences are shown in Figure 7.3. DDC makes decimal filing easier for users by always having three figures preceding the decimal point, so that there is no confusion between ordinal and decimal filing.

Function and purpose of notation

Keeping the order of classes is the main purpose of the notation, but in some schemes it shows other helpful characteristics. One important role of notation is to support the working of the classification, to enable number building, retrieval and other functional aspects of the scheme. We shall look at these aspects of notation in detail in the sections on specific schemes. More general properties **expressive notation**, and **mnemonics**, are considered below.

Expressiveness

When the structure of the notation corresponds to, or reflects, the structure of the classification itself, the notation is said to be **expressive**. The commonest type of expressiveness is where the length of a classmark reflects the position of the class in the hierarchy. At each step in the division of the hierarchy, an extra character is added to the classmark (as in Figure 7.4). This feature of the notation helps searching, as a searcher can broaden or narrow a search by lengthening or shortening the classmark. It's also easily understood by users, who see a natural logic in the system.

In a non-expressive notation (Figure 7.5) the only consideration is the order of classes, and notations of this kind don't always indicate that one class is a subdivision of another. This can seem illogical but there are advantages:

- classmarks don't have to be very long simply because the class is deep in a hierarchy
- short classmarks can be given to important subjects
- the notation can be more evenly distributed across the classes
- it is easier to insert new classes into the order.

```
5          Science
59            Zoology
599             Mammals
599.73             Artiodactyla. Even-toed ungulates
599.735               Ruminants
599.735.3               Antlered mammals
599.735.32               Moose
```

Figure 7.4 Hierarchy reflected in notation in UDC Class 5

```
S69        Access to the law
              * By the citizen or other party
S6A        Practice of law
S6A C        Malpractice
S6A D          Discrimination in the law
S6A E            Ethnic discrimination, racial discrimination in the law
S6A F            Sexist discrimination in the law
S6A H          Bribery in the law
S6A L        Evaluation of legal performance
```

Figure 7.5 Non-expressive notation in BC2 Class S

You can compare the difference between the expressive notation of UDC and the non-expressive notation of BC2 in Figures 7.4 and 7.5. UDC's classmarks get longer and longer with the hierarchy, whereas BC2 retains short classmarks for these important subjects by ignoring (notationally) the hierarchical relationships between classes.

Classmarks can also indicate the structure of the subject, where, in built numbers, the notation remains intact. Linking symbols can show clearly the position of different elements of a compound subject. In Chapter 18 on UDC, we'll look at how numbers are built using the colon as a linking device, and where you can see the separate parts that make up the classmark joined together like beads on a string.

Example

```
Australian marsupials and monotremes: an action plan for
their conservation / compiled by Michael Kennedy. -
Gland, Switzerland : IUCN, 1992

Habitat:          574.2
Monotremes:       599.11
Marsupials:       599.22

Classmark:        574.2:599.11:599.22
```

Mnemonics

A mnemonic notation is one that can be easily remembered. Mnemonic comes from the Greek word *mneme*, meaning recollection or remembrance. A notation is mnemonic when there's a direct correspondence between the characters in the classmark and the subject itself.

Literal mnemonics occur when there is a match between a notation using letters and the initial letters of the subjects represented. Bliss was very fond of mnemonics and lots of examples can be found in his scheme:

C   Chemistry
CE Electrochemistry
AM Mathematics
U   Useful arts

You can also see some nice examples of literal mnemonics at S6A D and S6A E in Figure 7.5.

Systematic mnemonics are more common, and happen where the code for a concept remains constant wherever it is used. Systematic mnemonics are very typical in schemes which allow for combination of concepts. Auxiliary tables in particular make use of this feature, as in this example from UDC, where (038) is always used to represent the concept of a dictionary:

53(038)   Dictionary of physics
339(038)   Dictionary of commerce

This example from the literature class of DDC shows a similar (but perhaps less obvious) example of system mnemonics in built numbers:

823 English novels   (from 820 English literature)
833 German novels   (from 830 German literature)
843 French novels   (from 840 French literature)

Summary
- Notation controls the order of classes.
- Notational characters may be numbers, letters or other symbols.
- The complete set of characters used is called the notational base.

Continued on next page

Summary *Continued*
- Numbers can file ordinally or decimally.
- Notation that reflects the structure of the schedule is called expressive notation.
- Mnemonic notation aids the memory of the user.
- It includes literal mnemonics and systematic mnemonics.

Flexibility and hospitality

Two essential characteristics of a good classification scheme are **flexibility** and **hospitality**. These characteristics are closely related to the notation and the way in which it operates.

Flexibility

Flexibility is the capacity of the classification to allow different arrangements of subjects to meet the needs of different users or situations. There are two main methods of achieving this:

- alternative locations for subjects
- alternative citation orders, or ways of combining concepts.

It goes without saying that the editors of the scheme must deliberately provide these alternatives. If you find that you can't decide in which of two classes you should place a document, because it could equally well go in either, that is called **cross-classification**, and is a bad thing. The alternatives should be clearly indicated as such.

Bliss's Bibliographic Classification is the best-known provider of alternative locations; the other schemes don't like them very much. UDC in particular aims to have only one possible place for a topic.

On the other hand, you'll find variations in citation order in most schemes. DDC, for example, has several different ways of arranging literature, and UDC is particularly flexible in its citation order, allowing classifiers to follow almost any pattern of combination that they wish.

When a scheme provides alternatives in this way (whether they're alternatives of location or of combination) you can't use them willy-nilly. You must decide at the outset which of the alternatives you are going to use, and strike out the others. Otherwise, if you hop from one alternative to another the classification will lose all sense of predictability, and the terrible sin of cross-classification will have occurred.

Hospitality

The **hospitality** of a scheme is its ability to accommodate new topics, whether these happen as a result of the interaction of existing subjects (as in the case of biotechnology or school league tables), or are completely new subjects that nobody had thought of before (such as the world wide web or extreme ironing).

New subjects of the first type can usually be accommodated in an analytico-synthetic or faceted scheme, where it is possible to join concepts together easily. The number of potential classes in such a scheme is very great, and many such new combinations can be inserted by the classifier without reference to editors of the scheme.

Completely new topics are more difficult, and their location will usually have to be determined at an editorial level. All of the big general schemes have facilities for letting users know about the provision for new subjects, normally in the form of updates or bulletins listing new classmarks, or changes in the scheme. Nowadays most systems do this updating via the internet.

How easy editors find it to insert new topics is largely related to the structure of the scheme. Well-constructed and logical schemes are usually easier to add to, because the proper location of new concepts is more evident.

The way in which notation is used also has a considerable effect on hospitality. Notation which files decimally (whether it uses numbers or letters) can be infinitely expanded to accommodate new classes, because more characters can always be added to the classmark. For example, the sequences shown in Figure 7.6 can be added to at any point to insert the new classes in the second and fourth columns.

Numeral sequence	Expanded numeral sequence	Letter sequence	Expanded letter sequence
1	1	BC	BC
12	12	BD	BCC
13	125	BE	BCK
14	126	BF	BD
147	13	BFG	BE
	14	BFH	BF
	143	BG	BFG
	147		BFGG
	1472		BFGL
	1473		BG

Figure 7.6   Decimal expansion of notation

When the notation is used ordinally, as it is in the Library of Congress Classification, gaps must be left in the notation to allow for the insertion of new classes. This is always a guessing game, and over time the notation may simply not allow for any more expansion. For example in the following sequence:

11, 12, 17, 18, 22, 24, 27, 30, 35, 40, 45,

once the two classes 25 and 26 have been inserted between 24 and 27, there is just no more room.

Summary
- Two important features related to notation are flexibility and hospitality.
- Flexibility can be achieved by alternative locations, and by alternative citation orders.
- In a given collection only one of a set of alternatives can be used.
- New topics may be new combinations of existing concepts, or they may be entirely new concepts.
- Analytico-synthetic and faceted schemes are able to accommodate new combinations.
- Entirely new concepts must be added by editors of the scheme.
- Sound logical structure is helpful in indicating the proper location of new concepts.
- Insertion into the sequence is affected by the notation.
- Decimal notation can be expanded indefinitely; ordinal notation has limited capacity for insertion.

8 Content analysis 1: document description

Before you can start to build a classmark or assign a subject heading to a document you must first decide what the document is about. This analysis of content is quite separate from any particular system of classification, and should be carried out independently of the system. You shouldn't be trying to fit the document into the classification scheme, but making an objective assessment of its content, and this chapter is about how you do that. (I've generally used the term 'subject content' to refer to what the item is about, but you may, in more theoretical works, come across the expressions 'intellectual content' and 'semantic content'. These are just more impressive ways of describing the subject.)

The problem of 'aboutness'; indexer consistency and subjectivity

The notion of 'aboutness' is an essential part of indexing, classification and subject cataloguing, but it contrasts markedly with the task of descriptive cataloguing. In the majority of cases it's not too difficult for the cataloguer to determine the author and the title of a book, and having found the author and title there is generally no dispute as to what they are. Sometimes the subject is similarly straightforward. Look at Figure 8.1: you can see that the author is Bruce Campbell, and the title is *Birds of coast and sea.* The title suggests that this is a book about birds, and there seems no reason to doubt that. Now look at Figure 8.2: you can see that the author is John Updike, and the title is *Hoping for a hoopoe.* But what about the subject? It seems at least possible that this book isn't about hoopoes, but how can you find out one way or the other? Unfortunately there's no part of a book which will tell you plainly and unequivocally what its subject is; you must decide this for yourself.

Deciding on the subject of a book can be tricky because it is a very subjective activity. What I understand to be the subject of a book may differ from your interpretation, and research has shown that if indexers think

Birds of Coast and Sea
Britain and Northern Europe

Illustrations by
RAYMOND WATSON
Text by
BRUCE CAMPBELL
Introduction by
ROBERT DOUGALL

Figure 8.1   *Birds of coast and sea*

HOPING   FOR   A
HOOPOE

POEMS BY
JOHN UPDIKE

LONDON
VICTOR GOLLANCZ LTD
1959

Figure 8.2   *Hoping for a hoopoe*

about the same item on two different occasions, they don't reach exactly the same conclusion about its content. Even experienced classifiers find it hard to describe accurately how they go about deciding on the subject of a book because it is largely an intuitive process.

Nevertheless, there are some techniques of content analysis which can be learnt, and which will help you to establish standards of good practice and produce effective subject indexing. In the following pages we shall consider:

- where to find indications of subject content
- how to construct a statement of subject content.

Where to look for content
The title
The beginner classifier often assumes that the best indicator of a book's subject is the title. Of course often the title *is* an accurate reflection of the content, and this is especially true of scientific publications. Take the following example from a set of conference proceedings:

Example

> Pineapple research in Brazil / J. H. Reinhardt and J. da
> S. Sousa <u>in</u> Proceedings of the Third International
> Pineapple Symposium: Pattaya, Thailand, 12-20 November
> 1998/ editors S. Subhadrabandhu, P. Chairidchai

The authors of this paper, when asked to describe the content, have assigned to it the descriptors, or subject keywords, 'pineapple', 'research' and 'Brazil', which correspond very closely indeed to the title. The following titles also demonstrate the descriptive quality of titles of scientific papers.

Examples

> Swimming sea cucumbers (Echinodermata, Holothuroidea) : a
> survey, with analysis of swimming behavior in four
> bathyal species / John E. Miller and David L. Pawson. -
> Washington, D.C. : Smithsonian Institution Press, 1990
>
> Anthropometric measurement of Brazilian feet / by Delfina
> Faco and Mario D. D'Angelo. - Manchester : Manchester
> Metropolitan University, Institute of Advanced Studies,
> 1993

You can fairly safely assume that the subjects of these documents are those stated in the titles. This is not always the case. *Hoping for a hoopoe* (Figure 8.2) doesn't look even at first glance as if it is a book about hoopoes; such a work would be more likely to be called something along the lines of:

Example

> Notes on the breeding of the Hoopoe (Upupa epops) in the
> county of West Sussex, June/July 1976 / John Dagger. -
> [U.K. : J. Dagger], 1976

In fact *Hoping for a hoopoe* is a book of poetry, and has nothing at all to offer the reader on the subject of hoopoes – it doesn't even contain a poem about hoopoes; the title is entirely whimsical. In many cases the titles of books are not helpful in indicating content, and sometimes can be downright misleading.

This is more likely to happen with books in the social sciences and humanities, particularly the latter, where authors often delight in producing witty titles, using wordplay such as puns or quotations, rather than titles which convey a sense of the book's subject.

This leads us to another fundamental law of classification – never classify by the title! In order to be confident about the real subject of a book, we need to examine it carefully for clues. Be observant when handling the book because information can be discovered in all sorts of places. (You should understand that the titles used for practice in this book have been chosen because they *do* accurately represent content, and that you're not expected to find original copies in order to carry out the exercises.)

The subtitle
Although the title of a book may itself be misleading, the author, having enjoyed his or her literary reference or clever joke, often helps the reader by explaining it. Subtitles usually provide a better indication of the content, as is shown by the example of *Gold was the mortar* (Figure 8.3); we can see the same thing in *The ark in the park* (Figure 8.4).

The dust jacket and covers
A rapid examination of the external parts of the book can also help you to identify aspects of the content that aren't immediately apparent from the title

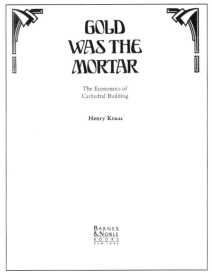

Figure 8.3 *Gold was the mortar*

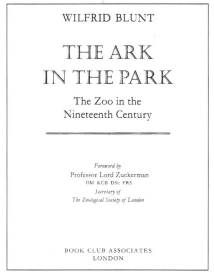

Figure 8.4 *The ark in the park*

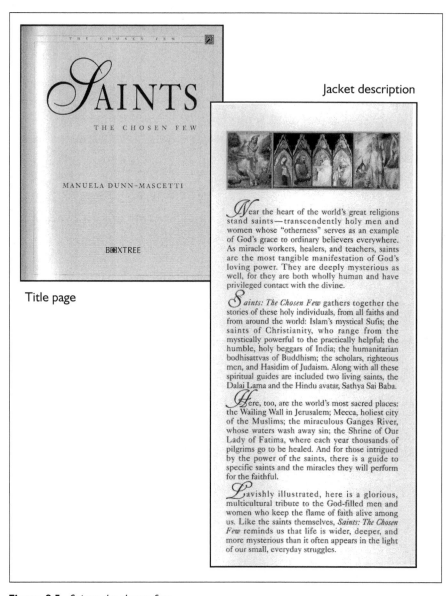

Jacket description

Title page

Figure 8.5 *Saints: the chosen few*

page. Figure 8.5, *Saints: the chosen few*, shows a book that appears initially, and because of the wording of the title, to be a book about Christianity, but the description on the dust jacket shows us that the work deals with a whole range of religions, and should be classified as a more general work on world faiths.

Figure 8.6   *Bird behaviour*

In Figure 8.6, *Bird behaviour*, the series title reveals that this is a book for children, but only the back cover of the book gives the age group targeted.

The contents page

If you're still in doubt about the subject of a book, the contents page provides you with a detailed list of the topics covered, and can clarify matters considerably.

Figure 8.7   *The British Museum book of cats*

Look at Figure 8.7, *The British Museum book of cats*. The title-page, with its subtitle of 'ancient and modern', suggests that this is a book about the history of cats, but the contents page tells you that, while there is some material about the cat in history, the book also deals with the biology of the cat, cat breeds and other general types of cat. In fact, it's just a general book about cats, and not really a history at all.

Reference sources

If you are completely stumped as to the subject of a book – perhaps it has a scientific or technical content quite beyond your experience – it's perfectly legitimate to seek someone else's opinion. There is no reason why you should be expert in every field of knowledge before you can assign a classmark. All libraries, if not the cataloguing department itself, should have a collection of reference works that will provide you with information about subjects, define terms and explain the structure of disciplines.

Other catalogue records

Nowadays most large general libraries as well as many special collections have online catalogues where you can search for an existing catalogue record for your book. The work of a more experienced classifier can help you to see how the book could be handled. Even if a different classification scheme is being used you will probably be able to work out what has been done, and in many instances subject headings will give you a clear indication of the book's subject. Beginner classifiers often think of this as cheating, but it's a sensible strategy when you are at a loss for what to do, and it's common practice among classifiers; you can even think of it as good practice to check your work with others from time to time. There's no need to feel obliged to reproduce exactly existing classification data – simply take what you need for your own purposes and situation.

Summary
- Examine the book carefully.
- Look at the title, but exercise caution.
- See if there are clues in the subtitle.
- Read the covers, jacket description and contents page.
- Consult works of reference if the subject is obscure.
- Seek confirmation from existing catalogue records if necessary.

Constructing the document description
What to include

Having looked at the various physical parts of the book we can now start to construct a proper description of the document content. The object of the exercise is to create a succinct statement of the document's content in a form that can be easily translated into a classmark or subject heading. Such a statement is called by a variety of names: subject string, subject summary and concept analysis all mean the same thing. In the following pages you'll see a number of examples of such objects.

Identifying the main class

The first stage in creating a document description is to decide on the broad subject area to which the book belongs. If you're using a classification scheme (as opposed to subject headings) this is absolutely unavoidable because the book must be physically located somewhere. You therefore have to make a decision about the main subject. Most of the time there won't be any difficulty about this. Look at Figure 8. 1, *Birds of coast and sea*. This is a book about birds, and you should put it in the biological sciences, under ornithology; there isn't any sensible alternative.

Examples

    Concise encyclopedia of Hinduism / Klaus K. Klostermaier.
    - Oxford : Oneworld, 1998

    Hittites and their contemporaries in Asia Minor / J.G.
    Macqueen. - London : Thames and Hudson, 1986. - (Ancient
    peoples and places)

These are more examples of relatively straightforward items; you would probably want to put the first one into the Religion class, and the second into Ancient History.

Exercise 8.1

Say what you think are appropriate general subject areas for the following titles:

1   *Archaeology in the lowland American tropics*
2   *Black American music: past and present*
3   *Colour atlas of AIDS in the tropics*
4   *Flora of the Russian Arctic*
5   *Jewish folk art: from biblical days to modern times*
6   *Mixed feelings: the complex lives of mixed race Britons*
7   *Winter garden glory: how to get the best from your garden from autumn through to spring*
8   *Women who made the news: female journalists in Canada, 1880–1945.*

Now look at Figure 8.8, *Railway architecture of Greater London*. Is this a book about railways, to be classified in the transport class, or is it a book about

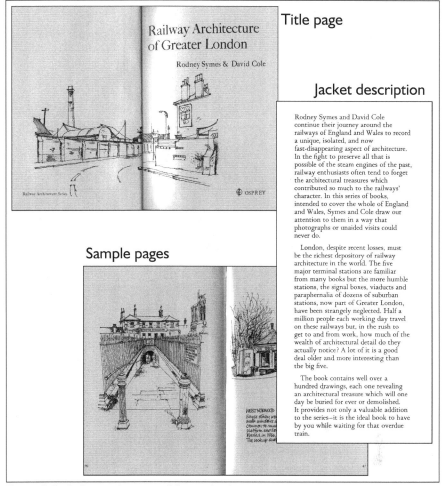

Figure 8.8 *Railway architecture of Greater London*

architecture which is in the arts class? *Gold was the mortar* (Figure 8.3) might be placed in the economics class, in architecture, in religion or in history. The subject area chosen will depend on who you think the book is intended for – who is the expected audience. A book about vegetables, for example, might be aimed at gardeners, farmers, botanists or cooks. Titles like those in Figures 8.8 and 8.3, which consider one topic from the point of view of a different discipline (railways considered for their architecture, cathedrals from an economic viewpoint), could potentially be placed with either. What are the possibilities for the following titles?

Exercise 8.2

Say what alternative general subject areas might be appropriate for the following titles:

1   *Teaching geography in secondary schools*
2   *Science and religion in contemporary philosophy*
3   *Food lobbyists: behind the scenes of food and agripolitics*
4   *Dionysus writes: the invention of theatre in ancient Greece*
5   *Antwerp in the age of reformation: underground Protestantism in a commercial metropolis, 1550–1577*
6   *Effects of nocturnal shift work on student nurses*
7   *Refugee women and their mental health*
8   *Scientists and the media: guidelines for scientists working with the media and comments on a Press Code of Practice/the Royal Society*
9   *Scots law for journalists.*

Significant concepts

Having established the general subject area of the book, the next task is to identify the important *specific* concepts contained in its subject. By this I mean those concepts:

• which best describe the content, and
• which a user is most likely to search for.

The idea of *sought concepts* is a very important one, since there's no point at all in classifying concepts that no one will look for. You should always remember to keep the readers in mind when you are classifying, and continually ask yourself what they will find helpful or informative.

Let's look at some examples to illustrate this.

Examples

```
Ale, beer and brewsters in England : women's work in a
changing world, 1300-1600 / Judith M. Bennett. - New
York ; Oxford : Oxford University Press, 1996
```

```
Flights of fancy : early aviation in Battersea and
Wandsworth / by Patrick Loobey. - London : Wandsworth
Borough Council, Recreation Dept., 1981
```

In the first example there are several topics for which a reader could be searching. 'Ale' and 'beer' are obviously important concepts, as are 'work', 'women' and 'England'; anyone wanting information on any of these topics could find this book useful. Although it doesn't appear as a word, the title also includes the notion of the mediaeval period in '1300–1600'. It's often necessary to translate *terms* from a title into more general *concepts* in this way. Again, try to keep in mind what will be looked for. In this case a search is much more likely to contain the word 'mediaeval' than a specific date.

At this stage we want just to identify the important concepts, and we could therefore list those as:

ale
beer
brewing
England
women
work
mediaeval.

In the second example there are some useful key words: 'aviation', 'Wandsworth' and 'Battersea'. The term 'early' has a ring of history about it, so we can include that as well. But terms such as 'flights of fancy' don't really say anything about the subject, and nobody is very likely to choose this as a phrase to search for. (This is in fact another good example of an unhelpful title.) Our final selection might therefore look like:

aviation
history
Wandsworth
Battersea.

Common categories of terms
Place and time
In the examples above, in addition to the subjects of brewing and aviation, we have included some terms to do with place (England, Battersea, Wandsworth) and some to do with period (history, mediaeval). Places and periods occur very commonly in the subjects of books, so much so that

classification schemes usually make provision for expressing these ideas in a classmark. *Flights of fancy* is not just of interest to students of aviation, but would also be relevant for someone researching the history of Wandsworth and Battersea. You should therefore always include any indication of place or time in your subject summary.

Be aware that place does not mean just political or administrative place, such as France, New York or Lancashire; it also includes physiographic regions, climatic zones and other sorts of spatial concepts (mountains, temperate regions, north and so on). Similarly, time covers broad chronological terms (mediaeval, renaissance), specific dates (1920s, 9/11) and other temporal concepts (post-war, nocturnal).

Examples

```
A study of hospital waiting lists in Cardiff, 1953-1954
: a report prepared for the Board of Governors of the
United Cardiff Hospitals / Fred Grundy, Robert Arthur
Naunton Hitchens, Ernest Lewis-Faning. - [Cardiff, 1957]
```

Concepts: hospitals
            waiting lists
            Cardiff
            1953/1954


```
The trombone in the Middle Ages and the Renaissance /
G.B. Lane. - Bloomington : Indiana University Press, 1982
```

Concepts: trombone
            Middle Ages
            Renaissance

Form

Another type of term which is very common relates to the form of presentation of the book or document. Form is not really a part of the subject of a book, but it can be a useful thing for the reader to be aware of, and most schemes make provision for expressing form. Form comes in two varieties:

- the physical format of the document: book, video, three-dimensional object, digital object, website, etc.

- the form in which the information is presented: encyclopaedia, bibliography, table, conference paper, textbook, etc.

These are sometimes referred to as 'outer form' for the first group and 'inner form' for the second. In some classification schemes inner form can be extended to include the language in which the document is written.

Examples

```
Third International Hedgehog Workshop of the European
Hedgehog Research Group 29-30 January 1999 / edited by
Nigel Reeve. - London : Roehampton Institute London, 1999
```

Concepts: hedgehogs
               conference proceedings

```
Six-language dictionary of plastics and rubber technology
: a comprehensive dictionary in English, German, French,
Italian, Spanish and Dutch / compiled by A.F. Dorian. -
London : Iliffe, [1965]
```

Concepts: plastics
               rubber
               technology
               dictionary
               polyglot

Note that a document could have both forms of presentation at once, for example a digital encyclopaedia or an online bibliography.

Persons

The example of *Ale, beer and brewsters* includes a 'persons' concept – that of 'women'. Persons are another frequently occurring idea, and their types can range across gender, age, ethnicity, nationality and other diverse characteristics.

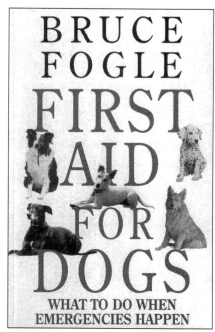

Figure 8.9 *Etiquette for men*   **Figure 8.10** *First aid for dogs*

Example

> Smoking among secondary school children in 1996 :
> Scotland : an enquiry carried out by Social Survey
> Division of ONS on behalf of the Scottish Office
> Department of Health / Jeremy Barton and Lindsey Jarvis.
> - London : Stationery Office, 1997

Concepts: smoking
             schoolchildren
             Scotland
             1996

A modification of the person as part of the subject is the idea of the person for whom the book is intended. Women and children are the most frequently encountered 'audiences', with titles of the type *Motor maintenance for women*, and *Chess for children* being relatively common. Figure 8.9, *Etiquette for men*, is a nice example of a book more unusually aimed specifically at men, although Figure 8. 10, *First aid for dogs*, might not be a valid example of a book for a target audience.

Ordering the subject string

When compiling the subject description it's a good idea to get into the habit of thinking about the order of concepts – remember the idea of citation order discussed in Chapter 3. Try to place the most important concepts first (or what you think are the most important concepts). In other words you should try to introduce some sense of the best citation order for the subject. You won't always be able to carry this through, because the classification scheme which you're applying may not allow you to do exactly what you want, but in some systems there are alternative treatments available, and you need to think about how the subject is structured.

Summary: checklist for making the subject string
- Identify the main class.
- Write down the important subject terms – remember to think about what users might be searching for.
- Are there any place or time concepts?
- Are there any concepts relating to persons?
- Is the document in any particular form?
- Is it intended for a particular audience?
- Put the concepts into order with the most significant first.

Now you should be able to begin to create document descriptions for yourself, and the following exercise is provided for practice.

Exercise 8.3

Create subject strings for the following titles, remembering to indicate the general subject area:

1   *Archaeology in the lowland American tropics*
2   *Black American short story in the 20th century: a collection of critical essays*
3   *Colour atlas of AIDS in the tropics*
4   *Images in ivory: precious objects of the Gothic Age*
5   *Ivory carvings in early medieval England*
6   *Sexual life of the Belgians 1950–1978 [Video recording of a BBC2 programme – in Flemish with English subtitles]*
7   *Web of adaptation: bird studies in the American tropics*
8   *Women who made the news: female journalists in Canada, 1880–1945.*

Answers to exercises

Remember the first law of classification – that there are no 'right answers'. The following are suggested answers to the exercises, and are meant to provide guidance. If you have a different answer but understand how you arrived at it, and have good reasons for your decision, you can count that as correct.

Exercise 8.1

1   Archaeology
2   Music
3   Medicine
4   Botany
5   Art
6   Sociology
7   Horticulture
8   Journalism

Exercise 8.2

1   Geography, education
2   Science, religion, philosophy
3   Politics, agriculture
4   Classics, performing arts
5   Religion, Dutch history
6   Medicine, employment
7   Sociology, psychology
8   Science, media studies
9   Law, journalism

Exercise 8.3

1   Archaeology: America   lowlands   tropics
2   Literature: short stories   20th century   America black essays
3   Medicine: AIDS   tropics   atlas
4   Art: ivories   Gothic   period
5   Art: carvings   ivory   England   medieval period
6   Sociology: sexual behaviour   Belgium   1950/1978   video
     Flemish/English
7   Zoology: birds   America   tropics
8   Journalism: Canada   1880/1945   women

9 Content analysis 2: practical constraints

In the last chapter we looked at how to make a document analysis on an objective basis, identifying all the likely sought terms and arranging them in an 'ideal' order.

In the real world two things will cause you to make some modifications to your ideal statement of content:

- the operating rules of the classification you're using
- the needs of the users as reflected in the library's own practices.

The first of these will be covered in the chapters on how to apply particular classifications. In this chapter we shall look at how to modify your objective statements to meet local requirements.

Broad and close classification

The problem of how exactly books need to be arranged is an old and thorny one. Librarians have usually decided to make precise classmarks for their books, whereas booksellers make broader groupings. The philosophy underpinning this is doubtless that the bookseller wishes the customer to browse, and to look at as many books as possible. Librarians, on the other hand, want readers to find the book most closely related to their information needs.

When the retrieval function is more important than browsing, documents must be given classmarks that reflect as nearly as possible their subjects. We call this **close classification**.

In the UK in the 1980s, a fashion arose for much less precise classification, the remains of which practice can be seen in many public libraries today. Instead of applying a conventional classification such as DDC, books were allocated to a category such as travel, sport or hobbies. Such a system was known as **categorization** or **reader interest classification**. The case for such schemes was founded on users' alleged lack of understanding of traditional classification (which is probably true), but savings in time and money undoubtedly played a part. A balance was being struck between the effort expended in cataloguing books and the perceived lack of need for this at the consumer end.

This is an extreme example of the conflict between broad and close classification, between browsing and retrieval, but many libraries nowadays will give some consideration to how much time they spend on creating records and whether the work involved is really necessary. Traditionally, library classification has been of the close variety, and many libraries operate a **rule of ten** policy, which requires that if more than ten books are located at the same class number, some means of further dividing them must be found. The inverse of this rule often leads to broad classification in a subject area where the library has few books, even if the books themselves have quite specific subject content. For example, if a library has only twenty books on mathematics, they will be given the general classmark for mathematics, even if the individual books are about differential calculus or binomial theorem or algebraic groups.

Dewey himself advised against this sort of practice, on the grounds that if a book is initially given the correct classmark for its subject you will never have to reclassify it. Certainly, if you adopt the broad option and your collection grows you will have to do your subject cataloguing again. My own objections are based on the searching behaviour of users. Most readers will search for what they want fairly precisely. Someone who wants a book on parrots will use 'parrots' as a search term, rather than 'birds'. They will miss the book on parrots that you have classified as a book on birds, unless they decide to browse the entire bird collection.

Nevertheless, there are some advantages to broad classification. It can save time, it avoids the problem of sorting out unfamiliar subjects, and, from the users' point of view, shorter classmarks can be easier to understand and to locate.

Specificity and exhaustivity

There are two properties of subject description that can be varied in order to make classification broader or closer. These are called **specificity** and **exhaustivity**.

Specificity

The specificity of subject description refers to the precision with which you place a subject in the hierarchy. If you classify a book at a more general class than it really warrants, then your classification lacks specificity. Look at Figure 9.1, *Inside out: a brief history of underwear*. What do you think is the main subject of this book? If you think it is 'underwear', your answer is specific; if you want to put it in the class for 'clothing' or 'costume', your answer is unspecific.

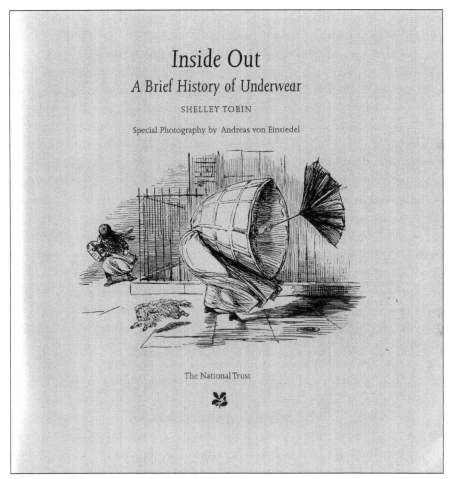

Figure 9.1   *Inside out: a brief history of underwear*

The usual departure from specificity is when the classifier makes the classification broader, or less specific, than the subject of the book, but sometimes a misleading title can cause you to choose too specific a class. Look

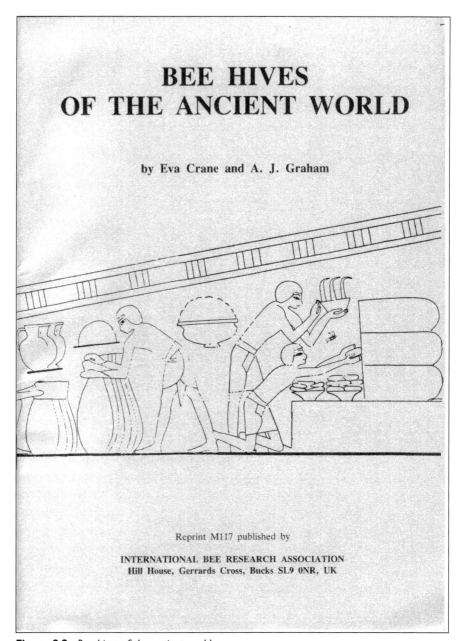

Figure 9.2   *Bee hives of the ancient world*

at Figure 9.2, *Bee hives of the ancient world*: the text of the introduction suggests that this is a book about bee-keeping generally, as well as the hives themselves, and that to classify it as 'beehives' is too specific.

Remember that hierarchies are not just restricted to entities; you can have hierarchies of actions and processes as well as places and times.

Exercise 9.1

Suggest (i) less specific, and (ii) more specific, terms for the following subjects:

- beer
- Bible
- dance
- 11th century
- ethics
- gemstones
- houses

- knitting
- marsupials
- roses
- Scotland
- seashore
- socks
- spoons

Sometimes broadening of the classification will be a deliberate decision; at other times the classification will drive the specificity.

Examples

```
Fun with land hermit crabs : a guide to their well-being
& general care / Daniele Scermino. - St. Petersburg,
Fla. : Palmetto Pub. Co., [1978]


Wife battering : a systems theory approach / Jean Giles-
Sims. - New York : Guilford Press, 1983
```

If you were trying to classify the first example using UDC you would be unable to select a number specifically for land hermit crabs, and would need to put it at the more general class 595.384.8 Anomura.

Similarly, the second title here is classified by LCC at HV6626, the class for Domestic violence, and you're not able to specify who is the victim of the violence.

Exhaustivity

While specificity in indexing refers to the exactness with which you place the main subject, exhaustivity deals with the extent to which the various parts of a compound subject are acknowledged. In making subject analyses we were careful to identify all the aspects of a document which might be searched for, whether these were the main topic, secondary topics, or concepts of place, time, persons, form, and so on.

Classification or indexing is said to be **exhaustive** when this process is translated into the final classmark.

Examples

```
The beast in the boudoir: pet keeping in nineteenth-
century Paris / Kathleen Kete. - Berkeley ; London :
University of California Press, 1994

The dictionary of picture postcards in Britain 1894-1939
/ A.W. Coysh. - Woodbridge : Antique Collectors' Club,
1984
```

Exhaustive subject strings for these books would look something like:

pets – care – Paris – 19th century
postcards – Britain – 1894/1937 – dictionary

The final classmarks would only be exhaustive if the classification used was able to denote the time, place and form elements of these titles.

Exercise 9.2

Construct exhaustive strings for the following titles:

1 *Jewish schools in Poland, 1919–39*
2 *Race, place and medicine: the idea of the tropics in nineteenth-century Brazilian medicine*
3 *Dictionary of proverbs in England in the sixteenth and seventeenth centuries*
4 *South African merchant ships: an illustrated recent history of coasters, colliers, containerships, tugs and other vessels*
5 *Vasantotsava: the spring festivals of India: texts and traditions*
6 *Marsupials in New Zealand: 1st Symposium*
7 *Pathological evidence in newborn children from the sixteenth century in Huelva (Spain)*
8 *Wooden churches of the Carpathians.*

The properties of specificity and exhaustivity operate side by side, so a description can be specific, but not exhaustive, and vice versa.

Example

```
Cultivated plants of Southern Africa : botanical names,
common names, origins, literature / H.F. Glen. –
Johannesburg, South Africa : Jacana in association with
the National Botanical Institute, 2002
```

A description of this book that is specific, but not exhaustive might be:

cultivated plants

Exhaustive but non-specific could be:

plants – Africa

Both exhaustive and specific indexing would require:

cultivated plants – South Africa

Just as the specificity of subject description is affected by the level of detail available in the classification, exhaustivity depends on the operating rules of the classification. If there are no facilities for compounding, or no auxiliary schedules, classification can't be exhaustive, whatever the classifier would like to do in theory. As a general rule you should aim to be as specific and exhaustive as the classification will allow.

Exercise 9.3

Indicate whether the following descriptions are specific and/or exhaustive:

1   *Beekeeping in rural development: unexploited beekeeping potential in the tropics with particular reference to the Commonwealth*
    Beekeeping – Commonwealth
2   *Astronomically speaking: a dictionary of quotations on astronomy and physics*
    Science – quotations - dictionary

Continued on next page

Exercise 9.3 *Continued*

3   *Web of adaptation: bird studies in the American tropics*
    Zoology – Americas
4   *Encyclopaedia of the umbelliferae (carrot/parsley) family of the British Isles*
    Umbelliferae – British Isles – encyclopedia

Summary
* Classification can be broad or close.
* Broad classification is adequate for browsing purposes.
* Retrieval requires close classification in order to be successful.
* Close classification has two factors: specificity and exhaustivity.
* Specificity means the exactness with which a subject is located in the hierarchy.
* Exhaustivity means the identification of all the parts of a compound subject.
* Both specificity and exhaustivity may be affected by the classification scheme used.

Some difficult subjects

The matter of specificity and exhaustivity in indexing leads us into an area of difficult content analysis. This is the problem of how we deal with subjects that constitute a class of one, and it is best exemplified by biography.

The location of biography is often the subject of debate. A strict subject content approach to classification demands that we always put a biography with the subject field of the 'biographee'. Thus a biography of Mozart goes in the music class, one of Nietzsche in philosophy, one of Marilyn Monroe in cinema, and so on. There are several arguments against this position. Firstly, a life of Marilyn Monroe may tell us more about 20th-century American history than about cinema. Advocates of this view consider biography as a sub-discipline of history, and a class in its own right. They would be supported by the army of readers who enjoy biography as a genre, regardless of the subject of the biography.

Another compelling objection to the 'subject' approach arises when the 'life' cannot be easily allocated to a single sphere of activity.

Example

```
Leonardo da Vinci / D.M. Field. - Rochester : Grange
Books, 2002
```

Where shall we put Leonardo? Undoubtedly, he's an important painter, but he is also an architect, sculptor, inventor, writer and scientist. Much of the literature about him focuses on only one of these aspects, and although he might be best known as an artist, one would not want to put books about his scientific writings in the art section.

Nor is he alone in this. Let's look at the case of Francis Bacon, Baron Verulam, Viscount St Albans, and Lord Chancellor of England under Elizabeth I.

Example

```
Sir Francis Bacon: a biography / Jean Overton Fuller. -
Rev ed. - Maidstone : George Mann, 1994

Subject headings:
Bacon, Francis, 1561-1626 - Biography
Statesmen - Great Britain - Biography
Philosophers - Great Britain - Biography
Great Britain - History - Elizabeth, 1558-1603
Great Britain - History - Early Stuarts, 1603-1649

LCC Classmark: DA358.B3 F84 1994
DDC Classmark: 192
```

The subject headings for this record on the Library of Congress catalogue include 'Statesmen' and 'Philosophers', and Bacon is also known as a literary essayist and scientific theorist. The classmarks on the Library of Congress record put Bacon with philosophers in DDC, but under the Elizabethan period in English history in LCC.

This latter classification raises another problem. The LCC classmark here conveys nothing about philosophy, science, belles-lettres or politics, but it does introduce the concepts of 'England' and '16th century' to describe Bacon. We thus have the problem not only of the general subject area, but also of what other characteristics are necessary to define the subject of the biography. The Library of Congress classification of this book has used 16th century and England; using a different system would we need to add 'male' or 'aristocracy' to these?

Unfortunately, the classification doesn't always help us in this respect. As with the question of broadness of classification, this sort of classificatory problem often has to be decided by a local policy. In a general library the problem is most evident in respect of artists and writers, and there are various solutions to the problem:

- subordinate the person to a sub-class defined by properties of, for instance, time, place, genre, and so on; in this case a book about Renoir would be classed as 'painting – France – 19th century'
- maintain a single alphabetical sequence of persons near the beginning of the main class
- place all studies of persons in a separate biography class.

The first option is probably the most helpful to serious students of art or literature but it raises the question of where one stops. Do we want also to say that Renoir is an impressionist? This would improve the grouping within the class, but could cause difficulties where an artist doesn't clearly belong to a particular movement. Schemes that give rules for this generally use two or three properties to define an individual, and where greater freedom is allowed in creating numbers (as, for example, with UDC), the classifier is best advised to keep to a similar, fairly simple and workable arrangement. It goes without saying that locally made decisions of this kind must be recorded and adhered to consistently.

The problem of what we do about biographical and critical material (usually known as secondary sources) is connected to where we place primary materials (the works *by* the individual, rather than works *about* him or her). Having a separate biographical sequence, whether in the subject class or in a biography class, will necessarily divide the two, and this may not be the most helpful arrangement.

A related problem occurs in respect of individuals whose lives spanned more than one century, or who were born in one country, but worked in another. Here the only sensible procedure is to make an arbitrary rule (use the date of birth, for example), and stick to it. It may not produce perfect linear order, but the basis of arrangement is clear, and the user can always be sure where a work will be found.

Example

```
The life of Christina the astonishing / by Thomas de
Cantimpré ; translated, with introduction and notes, by
Margot H. King ; assisted by David Wiljer. - 2nd ed. -
Toronto : Peregrina, 1999
```

To deal with this book we need to know that Christina was a Belgian saint, who lived from 1150 to 1224. We can describe the subject as:

Christianity – Saints – female – Belgium

but there is some doubt as to whether we use 12th or 13th century as the period concept. Either will do: what matters is that we choose either the date of birth or the date of death and apply it consistently to all biographical works. Similar doubts about nationality should be resolved in the same way, although in this case the country of birth is less open to debate than the country of major residence or most important work.

Other examples of 'individuals' as classes

The 'class-with-one-member' is not restricted to persons in the creative arts. It occurs whenever you encounter a 'one-off' phenomenon. Other obvious examples of such unique individuals include created works, historical events and geographical locations. Unless your classification contains named classes for these things you will need to work out where they belong; even if there is no need to create the classmark yourself, you will need to make a concept analysis to identify the correct class.

Just as the person in biography possesses all sorts of attributes, works of art, events and places may be defined by a number of different properties. Again a choice must be made as to how many, and which, characteristics should be used in subject description. And, as with books about people, books about these other unique entities probably give no clue as to their relevant properties in the title. You, as the classifier, must create the conceptual analysis yourself, on the basis of your knowledge of the subject, rather than by looking for clues in the title. This is one area where you may need to make use of reference sources to establish the dates or location or other details of your subject.

Example

```
The song of Hiawatha / by Henry Wadsworth Longfellow;
edited by Daniel Aaron. - London : J.M. Dent, 1993
```

In order to classify *The song of Hiawatha* we must decide how we're going to describe it. Since it is a work of literature, the most common concepts used are language, period and form. We'll therefore need to know where (United States) and when (1855) *Hiawatha* was written, and what form it takes (an epic poem). This would give a string for *Hiawatha* of:

American (literature) – 19th century – poetry

Although *Hiawatha* is in English it is usual to distinguish between the literatures of different English-speaking countries, so here we use 'American' as the concept. (This also applies to other comparable situations: e.g. you shouldn't regard French Canadian literature as French literature, but rather Canadian literature.)

As in the case of biography, it's not necessary to overburden the document description with concepts. The three above are enough for most purposes. In a poetry collection it might be useful to add 'epic', but there's not much of a case to be made for adding anything about the subject of Native Americans.

Exercise 9.4

Create subject strings for the following titles:

1 *Rembrandt: his life, work and times*
2 *Frank Lloyd Wright, architect*
3 *Mozart: a documentary biography*
4 *Browning: 'Men and women' and other poems*
5 *The winter's tale: critical essays*
6 *Remembrance of things past*
7 *The Divine Comedy of Dante Alighieri*
8 *The Battle of Hastings: sources and interpretations*
9 *The Boston Tea-Party*
10 *Mount Everest*
11 *The Great Wall of China*
12 *Aristotle's Ethics*

Having located our subjects in a class on the basis of some of their characteristics, it's common practice then to arrange individuals using alphabetical order. For example, in number 4 above, Browning will probably not be the only 19th-century English poet in the collection, but he is more easily distinguished from the others alphabetically than by introducing other subject criteria.

Summary
- Individuals of all kinds present difficulties in classification.
- The problem is to decide how many attributes need to be considered in defining them.
- Attempting very close classification does not always work well.
- Simple rules applied consistently ensure clarity and predictability.

Answers to exercises
Exercise 9.1
Remember that these are only suggestions; you might have equally good but different answers. Only worry if you can't see why these suggestions are suitable.

	Less specific	More specific
beer	alcoholic drinks	bitter, stout, lager
Bible	sacred books	Genesis, Psalms, Gospels
dance	performing arts	ballet, ballroom dancing, tap dancing
11th century	Middle Ages	1066
ethics	philosophy	business ethics, sexual ethics
gemstones	minerals	diamonds, emeralds, rubies
houses	buildings	cottages, bungalows, manor houses
knitting	needlework	Fair Isle knitting, machine knitting
marsupials	animals	kangaroos, wombats, koalas
roses	flowers	dog roses, ramblers, Peace

Scotland	United Kingdom	Edinburgh, the Cairngorms, Loch Ness
seashore	coast	rock pools, cliffs, beaches
socks	clothing	football socks
spoons	cutlery, utensils	teaspoons, wooden spoons

Exercise 9.2

1 schools – Jewish – Poland – 1919-1939
2 medicine – Brazil – tropics – 19th century
3 proverbs – England – 16th/17th centuries – dictionary
4 merchant ships – South Africa – history – illustrations
5 festivals – spring – India – texts
6 marsupials – New Zealand – conference
7 medicine – pathology – children – newborn – Spain – 16th century
8 churches – wooden – Carpathia

Exercise 9.3

1 This is specific (beekeeping, Commonwealth), but not exhaustive (no tropics).
2 This is exhaustive (science, quotations, dictionary), but not specific (science rather than astronomy and physics).
3 This is neither specific (zoology rather than birds) nor exhaustive (no tropics).
4 This is both specific and exhaustive.

Exercise 9.4

1 painting – Netherlands – 17th century
2 architecture – United States – 20th century
3 music – Austria – 18th century
4 literature – English – poetry – 19th century
5 literature – English – drama – 17th century – essays
6 literature – French – novel – 20th century
7 literature – Italian – poetry – 14th century
8 history – England – 11th century – battles
9 history – United States – 18th century – riots
10 geography – Nepal – mountains
11 geography – China – man-made structures
12 philosophy – Greek – 4th century BCE

10 Controlled indexing languages

So far we've looked at why we need to organize documents, at some of the fundamental problems in the process of organization and at how to decide on the subjects of documents. In the next part of the book we shall look at the tools which we need to bring those two operations together in the formal processes of classification and subject cataloguing.

Natural language indexing and searching

Indexing, classifying and the subject description of documents are on the whole very labour-intensive (and intellectually arduous) processes. This is one of the reasons why abstracting and indexing services, and bibliographic databases, are so very expensive to subscribe to. An obvious question is whether we really need to use complicated artificial systems of classification and indexing to describe documents. Why not use the language of our everyday speech, since surely this would make the assignment of the keywords much quicker and easier? And the titles of documents or the text itself could provide us with the terms that are needed for indexing. In any event, whatever cataloguers do, the end-users will choose search terms out of their own heads, and not from a classification scheme which they have never seen or heard of.

On the face of it, it would appear to be much easier to use this **natural language** approach to index documents, both for the initial indexing, and also for the retrieval process, particularly where machines can help with the process. When automation began to be used more widely in libraries in the 1970s it was generally thought that the immense power of the computer to scan the whole of a large store of information in a few seconds would obviate the need for all this expensive and exhausting brain work. Free-text searching and natural language indexing became the norm, classification and indexing were seen as moribund and pointless, and the study of classification disappeared from many library school curricula during the 1970s and 1980s.

Initially, the advent of the world wide web reinforced this attitude, since even the information illiterate can search and retrieve masses of information using only natural language. On the other hand, any acquaintance with web searching will have shown you how inefficient natural language searching can be, because the web is an information store so large that the juggernaut techniques of the early automated systems cannot solve the problems that searchers encounter. Masses of information may be retrieved, but most of it will be irrelevant to the task in hand, and it's usually impossibly difficult for the novice searcher to construct a search which will produce a manageable number of appropriate items. This happens at least in part because of the considerable difficulties attached to the use of words: wherever natural language is employed we have to contend with a variety of problems.

There are of course some real advantages in the use of natural language: it's quick and easy for the cataloguer, and intuitive for the user. Nobody has to learn cataloguing rules, or how the system works, and indexing can be carried out by untrained staff; in some cases authors can provide their own keywords. One school of thought maintains that language derived from the literature itself is more accurate, representative of the subject, and up-to-date than that of classifications and other subject tools. New terms and ideas are added to the language as they appear in the documentation, and as terms become obsolete they naturally disappear from use; such language needs no costly maintenance regime, and it is free to the user. (This of course is the basis of the vocabulary used by search engines, where search terms are harvested from the 'documents' themselves.)

Nevertheless, the disadvantages of natural language are also very considerable, and we'll look at some of them in detail here and in the next chapter – differences in how people understand the meaning of words, variation in the use of a word in different contexts, problems of synonymy and homography, and of course different orthographic (spelling) systems. Added to this is the problem of how we deal with indexing and retrieval across different natural languages. All of these difficult aspects of words, their vagueness and imprecision, affect indexing, and more particularly they affect searching.

What words mean

A major initial difficulty in subject description is in the area of meaning and definition of words – what a colleague of mine once called the 'slipperiness' of words. We can never be entirely sure that what you and I mean by a word is the same thing, and this uncertainty is multiplied when we cross national boundaries and the barriers of culture and language; even schools of thought within disciplines can use terminology in different ways. The following very simple example (Figure 10.1) illustrates this neatly: a colleague received a letter one morning, and, as is commonly the case, it had been stamped with a public service logo alongside the postmark. The logo looked like this:

Figure 10.1 *'Your Reading – keep it clean'*

When you know that the letter was posted in Reading in Berkshire, the message takes on an entirely different meaning.

This problem of understanding what words mean is a very considerable one. We're all familiar with variations in the meanings of words in British and American English: terms such as gas, hood, subway or soda indicate quite different things on either side of the Atlantic. In the UK a gas-driven car (not automobile) is quite distinct from one with a petrol engine, and no one would want to put an American soda in his Scotch whisky.

The following example of classes in the Dewey Decimal Classification shows how some terms relate to quite separate notions in the US and UK sectors.

373.222   Private secondary schools (Preparatory schools)
373.224   Public secondary schools

In the UK, of course, a preparatory school is an independent (or private) *primary* school, whereas a public secondary school is called a state school, or comprehensive school, because a public school is outside the public or state sector. Differences in understanding of this kind are quite common in different societies and cultures.

Synonyms

Words which have more or less the same meaning create one of the thorniest problems in indexing and searching. In a language such as English, which is rich in synonyms, the potential for confusion is very great. The *Oxford thesaurus* lists 79 synonyms for the common word 'group', 8 synonyms for the more esoteric 'hallucination' and 6 for the apparently specific 'photograph'.

When a concept has a variety of labels attached to it the classifier has difficulty in knowing which one to choose in describing a document, and the searcher has a corresponding problem in knowing which one to select for searching. The chance that they will both opt for the same term seems remote.

Homonyms

Homonyms present us with the reverse problem: words which look the same but have different meanings. Figure 10.1 shows a nice example of a word with two quite distinct meanings, but it is by no means unusual. Whereas the synonym causes us to miss relevant documents in searching, the homonym causes us to retrieve irrelevant ones.

Useful words

In addition to the problem of having too many words, or the wrong words, classifiers also have to think about whether the words they use are *useful* terms; that is, they need to be terms that searchers will use when they are trying to find material on a topic.

One of the earliest books on indexing, *Making an index* by Henry B. Wheatley, gives some splendid instances of the bad indexer at work. These examples from an index to the periodical *The Freemason* illustrate well the art of poor indexing:

An oration delivered
Another Masonic manuscript

Interesting extract from an old Masonian letter
Our portrait gallery
Recent festival

Other examples of quite useless entries are taken from the index to *Longman's Magazine* of October 1901:

According to the code
Some eighteenth century children's books

And finally, the last of this entertaining trio as cited by Miss Hetherington in her article 'The indexing of periodicals' in *Index to the periodical literature of the world* for 1892:

Creek in Demerara, Up a
Demerara, Up a creek in
Up a creek in Demerara

And all no doubt without a paddle!

Words such as 'an', 'another', 'our', 'according' and 'up' are not words that the searcher will look for – they are not **sought terms**. Although they will appear in the text of documents they don't tell us much about the content of documents, so indexers don't normally use articles, conjunctions or prepositions because they are not significant words. Adjectives and adverbs are not much favoured either, unless they form part of a phrase (such as 'rapid transit systems' or 'green politics'). Instead we use nouns and noun forms of verbs ('management', 'co-operation'), because these are the words that searchers will look for.

It seems then that if we leave the classifier or indexer to use natural language, there are far too many words to choose from, many of which have the same meaning, or share the same form, or are not words that anyone would look for. Using natural language makes efficient finding really very difficult. It would be much easier if we could limit the number of choices open to the classifier. It would be sensible to use instead what we call a 'controlled language' or **controlled indexing language**.

Controlled indexing language

This is a system for indexing or classifying documents that gets round some of the problems of natural language indexing. Common sorts of controlled indexing languages include thesauri and subject heading lists, as well as classification schemes. Rather than using the whole range of words in English or any other natural language, the controlled indexing language restricts the number of terms that the indexer can choose from. It does this by the following means:

- It cuts out synonyms and gives the indexer a single term for each concept.
- It excludes useless words that no one will look for.
- It helps to make sure that everybody uses the same words for the same ideas.

I've used words like 'idea' and 'concept' because it is often more helpful in classifying to think in those terms rather than in terms of 'words'. Words, as we've seen, can be treacherous, and it can be better to list concepts, and choose a single word to represent each concept. A classification scheme is one example of a controlled indexing language, and one which makes this conceptual approach central. Because the classification scheme arranges 'concepts' in a systematic structure, rather than words in an alphabetical list, it gets round most of the word-related problems. It also does two other useful things:

- It puts structure in the vocabulary to help the indexer choose.
- It uses codes to facilitate exchange across languages.

The structure of the classification acts as a map of the subject for the classifier. When classifiers look at a schedule they can see how the subject is broken down into classes; they can see the context of the class they've chosen, where it belongs in the overall scheme of things; they can see more general classes, and more specific classes on the page in front of them; and they can revise their thoughts about the subject in the light of what they see. In the next few chapters we'll look at the structure of classifications, and how this process of searching the structure is carried out, in much more detail.

The use of notational codes to represent classes is also very important since, to some extent, it allows us to dispense with words altogether. Because we work with notations we can put a great number of words into the class description to explain the scope and meaning of the class, since those words don't have to be attached to the document itself. The same is true of class descriptions which wouldn't make very good indexing terms, such as this one from UDC:

> **636.96**   **Various small land mammals. Including: Hedgehog. Ferret. Mongoose.** Except those at 636.91/.93, and primates.

Because we're always going to use 636.96 to represent this class, the verbal description can be as unwieldy as we like.

The use of notation has an additional advantage in an international environment since the codes can be used to represent subjects independently of natural languages. It really doesn't matter if you or I call that furry animal with the long ears *rabbit, lapin, Kaninchen, coniglio, conejo, usagi* or *krolik*, if we're agreed that it can be represented by 636.92. Classified documents can be searched for and retrieved irrespective of the language of the document, or the language of the indexer, since the codes are language independent. In this sense a classification is truly a language since it permits communication and the exchange of information.

Standards for document description

One final advantage of using a controlled indexing language is that it improves consistency on a very large scale. Limiting the use of synonyms and giving rules for describing documents undoubtedly makes searching and finding much better within the library or document centre, but there is a much broader dimension to this. In these days of web-enabled OPACs and of shared cataloguing there are real management and financial benefits in using standardized systems, rather than operating home-made or in-house regimes.

When trying to describe the subjects of documents, on the whole it's better if we impose some rules and restrictions on the process. There are considerable advantages in using systems with rules and controls, and it's clear today that controlled indexing languages have the edge over natural language indexing, and that even when using word-based systems, some limits and constraints have to come into play.

So far we've considered only the 'vocabulary' part of the indexing language, but indexing languages, like natural languages, also have rules for joining the words together, what is called syntax. The syntax of a classification scheme is one of the most distinctive things about it, and we shall be exploring that aspect of classification in some depth; you'll see that the various schemes are as diverse as natural languages, and their study quite as interesting.

Summary

- The use of natural language in classification and indexing creates some problems for classifiers and searchers.
- Variations in the meanings of words and in different interpretations mean that natural language isn't precise.
- Some words aren't useful or likely to be sought by users.
- Controlled indexing languages limit the number of indexing terms and control the form and type of words used.
- They improve consistency and effectiveness of classification or indexing.
- The use of such standards allows for the sharing of records between different organizations and the exchange of information in different languages.

11 Word-based approaches to retrieval

So far, we have looked at a number of general problems of the subject approach to information in general and to classification more narrowly. We have considered why we need a subject approach, the difficulties of handling and placing complex and compound subjects, how to identify the subject content of a document, and how the view of knowledge has moved from an idea of the unity of knowledge to a view based on the nature and relations of terms in various subjects.

We have assumed that these subject-related matters will be dealt with by using a classification scheme of some sort. That is to say a systematic arrangement that groups like with like, and locates related subjects next to each other. The emphasis is on the use of conceptual **classes**, rather than **terms**, and a notation is used to maintain order. See Figure 11.1.

A classification scheme:

- is systematic in its arrangement
- groups things according to subject content, placing like with like
- uses classes rather than terms
- uses a notation to maintain order.

Figure 11.1 Features of a classification scheme

It's possible, however, to use another approach to the subject management of information, and that is the alphabetical approach, the use of subject heading lists and thesauri.

Subject heading lists

Subject heading lists consist of single words or phrases that can be used to represent the subject content of documents. Instead of a using a notational code from a classification scheme, the subject of the document is described in words. Typical subject headings can be very simple.

Example

Simple subject headings:

Aeronautics
Biology
Birds
Chemistry
Children
Cookery
Football
France
Mermaids
Rabbits
Religion
Spaghetti

Other subject headings may need to be more complicated, to represent the content of more complicated documents.

Example

Compound subject headings:

Brain surgery
Chinese cookery
Cocker spaniels
English literature
Ice hockey
Metal fatigue
Modern art

In some cases, headings may consist of several words, or they may have sub-headings, which give a more structured appearance.

Example

Complex subject headings:

Boats and boating
Books for children
Dogs in literature

First aid for animals
Humorous songs
Zulu radio plays

Structured subject headings with sub-headings:

Bronze Age – Great Britain
Church fund raising – History
Greek language – Etymology
Turkey – Antiquities

Compound headings like this are said to be **pre-coordinated**, just like the pre-coordinated classes in an enumerative classification.

A system of subject headings can't be used as the sole means of subject organization, but has to be used in combination with a classification or other shelf-ordering scheme. Although there isn't any theoretical reason why subject headings could not be placed on the spines of books, in practice this would be very unwieldy to manage, and probably not very easy for users to understand. Therefore, the subject headings aren't attached to the items themselves but to the catalogue records for those items; they are used to provide a subject index to the catalogue rather then to organize the items in the collection physically. The purpose of subject headings is to improve subject searching of catalogues by providing additional subject information on the catalogue record. They can be particularly useful when the classification is not very detailed or doesn't cater for compound subjects.

In the days before automation, in the UK subject headings would be used to create a separate subject catalogue. In North America it was the practice to combine the subject heading entries with author and title entries to give a single alphabetical sequence known as a **dictionary catalogue**. Now that we have online catalogues, all these different means of entry are necessarily integrated into a single catalogue with many points of access: author, title, subject, publisher and so on. The subject headings enable more sophisticated subject searching than is possible using keywords from the title.

For example, in the following catalogue record, for Harriet Ritvo's *Platypus and the mermaid*, the subject headings reveal that the book is about zoological classifications, natural history and popular culture, rather than about platypuses and mermaids (although these do feature in the book).

Example

```
The platypus and the mermaid, and other figments of the
classifying imagination / Harriet Ritvo. - Cambridge,
Mass. : Harvard University Press, 1997

Subject headings:
Zoology - Great Britain - Classification - History
Natural history - Great Britain - History
Popular culture - Great Britain - History
```

The use of subject headings in the UK has increased dramatically with the spread of automation in libraries, and you can now find them in the majority of academic and special libraries. It is for that reason that we're considering them here, as the classifier is now more likely to encounter Library of Congress Subject Headings than a particular scheme of classification.

Thesauri

Like the subject headings list, the thesaurus is used to improve machine retrieval, but is more commonly used by archivists and documentalists than by librarians. The terms in the thesaurus are much simpler than in most classifications, and are not combined or pre-coordinated in the thesaurus itself. The thesaurus is normally used in a **post-coordinate** way. In other words, the indexer takes the keywords, or descriptors, from the thesaurus, and attaches them to the catalogue record as individual terms; they're not linked or combined in any way, and they don't have notation. They are brought together only during the search process, when the catalogue software attempts to match the terms in the searcher's query with the descriptors on individual records.

Alphabetical arrangement

It might seem that it is much easier to use words as the basis of indexing and searching than notational codes. Words are much more intuitive, are understood by everybody, and are anyway what the end user will start with when conducting a search. Nevertheless, there are some difficulties associated with the alphabetical approach.

Consider the following list:

Animals	Mice
Architecture	Monasteries
Art	Mountaineering
Artichokes	Museums
Buildings	Painting
Bulldogs	Parrots
Carrots	Rats
Cataloguing	Rembrandt
Dogs	Reproduction
Mammals	Rococo
	Rodents

Does anything immediately strike you about the terms in the list? The alphabetical order means that it's quick and easy to locate a specific term, but what about the sort of ordering that we looked at in Chapter 5, and what has happened to the grouping that is an essential part of classification?

Clearly, there are all sorts of relationships between the terms here that aren't expressed in the sequence or display. The alphabetical arrangement disperses or distributes related terms (such as rats, mice and rodents), and juxtaposes completely unrelated topics (such as buildings, bulldogs and carrots).

Consequently you must have some mechanism to enable users to find other terms that might be useful in searching, because these terms aren't grouped together in the way that they are in a classification. In other words in the list of headings you must have a system of cross-references, that lead the searcher from one heading to other related headings.

Exercise 11.1
Suggest some pairs (or sets) of terms in the list above where you think you would need to make cross-references.

These cross-references allow classifiers to navigate the headings list, finding additional terms to those they have initially chosen. The references fall into three basic categories:

- broader term (BT), or a term that is more general in scope
- narrower term (NT), or a term that is more specific
- related term (RT), or a term that is linked in some way other than that of broadness and narrowness.

If you think back to the section on hierarchical relationships (Chapter 5), you will see that the broader and narrower terms correspond to the different levels of the hierarchy. The classifier using broader and narrower terms is effectively 'browsing' the hidden hierarchy of the subject headings list.

If we look at our list of terms again we can identify examples of these different sorts of references.

Example

Reference to a broader term:

Mouse ➜ Rodent
Mammal ➜ Animal

These are referred to as 'upward references' and are usually written in the form:

Mouse
　　BT Rodent

Mammal
　　BT Animal

Example

Reference to a narrower term:

Dog ➜ Bulldog
Rodent ➜ Rat

These are called 'downward references' and are written as:

Dog
　　NT Bulldog

Rodent
　　NT Rat

Related term (RT) is used for terms that are at the same level in the hierarchy, or in the same **array**. These may also be called co-ordinate references:

Rat
  RT Mouse

The other main sort of RT is where the relationship isn't a hierarchical one. These could include an entity and its related activity: for example, 'Songs' and 'Singing', or 'Bicycles' and 'Cycling'. Other pairs of RTs are comparable to the syntactic relationships that we looked at in Chapter 5, and some of those pairs, such as 'Swimming' and 'Pools' or 'Football' and 'Boots', are also RTs. Just as the broader and narrower terms in a subject headings list mirror the hierarchy of the classification, so the related terms correspond to its non-hierarchical or syntactic relationships:

Painting
  RT Rembrandt

Animals
  RT Reproduction

Synonymy and other meaning-related matters

The second major problem of alphabetical systems of subject description occurs when we have several words for the same thing. This is a particular problem in English because of the great size of the word-stock (there are 600,000 words defined in the *Oxford English dictionary*).

Anybody who has tried to search the internet will know of the problems caused by this phenomenon of synonymy. Because a search engine doesn't search conceptually, but looks for matching character strings in the query and in the text to be searched, any and all synonyms must be searched for separately. Similarly, different meanings of the same word cannot be distinguished.

For example, if I want to look for material on 'cats' and use this as a search term, I'll probably retrieve items about the large cats as well as domestic cats. I need to consider whether I would do better using Latin names, but while this might work well for the larger species, it is probably less useful in the case of the pet cat. Texts which use familiar names for the cat, such as 'pussy' or 'moggy', won't be retrieved, nor indeed will the term feline, for which a separate search must be conducted. Other meanings of the word cat (which might cause irrelevant items to be retrieved) include a lash or whip (cat-o'-nine-tails); a spiteful person; a kind of boat; a kind of burglar; a kind of fortification; and, of course, the musical *Cats*.

There's little to be done about these semantic difficulties on the web, but in the controlled environment of the catalogue we can agree on certain rules to make indexing and searching easier. In this area of the meaning of words, an important strategy is to control the synonyms: this is done by selecting one of a set of synonyms, or near synonyms, as the preferred term to be used in indexing. The classifier is told to use only this term, and other synonyms are referred to it.

Example

Chickens	USE	Poultry
Domestic fowl	USE	Poultry
Hens	USE	Poultry

The unused synonyms are gathered under the preferred term in the following manner (where UF stands for 'use for':

Poultry
> UF   Chickens
>
>   Domestic fowl
>
>   Hens

In the situation where two words look exactly the same but have different meanings (homonymy), **qualifiers** (or words denoting context) are placed in brackets after the word.

Example

```
Boxers (Sport)
Boxers (Dogs)

Mules (Animals)
Mules (Footwear)
Mules (Drug carriers)
Mules (Spinning machines)
```

When these rules are imposed on the indexing it makes it much more likely that classifier and searcher will use the same term, and the retrieval rate will be greatly improved as a result.

These different conventions in alphabetical indexing enable us to avoid the worst disadvantages of using words, and they form an important element in what is known as **vocabulary control**. This is one of the important functions of a controlled indexing language. It imparts structure and logic into a subject headings list and increases predictability in retrieval.

A summary of the properties of a word-based system, as opposed to a classification, is shown in Figure 11.2.

The word-based subject tool:

- is alphabetical in its arrangement
- does not display relationships in the linear sequence
- uses words as opposed to concepts
- does not require a notation to maintain order
- requires a system of cross-references to indicate structure.

Figure 11.2 Features of the word-based tool

The form and structure of subject headings

The primary source of principles for managing subject headings is Charles Ammi Cutter's *Rules for a dictionary catalog*, which was published in 1876, the same year as the first edition of Dewey. The Library of Congress Subject Headings are based on Cutter's rules, and they have been very influential on other systems of subject headings.

Cutter's rules were mainly concerned with the form and structure of headings, and some of the more important ones were as follows:

- natural language forms were to be preferred
- established use was the guideline, based on literary warrant and educational consensus
- word order was to be reversed only if the second term was definitely more important, e.g. 'Art, modern' rather than 'Modern art'. (This of course is related to the needs of the card catalogue, with its single linear sequence. The 'most important' term in a compound, i.e. the one that a reader was most likely to search for, must be put in the lead position. This is less important in the days of automated catalogues and keyword searching, and nowadays we prefer to use normal word order.)

Since subject headings tended not to be very specific, it was quite common to use more than one heading for any book. For example:

> 19th-century poetry
> English poetry

rather than

> 19th-century English poetry

Cutter's approach created a subject heading list very similar in style to the enumerative classification, with lots of pre-coordination and some faults in the logical structure of the headings list as a whole. This is because his concern was mainly with the structure of individual headings rather than their interrelations.

Modern developments in alphabetical subject indexing

Since Cutter's time there has been a development in the theory of alphabetical subject indexing comparable to the development of classification theory and the change from enumerative to faceted classifications. At the beginning of the 20th century professional indexers started to look for some better basis to the order of terms than the natural language considerations, or the idea of relative importance of terms that Cutter had used.

Rather than using pre-coordinated headings such as 'Preservation of manuscripts' or 'Rehabilitating juvenile offenders' or 'Oxidation of metals', it was considered more helpful to write 'Manuscripts – Preservation' or 'Juvenile offenders – Rehabilitation' or 'Metals – Oxidation'. This makes the composition of the heading clearer, and in a long list the relations between subjects are more evident than with pre-coordinated headings. This led indexers to look for a pattern in the structure that would help them to create logical and predictable headings. All the above examples conform to a pattern of Object – Action. At the beginning of the 20th century, an American indexer called J. Kaiser noticed that these object and action combinations were very frequent. He named the categories 'concretes' and 'processes', and suggested that concretes should always precede processes in the heading – an application of the idea of citation order to subject headings. He identified 'place' as a third common and significant category, also to be placed third in the citation order.

Later in the century librarians such as Eric Coates and Derek Austin would build on the theories of Kaiser, and on Ranganathan's facet analytical theory to create alphabetical indexing systems for the *British Technology*

Index and *British National Bibliography*, which used up to 16 different categories in indexing.

We don't need to consider any of these systems in detail, but I include them to demonstrate the parallel application of categorical analysis to alphabetical subject headings as well as to faceted classification schemes. The same sorts of principles are equally applicable to the handling of words in alphabetical schemes as to the handling of concepts in systematic structures. The idea of citation order is also implicit in the ordering of terms in subject headings.

The purpose of all this is to ensure predictability, which is the essence of retrieval. The builders of schemes may never find a perfect solution to your problems, but they can attempt to provide a reliable and predictable mechanism which is structurally coherent and which will function efficiently.

Summary
- Alphabetical tools such as subject heading lists and thesauri provide an alternative to the classification scheme.
- Subject headings can't be used for physical arrangement but are added to catalogue records.
- Subject heading lists need good cross-referencing to help the classifier find suitable headings.
- Broader, narrower and related headings are usually provided.
- Vocabulary control deals with synonyms and other word-related problems.
- It helps to make the subject headings more effective.
- The form and structure of early subject headings were influenced by Cutter's *Rules for a Dictionary Catalog*.
- Modern developments in subject indexing correspond to the changes in classification theory, particularly that of facet analysis.

Answers to exercises
Exercise 11.1

These are some suggested answers to the exercise. You can see that even within this short list of terms there are lots of potential references to be made, and you can probably imagine the scale of cross-referencing within a large set of subject headings. Note that reverse references are also made from the second term to the first: these are called reciprocal references, and they make sure that a user can navigate the collection in all directions.

Animals
→ Bulldogs
  Dogs
  Mammals
  Mice
  Parrots
  Rats
  Reproduction
  Rodents
Architecture
→ Art
  Buildings
  Monasteries
  Museums
  Rococo
Art
→ Architecture
  Museums
  Painting
  Rembrandt
  Reproduction
Buildings
→ Architecture
  Monasteries
  Museums

Dogs
→ Animals
  Bulldogs
  Mammals
Mammals
→ Animals
  Bulldogs
  Dogs
  Mice
  Rats
  Reproduction
  Rodents
Mice
→ Animals
  Mammals
  Rats
  Rodents
Painting
→ Art
  Museums
  Rembrandt
  Reproduction
  Rats
→ Animals
  Mammals
  Mice
  Rodents

12 Library of Congress Subject Headings 1: basic headings

In the last chapter on alphabetical subject access we looked at some of the general considerations of alphabetical subject work and the problems (and their solutions) that arise when we use words as the basis of retrieval. While it's perfectly possible to develop an in-house subject indexing system based on the concept analyses for individual documents, the intellectual effort involved and the high cost of maintenance required mean that most libraries opt to use a published standard. In the vast majority of cases that standard will be the Library of Congress Subject Headings. During the last twenty years of the 20th century many academic libraries in the UK began to use LCSH, even if they were not using the Library of Congress Classification. This is in addition to its long-established use in the United States and Canada. The only other set of general subject headings in common use is Sears' *List of subject headings for a small library*, which, as the name suggests, is much less extensive than LCSH.

What is LCSH?
LCSH is an alphabetical list of the headings that are used in the subject catalogues of the Library of Congress, together with 'thesaural' cross-references that enable classifiers to find other appropriate headings. A typical section of LCSH looks something like this:

Umbrellas (May Subd Geog)
> UF   Bumbershoots
>   Umbrellas and parasols [Former Heading]
> BT   Weather protection — Equipment and supplies
> NT   Parasols

Umbrellas and parasols
> USE   Parasols
>   Umbrellas

NT   Umbrella industry

Umbrellas and parasols in art
    USE   Parasols in art
            Umbrellas in art

Umbrellas in art (Not Subd Geog)
    UF   Umbrellas and parasols in art [Former Heading]

Umbrellas– –Tariff
    USE   Tariff on umbrellas

When we come to the section on practical application of LCSH we'll look in detail at the layout, and at what the different cross-references and typographical variations mean, so you don't need to worry about these at this stage.

LCSH is a controlled indexing language, which means there are strict rules for the way in which headings can be used. It's also a standard, which implies that all its users should conform to those rules so that LCSH is consistently applied in all the libraries that use it. This means that searches can be carried out on more than one catalogue (or in merged catalogues) and get comparable results for the same query. It also means that individual libraries shouldn't change the headings or interpret them to meet local needs, although undoubtedly this does happen quite often.

History of LCSH

The Library of Congress developed LCSH as the principal means of subject access to its own collections. The first published list of LCSH was in 1914, under the title *Subject headings used in the dictionary catalogs of the Library of Congress*. Since then it has gone through many editions, both in print, and latterly on CD-ROM as part of a package called *Classification plus*. It is now available (together with the Library of Congress Classification) in an online format, *Classweb*, and the examples used in this book are taken from that version and from the online catalogue of the Library of Congress.

The print version of LCSH comes in four volumes containing the headings themselves (sometimes called the red books) and a volume of the rules for application, the *Subject cataloging manual* (or the green book). Beginners often find the printed volumes easier to use than the online version, since it gives them a broader view and a better sense of the context of headings. When you're more familiar with the scheme, the online LCSH is undoubtedly quicker and easier to search, and it uses hypertext to link directly to the classification, which is immensely helpful if you're using both.

The Cataloging Services Division at the Library of Congress maintains LCSH and produces the published version. Updates of the print version appear on an annual basis and *Classweb* can be continuously updated. The *Cataloging services bulletin* details changes and additions to LCSH.

As we shall see in due course, the Library of Congress Classification is a very broad classification. Although it aims to provide a unique location for every book, this is achieved by using author names and dates of publication as additions to the classmark, rather than by any great detail in the classification schedules. The Classification is used primarily as a shelf location device, rather than as a tool for subject searching and retrieval. The Library of Congress expects that readers looking for material on particular subjects will use the subject headings for that purpose. LCSH is consequently a very extensive and a very complex tool.

Theoretical basis of LCSH
In the introduction to the fourth edition of LCSH in 1943, David Haykin stated that there were no guiding principles, or theoretical basis to the subject headings, and this is largely true; they were just developed as needed. But it is also true to say that Cutter's *Rules for a dictionary catalog*, and the American Library Association subject headings which were published as an appendix to the *Rules* in 1895, were influential on the style and direction of LCSH. It does suffer from the fact that it was not originally based on any clear structural principles, but it is now too large for the problem to be addressed in a systematic way. Nevertheless, it is an immensely useful working tool, as well as a real treasure house of the weird and wonderful in document description. It is hardly possible to open any page of LCSH without finding something to surprise and delight.

The Library of Congress and literary warrant
If there are no philosophical principles underpinning LCSH, there is a very strong influence on its content and coverage, and that is the Library of Congress itself. LCSH was developed for the subject cataloguing of books at Congress and remained exclusively so for a long time. New headings were

added as needed for cataloguing items in the collections there, rather than to fill in gaps in a theoretical structure. Inevitably this means that the content of LCSH mirrors the content of the Library of Congress, and more importantly, it reflects any weaknesses in that collection.

This might seem not to be too enormous a problem in a great national library (the largest in the world), and indeed there are no serious short-comings in terms of the content of LCSH. Some subjects, however, are not collected by the Library of Congress (medicine and agriculture, for example, are the responsibility of other US national libraries) and the headings for those subjects are correspondingly fewer and less detailed than in 'strong' Library of Congress subjects, such as history and politics.

Critics of LCSH sometimes condemn its American bias, but that seems to me largely unimportant. There's certainly a proliferation of all things American: place names; names of individuals; details of events in US history; and an avalanche of US family history headings (which, one imagines, no one outside the family concerned will ever want or need). This could hardly be otherwise, and in any case, LCSH, like love, is not rationed. These headings don't exclude other, more generally useful, ones, and you can simply ignore the ones you don't need.

The existence of cultural bias and political incorrectness seems a more serious criticism, and LCSH has suffered a number of attacks on this front over the years. It is quite easy to find headings which infringe all sorts of unwritten laws, and many current written ones. There is considerable gender bias: there have been headings for **Women as judges, Women as composers, Women as astronauts**, perhaps inevitably **Women as automobile drivers** and even **Women as librarians**, without any mention of men in the same roles. The criminal fraternity is packed with minorities: apart from **Women criminals**, there are **Alien criminals, Chinese American criminals, Jewish criminals, Catholic criminals, Deaf criminals**, even **Aged as criminals**. Needless to say, no white, male Anglo-Saxons feature as criminals, although this may of course be the default definition for criminals.

Of course, no one at the Library of Congress, now or in the past, decided to create these headings out of malevolence or a sense of mischief. We know that LCSH is not built on a philosophical model, and that headings only come into being on the basis of need. These particular headings exist to accommodate a literature produced before such attitudes became unacceptable, and, because the literature will continue to exist, so will the offending subject headings. It is a problem of the material rather than the system used to organize it.

Nevertheless, the Library of Congress has taken notice of its critics, and in recent years has changed many of the headings to more acceptable forms. Most of the **Women as authors** type headings have been replaced by **Women authors**, or similar, and a few **Men** . . . headings have come in, although these are usually attached to unusual male occupations such as **Men caregivers** or **Men elementary school teachers**.

You can easily test the literary warrant of LCSH by matching new headings from the *Cataloging services bulletin* against the Library of Congress catalogue. The appearance of a new heading is usually accompanied by a new item requiring that heading. Indeed, looking at the catalogue will normally account for all the oddities of LCSH. A recently added curious heading is **Dog scootering**, the meaning of which initially escaped me; if you run a subject search on the Library of Congress for this heading you'll find the document that brought it into being, and be able to discover what dog scootering is. Other headings which have arisen in this way include **Feet in the Bible, Ear plugs (Whales), Leg (The Polish root), Wooden Leg, 1858–1940** and the delightful **One-leg resting position**. This was originally created for a book about standing on one leg, which has since had its record amended, although One-leg resting position remains a valid heading, should you need to use it.

Principles of Cutter's *Rules* for subject entry

Cutter himself was quite clear why one made a subject catalogue. It was:

- to enable a person to find a book of which . . . the subject is known
- to show what the library has . . . on a given subject [and] in a given kind of literature.

Today, when catalogues are mainly automated and many libraries have remote access to electronic materials rather than holdings of them in the collection, we might want to amend those statements. It might be more useful to say 'a resource' rather than 'a book', and to show what 'is available' rather than what 'the library has'. Nevertheless, the underlying philosophy still holds good. The subject catalogue allows us to find a particular known item from its subject (as opposed to its author or title), and it also lets us search in a more general way for information about a subject and to find items we don't already know about.

Form of entry

Cutter's *Rules* was the first attempt to lay down some systematic principles for subject entries in the catalogue, but it is concerned mainly with the style of the individual heading, rather than the structure of the headings list as a whole, or the relationships of the subject headings to each other.

Cutter's principles place a strong emphasis on intuitive use of the headings. He was in favour of the use of natural language, expressed in natural word order wherever possible, and the avoidance of technical and scientific terminology or jargon. The aim is to create headings that will correspond to the way in which users search for books. Most of Cutter's ideas about the form of entry are still in operation in LCSH today. Here are some of them:

- language that is familiar to the user should be used wherever possible
- popular names should be used in preference to scientific names
- foreign words should be used only where there is no English equivalent
- words should be removed when they become obsolete
- natural word order should be used except where a significant word needs to come into the lead position.

This last requirement is to some extent redundant now that we have automated catalogues. Early on LCSH had many 'inverted headings', that is, headings in which the word order is reversed: for example, **Art, Modern**, or **Chemistry, Organic**. When card catalogues were the norm it was essential that records weren't lost to the user because they had been entered under vague or unhelpful terms. It was the practice to bring the most important word to the front to make sure that the user would find the record. Now that automated catalogues can find search terms wherever they are in the record this is no longer a problem (except where the searcher wants to browse the indexes). The inverted headings in LCSH are gradually being converted to normal word order, but this is a long process, and very many of them still remain.

The need to discuss inversion and natural word order in the heading tells us that headings need not consist of only one word, and there are lots of examples of compound headings of various sorts. Headings of this kind are called pre-coordinated, and they are used liberally in LCSH. Adjectival phrases are very common, as are prepositional phrases and headings of the 'A plus B' kind. Headings that link a topic with its audience are frequent, as are those that combine a subject with another discipline. Some headings have elements of several of these. Here are some examples of compound headings:

- adjectival phrases:
  Egyptian literature
  Ecclesiastical embroidery
  Maiden aunts
  Golden parachutes
- prepositional phrases:
  Tariff on umbrellas
- 'A plus B' headings:
  Bear deterrents and repellents
  Salt-mines and mining
- topic for a specific audience:
  Gardening for teenagers
  Ballet dancing for men
- topic within a specific discipline:
  Stupidity in literature
  Kangaroos in art
  Dogs in the Bible
  Space flight on postage stamps
- more complicated headings:
  Tea making paraphernalia in art
  House built upon a rock (Parable) in art
  Gliding and soaring on postage stamps
  Hogwarts School of Witchcraft and Wizardry (Imaginary place)

Choice of heading

An important idea here is that of the **uniform heading**. Don't confuse this with the uniform title found in cataloguing (which is used to bring together in the catalogue any variant forms of the *title* of a document), although the general purpose of the uniform heading is quite similar in spirit with regard to the *subject* of the document.

The principle behind the uniform heading is to ensure that there is only one heading available for a particular subject (just as the uniform title ensures that there is one title heading for different versions of a title). Books on the same topic should not be scattered about under different headings because there should not be any alternatives available. So, if you have a lot of books about standing on one leg, you need to be certain that they will all end up with the same heading, **One leg resting position**, and that there are no alternative versions such as 'Standing on one leg' or 'Balancing on one foot' which will scatter the books and prevent them being found in a single search.

Three things need managing to keep the headings uniform:

* synonyms must be controlled
* alternative spellings and word forms must be dealt with
* a choice must be made between natural word order and inversion.

We've already looked at some of the ways in which Cutter's *Rules* has affected the first of these. Obviously, popular and scientific terms for the same thing cannot both be used or the uniformity of headings would be lost. Following Cutter, the preference is always for the normal everyday form of words, with technical terminology, foreign words, and archaic forms kept to a minimum. So we have:

> **Giraffe** rather than *Giraffa camelopardalis*
> **Carnival** rather than Mardi Gras
> **Radio** rather than Wireless

Sometimes, of course, the technical can't be avoided: if you have a book about tapirs, rhinoceroses and horses as a group, the Latin term **Perissodactyla** has no English equivalent.

Alternative spellings are more easily dealt with. *Webster's third new international dictionary* is used as the authority for spelling, and although this may sometimes cause minor difficulties for users of British English, at least there can't be any argument about the correct form.

We have already mentioned the problem of inverted headings. While quite a lot of these still exist, and it is virtually impossible to predict which way round a compound heading will go, it is at least clear that you can't have it both ways. If the heading comes in the form **String bags** or **Bog ecology**, there simply cannot be other headings 'Bags, string', or 'Ecology, bog'.

Occasionally you'll encounter a situation where, rather than having two headings with the same meaning, one heading has two or more meanings. Headings such as these are usually single words known as homomorphs, or words with the same shape. An example would be Reading (the place in Berkshire) and Reading (the act of scanning a text). In cases such as this the different meanings of the heading are indicated by a brief indication in parentheses after the heading, e.g.:

Reading (Activity)
Reading (Place)

These terms in brackets are known as **qualifiers**. Sometimes a heading has bracketed terms which are not qualifiers in the normal sense, e.g. **Cookery (Rabbits)**, but these are fairly uncommon.

Of course the classifier can't affect any of this: the editors of LCSH make these decisions. The point of working to a standard is that these decisions are already made, and so everyone using the standard gets the same result.

Practical application of LCSH: simple headings

Because LCSH is such a complex tool, we'll begin by looking at simple headings – that is, headings which are taken straight from the list, rather than being structured by the classifier.

Content analysis and LCSH

Everything that we did in the chapters on content analysis and document description applies to the use of LCSH. Although we're not using a classification scheme we still have to examine our document carefully and make a summary of those elements that we want to express for the reader. Our readers will still be using the subject description for retrieval or for browsing, although in the latter case they'll be browsing the indexes to the catalogue rather than the shelves.

Finding appropriate headings
Valid headings

Let's go back to our original sample of headings at the beginning of the chapter (p. 103). The headings in bold type are the ones that you use; these are sometimes called valid headings. The 'headings' in lighter type are not valid headings; they are simply there because they are words or phrases that classifiers or users might look up. The USE instruction tells the classifier to use another, or 'preferred' heading. For example, in this section we can see that there is no heading for umbrellas and parasols together; either of the headings **Parasols** or **Umbrellas** must be used instead. Situations like this usually arise because there has been an earlier heading (A plus B) which has been cancelled and replaced with two separate headings for A and B.

In *Classweb* the cross-references to valid headings are hypertext links so that the classifier can jump straight to the correct place in the list. You will also see under **Umbrellas** a link to the class for umbrellas in the Library of Congress classification schedules. The printed versions also contain these classification cross-references.

Cross-references

Because LCSH is such a very large vocabulary, the biggest problem for you as a beginner classifier is simply to find your way around it. The novice usually has no sense of what might be a suitable heading, nor any feel for the LCSH conventions in the form of headings or the choice of words. The only answer to this is to launch yourself upon the uncharted waters, and you'll soon discover that there are some navigational aids. Each heading is accompanied by a set of cross-references which help to put it in context, and also lead you to alternative headings. Look at Figure 12.1, which shows an example of a heading with its accompanying thesaural cross-references; you'll remember that we looked at these in the previous chapter. Because of the lack of a strong structural basis to LCSH, the cross-references are not used with the precision that they would be in a well-constructed thesaurus, but

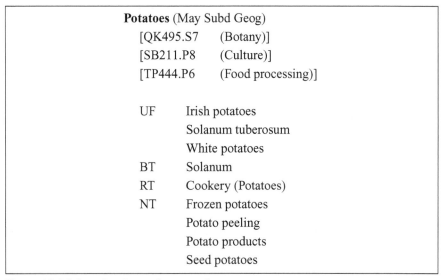

Potatoes (May Subd Geog)
[QK495.S7   (Botany)]
[SB211.P8   (Culture)]
[TP444.P6   (Food processing)]

UF   Irish potatoes
          Solanum tuberosum
          White potatoes
BT   Solanum
RT   Cookery (Potatoes)
NT   Frozen potatoes
          Potato peeling
          Potato products
          Seed potatoes

Figure 12.1 Subject heading with cross-references

none the less you should find them very useful. The list begins with some synonyms and near synonyms for potatoes, introduced by the relator **UF**, or Use For; this tells you that **Potatoes** is the preferred term, and that you shouldn't use 'Irish potatoes' or 'White potatoes' as a heading. Under those headings there will be a **USE** reference directing you to the heading **Potatoes**. You can also see that the Latin name for potatoes, *Solanum tuberosum*, has been rejected in favour of the common word potatoes, in line with LCSH policy.

After the synonym controls come cross-references that deal with the hierarchical structure, broader term (BT) and narrower term (NT). These allow you to decide whether you want to alter the level of specificity from your initial decision. Cutter's *Rules* restricted the use of cross-references to downward links, that is NTs, but today LCSH uses the upward, or BT, link as well. The BT here is **Solanum,** the family to which potatoes belong; there isn't a popular equivalent to this, so the Latin term must be used.

The NTs include some kinds of potatoes (**Frozen potatoes** and **Seed potatoes**) but they also include other terms that appear to be RTs (**Potato peeling** and **Potato products**) in addition to the straightforward RT **Cookery (Potatoes)**.

LCSH doesn't usually deal very well with distinguishing between NTs and RTs, and you can find lots of examples of confusion between the two. Look at the splendid selection of NTs for the heading **Girls** in Figure 12.2. In this example most of the NTs are really RTs: clearly there are some *kinds* of girls represented here (which we don't need to go into), but many of the headings are about *activities* of girls, or *relationships* of girls, and hence syntactic and not hierarchical relationships.

Despite these criticisms, the cross-references are still absolutely essential to navigating LCSH, which would be very difficult to use without them. You would have to guess all the time about any other headings that you might use, and spend ages searching for them. They also perform a vital function in helping you to get the correct level of specificity in subject description.

Selecting headings

You'll remember that in Chapter 9 we carried out some exercises on the level of specificity of the description, and on placing the document in the correct level in the hierarchy. The first rule to remember when selecting headings is to get as close to the subject of the document as possible. LCSH

Girls (May Subd Geog)
BT	Children
RT	Young children
NT	Christian education of girls
	Fathers and daughters
	Games for girls
	Gifted girls
	Grooming for girls
	Handicraft for girls
	Homeless girls
	Indian girls
	Infant girls
	Jewish girls
	Money-making projects for girls
	Mormon girls
	Mothers and daughters
	Muslim girls
	Nymphets
	Poor girls
	Puritan girls
	Religious education of girls
	Sex instruction for girls
	Sports for girls
	Teenage girls

Figure 12.2 Narrower terms in LCSH

is quite plain about this: the heading that most closely represents the subject of the document should be the one chosen.

Example

```
Pendulum magic for beginners : power to achieve all
goals / Richard Webster. – St. Paul, Minn. : Llewellyn
Publications, 2002
```

This is a book about divination using a pendulum. Although there are headings for **Pendulum** and **Fortune telling,** they should be rejected in favour of the heading which exactly matches the content, that is, **Fortune telling**

by pendulum.

The biggest mistake that beginners make is to assign headings that are too broad.

Example

```
Bees without frontiers : proceedings of the Sixth
European Bee Conference, 1-5 July 2002, University of
Wales Institute, Cardiff, Wales / convened by the
International Bee Research Association. - Cardiff :
International Bee Research Association, 2002
```

The main subject of this document can only be 'Bees', and this is indeed the heading that the Library of Congress assigns to it. (In the next chapter we'll look at how to add something about 'Europe' and 'conferences'.) Don't be tempted to use headings such as **Insects** or **Entomology**, because this really won't help the reader to find what he or she wants; in fact it is misleading.

Having chosen the correct heading **Bees** you should resist the temptation to add to it the broader headings. Again, many beginner classifiers do this in the mistaken belief that it's helpful to the searcher, but the reverse is true.

Imagine that you have a collection of documents on the subject of art. Some of them will be general books on art, but most will be more specialist, covering mediaeval sculpture, Picasso, post-modern architecture, watercolour techniques, the Impressionists and so on. You decide to attach to each book the appropriate subject heading, plus one for art. Now imagine that you're carrying out a search for books on Picasso. This shouldn't give you any particular problems: you'll retrieve all the books with the Picasso heading on the record. Now try to search again for all the general books on art. What do you think will happen? Of course the computer will give you a list of all the books in the collection, rather than just those which are at a general level. If you add overly broad headings in this way, you swamp the indexes with them and you make accurate searching much more difficult. So don't do it.

Exercise 12.1

Try to select appropriate headings for the following titles:

1   Step-by-step book about stick insects / David Alderton.
    – Neptune City, N.J, : T.F.H. Publications, 1992
2   Horizon book of great cathedrals / by the editors of
    Horizon magazine ; editor in charge, Jay Jacobs. – New
    York : American Heritage, 1984
3   Boat book / Helene Gaillet de Neergaard ; edited by
    Marcia D. Wiley. – Stamford, Conn. : Westcott Cove, 1994
4   My dog likes to run, I like to ride: how to train your
    dog to pull you on a scooter on city sidewalks & country
    paths / Daphne Lewis. – Seattle, Wash. : Bamboo People,
    1997
5   One-leg resting position (Nilotenstellung), in Africa
    and elsewhere / by Gerhard Lindblom. – Stockholm :
    Statens etnografiska museum, 1949

Selecting multiple headings

These are fairly straightforward titles, each requiring only one heading, but often more than one heading is needed to complete the document description. Look at Figure 12.3, *Knitting with dog hair.*

Figure 12.3 *Knitting with dog hair*

Example

```
Knitting with dog hair : a woof-to-warp guide to making
hats, sweaters, mittens, and much more / Kendall Crolius
and Anne Black Montgomery. - New York : St. Martin's
Press, 1994
```

A concept analysis for this book might be 'Knitting – dog hair'. There is no heading for 'dog hair' as such, so the closest match is **Animal fibers**. We can add this to the heading **Knitting** to give a more complete subject description for the book.

Note that you *cannot* combine the two headings into one. We shall look in the next chapter at the ways in which more complicated headings can be constructed, but adding headings together is not one of them. The headings must be listed separately, thus:

Knitting
Animal fibers

Using more than one heading like this is very common, and it gets round the problem of being unable to represent the whole subject of the document in a single heading. LCSH recommends that you shouldn't use more than six headings for one document, but this is usually more than enough to meet your needs – if, on occasion, it really isn't, then rest assured that the Library of Congress exceeds its own limit from time to time. You can use your concept analysis of a document as a basis for deciding which headings to use, making sure that each component of the analysis is represented in a heading.

Example

```
Fanfare : fourteen stories on a musical theme / edited
by Duncan Minshull and Helen Wallace. - London : BBC,
1999

Concept analysis: Literature - English - short stories -
music

Headings: Music--Fiction
          Short stories, English
```

Since there is so much pre-coordination of terms, you won't necessarily use a heading for every single part of the concept analysis.

Entering headings onto a record

Because you may have several headings attached to each document, you'll need to think about how to arrange them. You'll normally put them into some sort of list. The Library of Congress advises you to put first the heading that approximates most closely to the subject, but otherwise there is no order of preference. Many libraries number the headings, and it's also common to put a full stop (period) at the end of each heading.

You also need to pay careful attention to the layout and construction of the headings. Mostly, you have only to copy the heading , but it's surprising how many beginner classifiers do this carelessly, without any regard for punctuation, capitalization or spelling. Errors here can cause mis-filing, poor collocation of records and consequently poor levels of retrieval. Because LCSH is a standard and internationally used, one of its great advantages is as a search tool within merged catalogues; if it's not used accurately that advantage is undermined, and users are confused by the variations.

Although you need to copy out the heading exactly, there are some common conventions to help you:

- capital letters are used at the beginning of headings, e.g.:

    Traditional ecological knowledge
    Dwarfs in motion pictures
    Coarse woody debris

- in a structured heading (which we'll encounter in the next chapter), each element starts with a capital letter, e.g.:

    Espionage– –Biography– –Dictionaries
    Astrology and pets– –Humor

- in an inverted heading the word after the comma (the original lead word) has a capital letter, e.g.:

    Artificial satellites, Chinese
    Body, Human
    Colors, Liturgical

- otherwise capitals are used only where one would always use them (for proper nouns, etc.):

Lone Ranger films
Submarine topography– –Pacific Ocean

Summary
- Never try to combine two headings into one.
- Use as many headings as necessary to cover the content of the document.
- List them with the one closest to the subject of the document first.
- Use any local conventions, such as numbering or terminal full stops.
- Remember to reproduce accurately any capital letters, spaces or punctuation contained in the heading.
- Speakers of British English should look carefully for variations in spelling.

The biggest difficulty that most beginner classifiers will have in applying LCSH to a document is simply to know where to start. However well you understand the principles of LCSH, knowing which headings to pick can often be a time-consuming guessing game at first. In this situation the most sensible thing you can do is look at what someone else has done. Very many OPACs now have LCSH on their records, and of course the biggest and most authoritative catalogue, that of the Library of Congress itself, is freely available on line. Not only can you check the Library of Congress's records, but you can also browse the subject indexes and check the Library of Congress authority files for further information about LCSH.

You don't have to take the Library of Congress's decisions as authoritative if your situation requires a different treatment, and you'll soon become aware that the catalogue is not free of errors; there are lots of examples of misspelt headings. However, the Library of Congress records can give you a starting point and suggest headings that you might not otherwise have thought of for yourself.

Answers to exercises
Exercise 12.1
1 Stick insects *or*

Stick insects as pets
2 Cathedrals
3 Boats and boating
4 Dog scootering
5 One-leg resting position

13 Library of Congress Subject Headings 2: structured headings

In the previous chapter we considered how to express the complete content of a document by using more than one heading. Most of the headings used to illustrate Chapter 12 were pre-coordinated headings, combining more than one concept, such as **Ecclesiastical embroidery** or **Wildlife conservation**. In fact it's quite hard to find headings that are not pre-coordinated in this way.

There is another way for you to combine concepts in LCSH, and that is through the use of structured headings. A structured heading, like a pre-coordinated heading, has two or more concepts combined, but instead of merging them into a natural language phrase, the conceptual structure is displayed using dashes, rather as we've done with the concept analyses or subject strings.

Examples

    Bumblebees– –Fiction
    Archipelagoes– –Guadeloupe
    Jigsaw puzzles– –Collectors and collecting– –United States
    Cucumbers– –Bibliography
    Tightrope walking– –France– –Case studies
    Measles in art– –Exhibitions
    Dentures– –Drama

The normal practice when typing out or entering structured headings is to use a double dash (**Bumblebees– –Fiction**). This is to distinguish the structured heading from one that simply contains a hyphen (**Water-color painting** or **Sugar-beet web-worm**).

Structured subject headings fall into three broad categories:

- headings with topical subdivisions
- headings with geographical subdivisions
- headings with free-floating subdivisions.

Topical subdivisions

Topical subdivisions, or subject subdivisions, are those subdivisions of a heading that are enumerated in the main list of headings. That is to say, LCSH gives us the subdivision, ready-made for use. Just as in the case of the main headings, valid topical subdivisions are shown in bold. Here are some examples:

Saturn (Planet)
> **Saturn (Planet)– –Exploration**
> Saturn (Planet) (in religion, folklore, etc.)
>> USE Saturn (Planet)– –Mythology
> Saturn (Planet)– –Influence on man
>> USE Human beings– –Effect of Saturn on
> **Saturn (Planet)– –Mythology**
> **Saturn (Planet)– –Orbit**
> **Saturn (Planet)– –Phases**
> **Saturn (Planet)– –Ring system**
> Saturn (Planet)– –Rings
>> USE Saturn (Planet)– –Ring system
> **Saturn (Planet)– –Satellites**
> **Saturn (Planet)– –Satellites– –Ephemerides**

This is just a selection of the topical subdivisions under **Saturn (Planet)**. I've left out some of the intervening text, so that you can see the structure more clearly; as a result the BTs and so on are missing here, but you can still see the references from unused terms (non-bold) to preferred terms (bold). This example from the online version actually puts both the heading and its subdivision together, and you need only to copy those you want. In the printed volumes the display looks more like this:

Swine
> UF Hogs
>> Pigs
>> Pig farming
> BT Livestock
> **– –Anatomy**
> **– –Breeding**
> – –Breeds

USE Swine breeds

– –Disease

– –Feeding and feeds

– –Herd books

USE Swine– –Pedigrees

– –Infancy

USE Piglets

The bold and feint headings still mean the same, but in this case you have to 'write out' the full form of the headings yourself, e.g. **Swine– –Anatomy**.

Exercise 13.1

Find appropriate subject headings for the following titles:

1 Controlled reproduction in sheep and goats / Ian Gordon. – Wallingford : CAB International, 1997

2 The biogeochemistry of iron in seawater / edited by David R. Turner, Keith A. Hunter. – Chichester : Wiley, 2001

3 Color in philately / R. H. White. – New York : Philatelic Foundation, 1979

4 The lawfulness of deep seabed mining / Theodore G. Kronmiller. – Dobbs Ferry, N.Y. : Oceana Publications, 1980

5 The butterflies named by J. F. Gmelin: Lepidoptera, Rhopalocera / by Richard Irwin Vane-Wright. – London : British Museum (Natural History), 1975

6 Fire assaying for gold and silver / by Sigmund L. Smith. – Tucson, Ariz. : Distributed by Jacobs Assay Office, 1979

7 Hearing loss after Eustachian tube ligation measured electrocochleographically. – St. Louis : Annals Pub. Co., 1978

8 Popes and church reform in the 11th century / H.E.J. Cowdrey. – Aldershot : Ashgate, 2000

9 Clinical aspects of iodine metabolism / E.J. Wayne, Demetrios A. Koutras, W.D. Alexander. – Oxford : Blackwell Scientific, 1964

Occasionally the topical subdivisions extend to more than one level of hierarchy, as in this (again compressed) example:

Mars (Planet)
BT   Inner planets
– –Exploration
RT   Space flight to Mars
– – – –Equipment and supplies
– – – –Juvenile literature

The further indentation here is shown by two double dashes. When using topical subdivisions of this kind you must take care here to reproduce all the levels of the hierarchy or elements of the heading. So:

Mars (Planet)– –Exploration– –Equipment and supplies
Mars (Planet)– –Exploration– –Juvenile literature

and not:

Mars (Planet)– –Equipment and supplies
Mars (Planet)– –Juvenile literature

Exercise 13.2
Write out in full the headings with topical subdivisions in the following sections of LCSH:

Mass media
– –Audiences
– –Employees
– – – –Labor unions
– –Law and legislation
– –Religious aspects
– – – –Baptists
– – – –Buddhists

Continued on next page

Exercise 13.2 *Continued*
Cattle
– –Aging
– – – –Prevention
– –Anatomy
– – – –Atlases
– –Biography
– –Breeding
– – – –Selection indexes
– –Carcasses
– – – –Grading
– – – –Handling
– – – –Information services

Pattern headings

Sometimes the topical subdivisions under one heading can be applied under other headings of the same type. Such a heading is known as a pattern heading. The heading **Cattle** is a pattern for all headings for animals, and you can take all the topical subdivisions of **Cattle** and add them to any other heading for a type of animal. The pattern headings are listed in the green book. Commonly used pattern headings and their categories are those for **Shakespeare** (literary authors), **Wagner** (composers), **Piano** (musical instruments) and **Copper** (metals).

The use of these topical subdivisions is very straightforward. You must simply take the usual care in reproducing them, and always make sure that the levels of hierarchy are fully represented.

Summary
- The simplest kind of structured heading is one with a topical subdivision.
- Topical subdivisions are included in the main list of headings.
- Valid subdivisions are formatted in bold type.
- Topical subdivisions can contain more than one level of hierarchy.
- When using the print version of LCSH you must be sure to put in all the levels of the topical subdivision when entering your heading.
- Some headings act as a pattern for others in the same category.
- Always separate the different parts of the structured heading with double dashes.

Topical subdivisions are very easy to use because the Library of Congress has created them for you, and you only have to copy (carefully!). However, there are some categories of structured headings that you can make up for yourself, using certain rules.

Geographical subdivisions

The commonest sort of 'made-up' heading is one containing a geographical place. You can put in a place subdivision wherever you see the instruction (May Subd Geog) after a heading, as in:

Double cathedrals (May Subd Geog)
Catahoula leopard dog (May Subd Geog)
Sea coconut (May Subd Geog)
Liposuction (May Subd Geog)
Catacombs (May Subd Geog)
Eskimo baskets (May Subd Geog)

There seem to be very few headings that aren't divisible by place, although you mustn't do it in the absence of the instruction. Occasionally there's a specific prohibition on putting in a place. For example:

Eskimo cookery (Not Subd Geog)
Winnie-the-Pooh (Fictitious character) (Not Subd Geog)
Fans in art (Not Subd Geog)
Puns and punning in literature (Not Subd Geog)
Near-earth asteroids (Not Subd Geog)
Rabbitt family (Not Subd Geog)

It's not very clear why it would be such a wrong thing to put in a place subdivision for these headings, although in the examples above there seems little likelihood that you would ever wish to.

Constructing geographic subdivisions

There are a few simple rules relating to the way in which you create the geographical subdivision:

- Countries or larger geographical units are added directly to the heading. This is called direct subdivision, e.g.:

Raffia work– –Belgium
Banana bunchy top disease– –Africa
Biogeography– –Pacific Ocean

• Smaller geographical units must have the country added first. This is called indirect subdivision, e.g.:

Plastic kitchen utensils– –France– –Paris
Floppy disks– –Iceland– –Reykjavik

Indirect subdivision applies to geographical features, historical regions, and to any administrative unit (not just a city), including island possessions close to the mother country:

Pyramids– –Egypt– –Nile Valley
Tourism– –Italy– –Sorrento peninsula

• The current name of the place should be used.

• The name in English should be used, unless there isn't one (in which case the vernacular name is used):

Croquet– –Italy– –Rome *not* Croquet– –Italia– –Roma

There are some exceptions to the indirect subdivision rule, where units smaller than a nation state are added directly to the heading:

• states of the USA, e.g.:

Ironing boards– –California
Hijacking of ships– –Massachusetts

• Canadian provinces, e.g.:

Molecular biology– –Manitoba

• constituent countries of the United Kingdom, e.g.:

Sunburn– –Scotland

To these are added four cities, or 'city-states': Vatican City, Washington, New York, and Jerusalem, e.g.:

Strabismus– –New York
Alphabetizing– –Jerusalem

Islands which are outside the ruling country's territory are also added directly, e.g.:

Public welfare– –Greenland
Postage stamps– –Falkland Islands

Exercise 13.3
Construct headings for the following titles:

1 *Wallpaper in America: from the seventeenth century to World War I*
2 *The place-names of Wales*
3 *The prospective development of Peru as a sheep-breeding and wool-growing country*
4 *The languages of Jerusalem*
5 *Music in Vienna*
6 *Kentucky mountain square dancing*
7 *Red Sea coral reefs*
8 *Road making materials in Basutoland*
9 *A history of tin mining and smelting in Cornwall*
10 *Prospects for Nigerian pineapple and mango in the international market*
11 *Evangelism in India: a survey*
12 *Jews and Judaism in a midwestern community, Columbus, Ohio*
13 *Duels and duelling: affairs of honour round the Wandsworth area*
14 *Naturalisation of Plants in Urban Auckland*

If more than one place is represented in the document, separate headings must be made for each place.

Example

```
Cactus odyssey : journeys in the wilds of Bolivia, Peru,
and Argentina / James D. Mauseth, Roberto Kiesling,
Carlos Ostolaza. - Portland, Or. : Timber Press, 2002

Concept analysis: Cactus - Bolivia - Peru - Argentina

Headings:      Cactus-Bolivia
               Cactus-Peru
               Cactus-Argentina
```

If geographical subdivision is allowed where there is also a topical subdivision, you must be careful to put the geographical part in the right place. For example:

Goats (May Subd Geog)
– – **Breeding** (May Subd Geog)
– – **Diseases** (May Subd Geog)
– – **Equipment and supplies**
– – **Pedigrees**
– – **Virus diseases** (May Subd Geog)

This allows you to construct headings:

Goats– –Scotland– –Diseases
Goats– –Diseases– –Scotland
Goats– –Scotland– –Equipment and supplies
Goats– –Scotland– –Pedigrees

but not: Goats– –Equipment and supplies– –Scotland

nor: Goats– –Pedigrees– –Scotland.

Summary
- You can create your own structured headings using geographical subdivisions.
- Most headings can be subdivided geographically; look for the instruction (May Subd Geog).
- Headings without this instruction or those labelled (Not Subd Geog) may not be subdivided.
- Countries or larger units are added directly to the heading (direct subdivision).
- Units smaller than a country must have the appropriate country inserted into the heading (indirect subdivision).
- States of the USA, Canadian provinces and the countries of the UK are added directly, as are New York, Washington, Jerusalem and the Vatican City.
- When topical subdivisions and geographical subdivisions are used together, be careful to put the geographical subdivision in the correct position.

Free-floating subdivisions

Free-floating subdivisions are non-geographical concepts that can be added to headings. Until 2003 they were contained in the green *Subject cataloging manual*, but they are now included in the red books; they are also published in a separate printed *Free-Floating subdivisions: an alphabetical index*. They are searchable as a separate subset of the online LCSH.

The free-floating subdivisions act rather like the auxiliary tables in a classification. Some can be added to any heading, whereas others are restricted to particular types of heading, such as those for individual authors which are used to specify the different texts, editions and secondary publications associated with an author.

Free-floating subdivisions comprise a variety of concepts: a large number are concerned with the form of the document, both inner and outer (**Encyclopedias, Specifications, Biography**), some refer to particular groups of persons (**Women authors, Juvenile fiction**) and others make provision for chronological treatment (**History– –16th century**).

Most deal with common subject subdivisions (**Law and legislation, Salaries, Songs and music, Research**) or with subject subdivisions for a particular class of headings, such as Animals, Plants, Parts of the body, Countries, Languages, Religions, Persons, Families, Chemical substances, Musical instruments and so on. The headings to which a free-floating subdivision can be applied are clearly explained in the lists, so you shouldn't be confused about this.

You may be confused about finding your way through the free-floating subdivisions. As in the case of the headings themselves, it can be difficult to determine what free-floating subdivisions there are, as you initially have to guess which terms have been used. I think this is a particular difficulty for British users, as some of the American terminology may not naturally spring to mind. There is not much that can be done about this problem, except to use the cross-references, and be comforted by the fact that familiarity improves the situation.

Applying the free-floating subdivisions

In the majority of cases only one free-floating subdivision can be added to a heading, e.g.:

> **Ice cream, ices, etc.– –Bibliography**
> **Sea horses– –Life cycle**
> **Cookery (Mexican)– –Exhibitions**

Rather like the topical subdivisions, some free-floating subdivisions have more than one element. The most commonly used example of this is for history, where the headings are of the form:

– –History– –16th century
– –History– –17th century

Except for these 'given' examples of compound free-floating subdivisions, free-floating subdivisions cannot be added together in the same heading, just as main headings cannot be combined. If a document requires more than one free-floating subdivision to cover the content, then separate entries must be made for each.

Example

```
Rhetoric and the pursuit of truth : language change in
the seventeenth and eighteenth centuries : seminar :
papers / by Brian Vickers, Nancy S. Struever. - Los
Angeles : William Andrews Clark Memorial Library, 1985

Concept analysis: English language - history -
          seventeenth century - eighteenth century


Headings
   English language--History--17th century
   English language--History--18th century
```

Exercise 13.4

Construct headings using free-floating subdivisions for the following titles:

1 *Accordionist's encyclopedia of musical knowledge*
2 *Autobiography of a geisha*
3 *The greatest weddings of all time* [with illustrations]
4 *Chimpanzee: a topical bibliography*
5 *Book of Merlin: insights from the first Merlin conference*
6 *Platypus and echidnas: selected papers presented at a symposium held at the Royal Zoological Society of New South Wales at the University of New South Wales in July 1991*

Continued on next page

Exercise 13.4 *Continued*

7 *Barbed wire: a political history*

8 *Self-assessment picture tests: avian medicine*

9 *Journal of the Society of Parrot Breeders and Exhibitors*

10 *The Dead Sea scrolls catalogue*

11 *The artful teapot: exhibition held May 16–Sept. 2, 2002, at COPIA: the American Center for Wine, Food, and the Arts, Napa, Calif. and other locations*

12 *How thunder and lightning came to be: a Choctaw legend*

Summary

- Free-floating subdivisions can be added to headings to improve the subject description.
- Most free-floating subdivisions are applicable to all headings, but some can be used only with certain groups of headings.
- The lists of free-floating subdivisions make it clear which restrictions apply.
- Only one free-floating subdivision can be added to a heading; if you need to use two, you must make two separate headings. Don't combine free-floating subdivisions.

If necessary you can have both geographical subdivisions and free-floating subdivisions in the same heading. In such cases the geographical subdivision comes immediately after the heading, followed by the FFS.

Using a combination of geographical subdivision and free-floating subdivisions allows you to construct quite complicated headings, sometimes with five or six elements in them. Here are some examples.

Examples

```
Keiller's of Dundee : the rise of the marmalade dynasty,
1800-1879 / W.M. Mathew. - Dundee : Abertay Historical
Society, 1998

Concept analysis: Marmalade -- manufacture -- Scotland --
            Nineteenth century


Heading:   Marmalade industry--Scotland--History--19th
           century
```

```
Country copper : the autobiography of Superintendent G.H.
Totterdell of the Essex County Police. - London :
Harrap, 1956

Concept analysis: Police - Essex - autobiography

Heading:   Detectives-England-Essex-Biography
```

Exercise 13.5

Construct headings for the following titles, using both geographic subdivisions and FFS.

1 *Tennis courts map of Santa Clara County [San Jose, Calif.]*
2 *Cruising guide to the west coast of Vancouver*
3 *Archival Morris films in the Vaughan Williams Memorial Library (Morris dancing in the South Midlands, Vol. 9)*
4 *Witchcraft and the Inquisition in Venice, 1550–1650*
5 *Musique à Paris sous la regne de Charles VI, 1380–1422*
6 *Zhongguo sha mo=Journal of desert research [Chinese]*
7 *Methods for Diminishing the rabbit nuisance. Reprint of the 1st (1877) ed. published in the Appendixes to Journals of the House of Representatives of New Zealand*
8 *Report of the East Anglian earthquake of 22 April 1884*
9 *American funeral vehicles, 1900–2003: an illustrated history*
10 *Budapest, 1896: the first great chess tournament in Hungary*

Name headings

There is another sort of heading that you can create, and that is a heading for a name. This might be a personal name, a geographical name, or the name of an organization. The need for these name headings often crops up, and you can see a great number of them already in LCSH:

Waterloo Bridge (London, England)
J. Paul Getty Museum
Everest, Mount (China and Nepal)
Ranganathan, S. R. (Shiyali Ramamrita), 1892–1972
Bush, George W. (George Walker), 1946–
Elizabeth I, Queen of England, 1533–1603
Big Bug Creek (Ariz.)
Laura C. Hudson Visitor Center (New Orleans, La.)

Name headings should be created using the appropriate section of the *Anglo-American Cataloguing Rules*. Remember that in the case of the personal name headings these are for works *about* the person, and not *by* him or her.

Otherwise you shouldn't create headings, although of course if you have need of a heading that isn't currently part of LCSH, you can contact the Cataloging Services Division of the Library of Congress and suggest that they incorporate it.

Answers to exercises
Exercise 13.1
1 Sheep--Reproduction
  Goats--Reproduction
  Sheep--Breeding
  Goats--Breeding
2 Sea-water--Iron content
3 Postage stamps--Color
4 Ocean mining--Law and legislation
  Ocean bottom--Law and legislation
5 Butterflies--Nomenclature
6 Gold--Assaying
  Silver--Assaying
7 Electrocochleography
  Eustachian tube--Ligature
  Deafness
8 Church history--11th century
9 Iodine--Metabolism

Exercise 13.2
  Mass media
  Mass media--Audiences
  Mass media--Employees
  Mass media--Employees--Labor unions
  Mass media--Law and legislation
  Mass media--Religious aspects
  Mass media--Religious aspects--Baptists
  Mass media--Religious aspects--Buddhists

Cattle
Cattle– –Aging
Cattle– –Aging– –Prevention
Cattle– –Anatomy
Cattle– –Anatomy– –Atlases
Cattle– –Biography
Cattle– –Breeding
Cattle– –Breeding– –Selection indexes
Cattle– –Carcasses
Cattle– –Carcasses– –Grading
Cattle– –Carcasses– –Handling
Cattle– –Carcasses– –Information services

Exercise 13.3

1   Wallpaper– –United States
2   Names, Geographical– –Wales
3   Sheep– –Peru
4   Multilingualism– –Jerusalem
    Hebrew language– –Jerusalem
    Sociolinguistics– –Jerusalem
5   Music– –Austria– –Vienna
6   Square dancing– –Kentucky
7   Coral reef biology– –Red Sea
    Coral reefs and islands– –Red Sea
8   Road materials– –Lesotho
9   Tin mines and mining– –England– –Cornwall
10 Pineapple industry– –Nigeria
    Mango industry– –Nigeria
11 Missions– –India
    Christianity– –India
    Evangelistic work– –India
12 Jews– –Ohio– –Columbus
13 Dueling– –England– –Wandsworth
14 Botany– –New Zealand– –Auckland
    Plant introduction– –New Zealand– –Auckland
    Weeds– –New Zealand– –Auckland

Exercise 13.4

1 Accordion– –Dictionaries
2 Geishas– –Biography
3 Celebrity weddings– –Pictorial works
4 Chimpanzees– –Bibliography
5 Wizards in literature– –Congresses
6 Platypus– –Congresses
  Echidnas– –Congresses
7 Barbed wire– –Political aspects
8 Avian medicine– –Examinations, questions, etc.
9 Parrots– –Periodicals
10 Dead Sea scrolls– –Catalogs
11 Teapots– –Exhibitions
12 Thunderstorms– –Folklore

Exercise 13.5

1 Tennis courts– –California– –Santa Clara County– –Maps
2 Boats and boating– –British Columbia– –Vancouver Island– –Guide-books
3 Morris dance– –England– –Midland– –Film catalogs
4 Witchcraft– –Italy– –Venice– –History– –16th century
  Witchcraft– –Italy– –Venice– –History– –17th century
5 Music– –France– –Paris– –500-1400– –History and criticism
  Music– –France– –Paris– –Fifteenth century– –History and criticism
  (Note that here the Period subdivisions are topical subdivisions, and not free-floating subdivisions.)
6 Deserts– –China– –Periodicals
7 Rabbits– –Control– –New Zealand– –History– –Sources
8 Earthquakes– –England– –East Anglia
9 Hearses (Vehicles)– –United States– –History– –20th century
  Hearses (Vehicles)– –United States– –Pictorial works
10 Chess– –Tournaments– –Hungary– –Budapest
   Chess– –Hungary– –Budapest– –Collections of games

14 Classification scheme application

When the content of the document is decided, and the concept analysis made, the time has come to translate this into the specific language of your chosen scheme. We shall examine several of the general schemes in detail, but first we are going to look at the general appearance and features of a classification scheme, and how to go about using one.

For the beginner classifier one of the greatest difficulties lies in simply navigating the scheme. This is because at the outset you have little idea of the overall order and structure of the scheme, and no expectation of what you might find in terms of the vocabulary or level of detail. This feeling is multiplied if you're not familiar with any scheme, since the general idea of which topics belong in which discipline tends to be common to them all – what we call consensus – and knowledge of one system is helpful in second guessing the location of classes in another.

Don't therefore be alarmed, if, when you start cataloguing, you spend a long time looking for things – this is quite usual and you will soon speed up when you get to know the scheme better.

In this chapter we'll look at the various parts of a published schedule, and examine some ways to help you find your way round a big scheme.

The composition of the classification scheme

A classification scheme consists of two parts: the systematic display (or schedules) and the index. Both are important in the application of the scheme, and you should examine both carefully when classifying.

The index

We'll begin with the index, because this is where, as a novice, you will have to start.

In Chapter 4 we discussed how an aspect classification scatters the various aspects of an entity, using the rabbit as an example. The index is very important because it is where the **distributed relatives** are brought together in an aspect classification and where you find out all the possible places to put a book about rabbits. Although you might make an educated guess at where your subject occurs, you will need the index to discover for certain the various places where your subject is provided for. If you go straight to the schedule you may miss a better location for your document.

For example, in the index to the Pocket Edition of UDC we find:

animals
as art subject	7.042
behaviour	591.5
companion	636.9
ethics in relation to	179.3
and environment	591.5
fossil	57.07
insurance	368.5
palaeozoology	562/569
performance	791.8
contests	798.9

These different classes represent all the possible places to locate a book on animals in UDC; the first question you should ask when classifying such a document is which aspect of the subject is being considered, and in which part of the classification you should place the document.

Bear in mind the difficulties of alphabetical searching, and, if you can't find your topic straightaway, try looking for more general or more specific terms. Remember to look for synonyms, and remember when using the index to a scheme published in America that it may use different spelling.

One of the main rules of classification is that you should never classify from the index, but it will be some time before you're able to dispense with it altogether.

The schedules

The schedules are often thought of as the most important part of the classification, and they are certainly what most classifiers regard as 'the classification'. See Figure 14.1 for an example. The schedules consist of three principal parts:

1 the classes themselves, the vocabulary, terminology or class names
2 instructions and explanatory text
3 the notation.

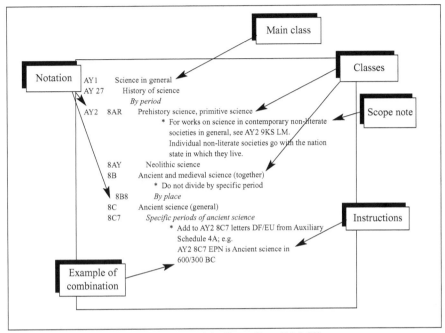

Figure 14.1 Parts of a classification schedule (from Class AY, BC2)

The vocabulary or classes

These constitute what most people think of as the classification proper, and they are what the document must be matched against when classifying. The assignment of a document to a class will involve selecting the 'best fit' for the subject of the document against the classes listed in the scheme.

In a classification scheme we are dealing with concepts rather than words, so the description of a class may include synonyms and near synonyms that relate to the concept. An individual class can therefore consist of several terms or phrases which together give the classifier an idea of the intended content. This group of concepts is called the class **heading** or **caption**. Some headings may be quite lengthy: in particular where there is no convenient broader class or group name for the sub-classes, the caption may consist of a list of the sub-classes.

When you have found an appropriate class for your document you need to scan the schedule preceding and following the class. This scanning allows you to establish the context of the class, and to confirm that you're in the right part of the forest. Some classifications provide an abridged hierarchy at the top of the page, and this will also help to get a sense of the context.

If you find more than one class for your subject in the index, be sure to look at the different possibilities in detail before finally making up your mind on a location.

The layout of the schedules

The layout (or display) of the classes is important. The major feature of the display is the order of classes, but most schemes show other relationships. The hierarchical structure of the classification is usually shown by indenting subordinate classes. By moving up and down the hierarchical order the classifier can easily identify broader (more general) and narrower (more specific) classes.

It is important that you scan the classes in the area of schedules you are using in order to see whether a broader or narrower class might be closer to your subject. If you have followed the method for document analysis properly you should have an appropriately specific concept for your document, but of course the classification schedule may not allow for the term you have selected. In this case, you will need to look for a class that does contain the concept you've chosen.

The conceptual nature of classification means that you can sometimes place a topic that isn't specifically mentioned, if the general intention of the caption seems to imply it. For example:

AY36	Practical scientific work
	Research by environment
AY7 WL	Special environments
X	Vacuums
XE	Subsurface .... Submarine ...

It is clear here that AY7 XE can be extended to include the class 'subterranean', since conceptually this is where that term would belong, even though it is not specifically included.

Instructions, explanations and other subsidiary text
Scope notes
Not all of the text in a schedule comes into the category of captions or headings. Sometimes a heading needs further explanation or definition. Such text is called a **scope note**, because it is meant to make clear the scope or content of the class. For example, in Figure 14.1 the note at AY2 8AR, makes it clear that this class only deals with primitive science in prehistory, and that another class (AY2 9KS LM) deals with primitive science in contemporary non-literate communities. Read scope notes carefully. They usually tell you where related topics are located in the classification, and which to choose (and why) when there is overlap, or where you might be in doubt about which to choose.

Instructions and examples of combination
You will also find within the schedule instructions about how to apply the classification, or how to build classmarks (as at AY2 8C7); very often, these instructions include examples of built classmarks showing you how to apply the rules. Such classmarks are called examples of combination.

Different schemes use a number of different ways to build classmarks, and any particular scheme may have several methods of doing this. It is very important that you read the instructions where they occur, and do exactly as you are told. It would be easy for beginner classifiers if you could be given a few simple rules to apply generally, but this is seldom possible. The big general classifications are complex structures that have expanded and evolved over many years. Notational allocation is a complicated affair, and most of them contain many variations from the general rule. You need to make certain that you apply the rules as intended, so read them carefully, and follow the examples.

The editors of schemes usually put scope notes and instructions in a different font from that used for classes proper, so they can be easily distinguished.

In our example in Figure 14.1 you can also see some other 'headings' which are in italics and which don't have a notation. Un-notated headings of this sort are structural 'signposts'. In this case, they indicate the **principle of division** which is being applied at that point, i.e. the characteristic which the following classes share. It goes without saying that you cannot use an un-notated 'heading' to create a classmark.

Summary

- Don't worry if you feel lost at first; this is quite normal.
- Use the index to find the possible locations for your subject.
- Examine the schedules for each location.
- Browse the schedules in each area to determine the context.
- Browse the schedules for more suitable broader or narrower classes.
- Read scope notes and definitions.
- Follow instructions carefully and don't invent classmarks.

15 Library of Congress Classification 1: basic classmark construction

The Library of Congress Classification is unusual among the general schemes in that it was originally a scheme intended for a single library, with no expectation that it would ever be used in any others. Today it is one of the two dominant classification schemes, certainly in the Western world (the other being the Dewey Decimal Classification). It's a popular choice for academic libraries, particularly university libraries, but also for specialist collections in some subjects. It is also used in one British public library (Edinburgh), but is more common in public libraries in the United States.

Undoubtedly the management advantages of using LCC have influenced modern libraries. The free availability of records on the Library of Congress catalogue, and big union catalogues which include LCC records (such as COPAC in the UK), as well as the excellent bibliographic services offered by the Library of Congress, are very attractive at a time when most libraries regard copy cataloguing as the norm, and do little original cataloguing work.

History of the Library of Congress Classification

The Library of Congress itself was founded by order of Congress in January 1802, by 'An Act concerning the Library for the Use of both Houses of Congress'. This provided for a room for the collection of 740 books (which had been purchased by Senator Samuel Dexter in the previous year), the establishment of rules for the use of the Library, and the appointment of the first librarian, John Beckley. In April 1802 he was able to issue the first catalogue, in which the shelf arrangement is recorded: this was by size.

In 1812 a subject approach was applied for the first time, the classification used being that of the Library Company of Philadelphia, an independent research library. This classification was based on an adaptation of Bacon's system used in the *Encyclopédie* of Diderot and d'Alembert. The Library of Congress used only 18 of Philadelphia's 31 main classes, and within each class the books were subdivided by size and arranged alphabetically.

In 1814 the Capitol, including the Library of Congress, was burned by the British, and most of the collection was lost. Thomas Jefferson offered to sell Congress his own library, which was organized by his own system of 44 main classes, again based on Bacon/d'Alembert. In 1815 Congress purchased the collection, and it remained in place until 1897, and a move to a new library building. At this time the Library considered the adoption of a new classification scheme, since there were now systems of bibliographic or library classification available, in addition to the philosophic schemas such as Bacon's. Serious contenders for use at the Library of Congress were Dewey's Decimal Classification, Cutter's Expansive Classification, and Hartwig's Halle Schema.

Of these the Expansive Classification was felt to be the most appropriate to the needs of Congress, and Cutter the most willing of the three compilers to make modifications to his system to accommodate the Library of Congress. Interestingly, DDC was rejected on the grounds that it was a 'system bound up in and made to fit the notation, and not the notation to fit the classification'.

A decision was made in 1901 to develop an entirely new classification system specifically for the Library of Congress, although it is clear that Cutter's Expansive Classification had a considerable influence on the new scheme.

Publication and management of LCC

The Cataloging Services Division of the Library of Congress is responsible for the maintenance and general management of the classification. The classification is a huge, multi-volume publication; even some individual main classes are published in parts because of the length of the schedules. Unlike DDC, the Library of Congress never produces a 'whole' new edition, but individual volumes are updated as necessary. In the past revision has been a very slow process with new schedules appearing very infrequently, but conversion to machine readable format has speeded up the revision process considerably. In the 1990s an electronic LCC was marketed to end-users in CD-ROM format, which was much easier to search and navigate. In 2002 this was replaced by *Classweb*, an online version of the classification and LCSH.

The Library continues to produce the print version and many users will prefer this, if only because local decisions and amendments can easily be recorded in the schedules. I also think that beginner classifiers generally find a paper copy easier to get to grips with than the rather 'peep-hole' view of the online classification.

Alterations and additions to the classification are recorded in the *Cataloging Services Bulletin*, published at regular intervals; changes are incorporated in *Classweb* as they are made. The website of the Library of Congress (www.loc.gov) is an excellent place to find information about LCC, and of course the catalogue of the Library of Congress is a wonderful source of classification data on bibliographic records.

The availability of free records and the bibliographic services provided by the Library of Congress undoubtedly affect the choice of this classification by many libraries. The stability of LCC's long-term future also gives it an advantage over less well supported systems.

General principles underlying LCC

It is quite hard to discern any strong theoretical principles underlying LCC, but nevertheless it has some quite distinct characteristics.

Firstly, the Library of Congress Classification is unique in that it is a classification developed with only one collection in mind. Its original creators were not at all interested in bibliographic classification for its own sake, nor did they imagine that anyone else would use the classification. Herbert Putnam, the then Librarian, writing in the Library of Congress annual report for 1916, makes this quite clear:

> the scheme adopted has been devised with reference (1) to the character and probable development of our own collections, (2) to its operation by our own staff, (3) to the characters and habits of our own readers, and (4) to the usages in vogue here . . . . There was no expectation that the scheme would be adopted by other libraries; much less was there any profession that it would be suited to their needs.

This would not matter greatly except for the fact that the Library of Congress is not quite like any of the other great national libraries. The classification was intended for a collection that is both a national library and the library for the national executive; as such it is quite distinct from, say, the British Library or the Bibliothèque Nationale, which were both developed with principally scholarly objectives.

LCC is best suited to large, comprehensive collections such as university libraries (or other national libraries). It's not really a logical choice for a public library, college or smaller academic library. Nevertheless, many of these libraries do choose LCC, not least because of the advantages it offers in managing the scheme, rather than for any inherent theoretical qualities. Special libraries in subjects where LCC is very detailed (such as law, politics and many humanities subjects) will find it a good choice of scheme.

Literary warrant

A particular feature of LCC is that it is constructed almost entirely on the basis of literary warrant. That is to say that classes are created to cope with the literature that must be classified by the scheme, rather than on the basis of any theoretical analysis of knowledge, either documentary or philosophical.

Now this is not necessarily a bad thing, since any bibliographic classification should reflect subjects as they exist in the material to be classified, rather than in an abstract view of the world. The problem arises because in LCC's case we are dealing with only one library. Where the collection is strong the classification will be strong, but where it is lacking, the scheme will reflect that weakness. Obviously the classification will also exhibit local deficiencies or over-developments, or reflect particular acquisition programmes.

The biggest difficulty is that the Library does not collect systematically in all subject areas. Specific subject strengths and weaknesses are as follows:

- there is obviously a very strong US bias; LC is a copyright deposit library, and as such receives all US publications, but it may not collect systematically outside the USA. This is perhaps less evident in the classification than in the subject headings, where there are large number of subjects of very local American interest
- there are weaknesses in subjects where the Library of Congress is not the principal institution for copyright deposit: obvious examples are those subjects which are the concern of another major library, such as medicine, agriculture or education
- because the Library is there primarily to serve Congress, the classification is very detailed in subjects such as law, politics and administration, and military and naval science, and less strong in science and technology.

You should also bear in mind that the arrangement of material within classes may also reflect this purpose, and may not be the best order for academic purposes.

Nowadays, with many more libraries using LCC, and with the Library's involvement in co-operative cataloguing projects, the external world has more influence on the Library of Congress than in the past. Libraries are able to make suggestions for alterations and for new classes and headings, and these are slowly being incorporated into the Library of Congress's systems. Indeed, if you compare *Classweb* with the Library of Congress Catalog you can see a difference in content between the two that would not have been evident even 20 years ago.

An enumerative classification

Its enumerative nature is probably the single most important feature of LCC. LCC is the prime example of an enumerative classification, that is, a classification that lists all its possible classes. This approach may be contrasted with that of analytico-synthetic systems such as UDC and BC1 (the first edition of the Bibliographic Classification), and faceted schemes such as Colon and BC2 (the second edition of BC). In schemes such as these you can build (to a greater or lesser degree) classmarks that reflect the constituent parts of a document's content, and so the number of potential classes is much greater than those actually listed.

In an enumerative scheme complex and compound subjects are already listed in the classification schedules, and you can't usually add to what is there already. This makes it difficult to deal with new topics until the Library of Congress officially adds them to the system; it also means that compound subjects that aren't represented in the schedules can't be synthesized.

In addition the schedules are much lengthier and more complex than in other classification schemes. This is mainly because of the frequent repetition of common concepts which could more economically be added from systematic schedules or tables; LCC habitually repeats even such common notions as form subdivisions and historical periods under individual subject classes.

Because only certain compounds are enumerated it is often difficult to say in which of two or three pre-coordinated classes a compound should be placed. For example, look at this section of the schedule for 'Economic conditions and history of the United States':

	By period
HC104	Colonial period
HC105	1776-1900
	1860-1869
HC105.6	General works
HC105.65	Confederate States
HC105.7	1870-1879
	1901-1945
HC106	General works
HC106.2	World War I, 1914-1918
HC106.3	Reconstruction, 1919-1939
HC106.4	World War II, 1939-1945
HC106.5	Reconstruction, 1945-1961
HC106.6	1961-1971
HC106.7	1971-1981
HC106.8	1981-1993
HC106.82	1993-2000
HC106.83	2001-

	Regions
HC107.A11	New England
HC107.A115	Northeastern States
HC107.A118	Atlantic States

If you have to classify a document on the economic conditions in New England in the colonial period, it is hard to decide whether to put it at HC104 for that period, or HC107.A11 for New England. When a compound subject can be quite easily (and legitimately) classed in more than one place, it is called cross-classification. Of course this is less likely to happen in this sort of subject where the combination of place and time will occur fairly frequently and classifiers will spot the problem and tackle it. In other areas cross-classification is more insidious and can happen without the classifier noticing.

The classification also lacks mnemonic value in that the notation for common concepts is not always consistent in the way that it normally is in other classifications.

On the positive side, the enumeration ensures that the classification is very simple to apply since the options are severely limited, and not much intellectual effort is required of the classifier.

Summary
Features of an enumerative classification:

- Compound subjects are pre-coordinated and listed.
- There is very limited if any synthesis.
- Classes which haven't been listed can't be constructed by the indexer, and so the system lacks hospitality.
- There is extensive repetition of concepts.
- The schedules are very lengthy.
- There is a danger of cross-classification.
- The scheme lacks mnemonic features.

But:

- The scheme is easy to use and requires minimal intellectual effort.

Alphabetization

A third significant characteristic of LCC is its extensive use of alphabetical order for subject arrangement. As far as the structure of the scheme is concerned it is really a very broad and shallow classification, with not much depth to the hierarchy. Division of a subject is usually restricted to some form subdivisions, common subject subdivisions such as 'philosophy' or 'study and teaching', followed by period and regional subdivision. As soon as any detail is required LCC usually opts for an alphabetical arrangement of topics. Of course this isn't really a systematic arrangement and the order achieved is not always very helpful, since it naturally doesn't put related subjects together.

The following list is taken from the literature class, and provides for poetry by subject. You can see all the difficulties of using words displayed here: the lack of meaningful associations, difficulty in knowing what words will have been chosen, and the impossibility of broadening or narrowing the search.

PR1195.J4	Jesus Christ
PR1195.J6	Jonson, Ben
PR1195.K4	Kerouac, John
PR1195.K48	Kilpeck (Hereford and Worcester)
PR1195.L3	Labor. Working class

PR1195.L33	Lake District, England
PR1195.L34	Landscape
PR1195.L37	Law and lawyers
PR1195.L6	London
PR1195.L8	Lullabies
PR1195.L85	Luther, Martin
PR1195.M15	Machinery
PR1195.M18	Maclean, John
PR1195.M2	Madrigals
PR1195.M22	Magic
PR1195.M24	Manners and customs
PR1195.M33	Medicine
PR1195.M53	Mice
	Military aeronautics see PR1195.A37
PR1195.M6	Monsters
PR1195.M63	Mothers
PR1195.M65	Mountains
PR1195.M67	Muktananda Paramhamsa, Swami
PR1195.M8	Mythology

The use of alphabetical order is very widespread in LCC once a broad level structure is established. In many cases even countries are arranged alphabetically (within, say, a continent), separating neighbours and members of political groupings. An advantage of alphabetical arrangement is that a new topic can usually be inserted into the order without much difficulty, but the disadvantages are very plain to see.

We'll return to the issue of alphabetization in the section on practical application of LCC to look at the way in which it is managed.

Notation

LCC uses what is known as a mixed notation, because it has a mixture of numbers and letters in the classmarks. No other symbols are used except a full stop or period, and occasionally a decimal point.

A typical classmark consists of two letters and a number from 1 to 9999:

TS1865	Umbrellas and parasols
BF1775	Popular superstitions
HE6183	Postage stamps

Very occasionally, in a very detailed class, such as Law, three letters may be used, and at the beginning of a main class there may be only one:

KDE540	Criminal law of Northern Ireland
KNP501	Administrative law of Taiwan
B42	French and Belgian dictionaries of philosophy
H57	Collective biography of the social sciences

The last two examples also illustrate very neatly the levels of pre-coordination in LCC; in other schemes form concepts, such as 'dictionary' or 'biography', and languages would be taken from auxiliary tables.

The numbers are filed ordinally, that is to say in order of their numerical value:

BR97	General works
BR98	Atlases
BR99	Dictionaries
BR99.5	Pictorial works
BR99.7	Information services
BR99.74	Computer networks
	Including the Internet
	Cf. BR115.C65 Christianity and computers
BR100	Philosophy of Christianity. Philosophy and Christianity
	For early works see BR120
	Cf. BL51 Philosophy of religion
	Cf. BT40-55 Philosophical theology
	Biography of Christian philosophers
BR102.A1	Collective
BR102.A2-Z	Individual, A-Z

Here you can see decimal subdivision in operation (under Biography of Christian philosophers), as well as the ordinal filing.

Because LCC has a wide notational base (it uses the alphabet plus the 10 numerals, giving 36 characters altogether) it has relatively short classmarks for quite specific subjects. The notation isn't expressive in any way, which means that important subjects can be given particularly short classmarks.

You'll notice that there are regular gaps in the notation: LCC accommodates new subjects by slotting them into these gaps. As the classification isn't very precise, finding a place is more important than achieving any finesse in the structure, and new classes can be put in at any reasonably sensible location. A large number of new topics will in any case be inserted into an alphabetical list.

In the great majority of cases the classifier has only to copy out the classmark; there is very little number building at all.

Summary
- LCC was devised specifically for the Library of Congress, but it shows the influence of Cutter's Expansive Classification.
- There are no real theoretical principles underlying LCC.
- The structure of the classification and the level of detail provided tends to reflect the strengths and weaknesses of the collections of the Library of Congress, although this is less the case than it used to be.
- It is a broad classification used principally for shelf arrangement; LCSH is the main means of subject retrieval at the Library of Congress.
- LCC is the classic example of an enumerative classification.
- There is much pre-coordination and very little synthesis of classmarks.
- Alphabetization is very commonly used as a means of subject arrangement.
- LCC is a difficult scheme to navigate, but an easy scheme to apply.

Practical classification using LCC

LCC is probably the easiest of all the general schemes to use in terms of constructing the classmarks. The major difficulty, as with LCSH, is that of locating an appropriate class. Because of the sheer physical size of LCC, hunting through the schedules in search of a suitable class is a difficult business unless you are already in roughly the right area, and it is really essential for beginner classifiers to use the indexes. Individual volumes have their own indexes, and the whole scheme is more easily searched now that it is available online as *Classweb*.

Having found the general location it's still important to scan the schedules to see what is there, how classes relate to each other, and to read any notes or instructions.

In comparison with a scheme like DDC, LCC has very little in the way of explanations or instructions, and gives limited help to the classifier. Something that puzzles many newcomers to LCC is the number of classes without a notation. The following schedule section is very typical:

	Women. Feminism
	Women's studies. Study and teaching. Research
HQ1180	General works
HQ1181.A-Z	By region or country, A-Z
	Biographical methods
HQ1185	General works
HQ1186.A-Z	By region or country, A-Z
	Feminist theory
HQ1190	General works
HQ1194	Ecofeminism
	General works
HQ1201	Early to 1800
	1800-
	Scientific. Psychology, etc.
	Cf. HV6046-6046.2222 Female offenders
HQ1206	English
HQ1208	French
HQ1210	German

The captions Women's studies, Biographical methods, Feminist theory and so on seem to have no classmarks. This is because a general work on any of these topics is classed at the subdivision 'General works'. This way of doing things is widely used in LCC, but it can look quite odd to those more familiar with the schedules of, say, DDC.

Because of the other regular LCC practice of listing common subject subdivisions before you get to general works, you might have to scan quite a lot of schedule before you get to the place where you actually find the classmark. This happens to Feminism, where study and teaching, biography and theory all precede the broader class Feminism – general works at about HQ1201. I say 'about', because the same thing now happens again, and there are no notated classes before HQ1206 – scientific works on feminism published after 1800 in English.

Exercise 15.1

Find appropriate LCC classmarks for the following titles:

1 *Ancient Roman jobs*
2 *The boat book*
3 *Business ethics: critical perspectives on business and management*
4 *Collect mammals on stamps*
5 *Essential guide to bird photography*
6 *Incredible secrets of vinegar*
7 *Land of plenty: a treasury of authentic Sichuan cooking*
8 *Leonardo da Vinci*
9 *New dictionary of liturgy and worship*
10 *Selected themes and icons from mediaeval Spanish literature: of beards, shoes, cucumbers, and leprosy*

In order to construct a complete LCC **call-mark,** we need to add some other elements to the basic classmark. A call-mark consists of three parts, only one of which (the classmark) has to do with the subject content of the book. The point of the call-mark at the Library of Congress is to provide an individual **book number** for every item, to enable the physical retrieval of items. (You'll remember that the subject headings perform the role of subject retrieval.) To create this unique number we need to add information about the author and about the date of publication.

Cutter numbers

The author information takes the form of an encoded number representing the author's name. This system of encoding names was invented by the ubiquitous Mr Cutter, and the resulting numbers are known as Cutter numbers, or sometimes simply as Cutters. Cutter numbers are not restricted to LCC, and US libraries in particular use them for author numbers in conjunction with DDC and other classification schemes.

Cutters are constructed using a little conversion table (Figure 15.1) that allows you to express the letters in a word as numbers. There is obviously a fundamental difficulty here as there are 26 letters and only 10 numerals, so one number is used to represent several letters. This makes use of the Cutters a bit less than exact, and in practice they often need manipulation to maintain the correct alphabetical sequence.

```
1. After initial vowels

For the second letter    b    d    1-m   n    p    r    s-t  u-y
Use number               2    3    4     5    6    7    8    9

2. After initial letter S

For the second letter    a    ch   e    h-i   m-p  t    u    w-z
Use number               2    3    4    5     6    7    8    9

3. After initial letters Qu

For the second letter    a    e    i    o    r    t    y
Use number               3    4    5    6    7    8    9

For initial letters Qa-Qt use 2-29

4. After other initial consonants

For the second letter    a    e    i    o    r    u    y
Use number               3    4    5    6    7    8    9

5. For further expansion

For the letter       a-d   e-h  i-l   m-o   p-s  t-v  w-z
Use number           3     4    5     6     7    8    9
```

Figure 15.1 Table for constructing Cutter numbers

The Cutter number consists of the initial letter of the author's name, plus numbers representing the next two or three letters. These numbers differ according to whether the first letter of the name is a vowel, S, Q or any other consonant. If further differentiation is needed, extra numbers can be added using section 5 in Figure 15.1.

The Cutter number for Broughton will be B76, derived as follows: B plus 7 (representing R after a consonant other than S or Q) plus 6 (representing further expansion of O). Similarly, the Cutter for Stendhal is S74, for Beethoven B44, for Ivan the Terrible I93 and for Quasimodo Q37.

Cutter numbers are usually taken to two numerals, although where not many books are to be arranged one number might be enough, and very large collections might need more than two numbers. The purpose at the Library of Congress is to give each book a unique number, but other libraries are not necessarily aiming for that and so won't bother with very long Cutter numbers.

Exercise 15.2

Construct Cutter numbers for the following authors' names:

1 Dickens
2 Shakespeare
3 Morris
4 Browning
5 Betjeman
6 Isherwood
7 Fowler
8 Stendhal
9 Eliot
10 Quiller-Couch

The above names are straightforward, but if you look carefully at the table you will immediately notice that some very necessary letters are not represented: for instance there is no provision for 'h' or 'l' following a consonant, despite the frequency of these letter combinations in English. Slavonic (and other non-Western European) languages have many letter pairs that are not provided for at all. In cases like this you have to invent a number that will get the Cutter to file in the right place alphabetically. This seems to me greatly to undermine the value of the Cutters, since different classifiers in different libraries will make up different numbers; over a period of time the adjustments necessary to maintain the correct order can move a long way away from the original table. It also worries beginners not to have a 'right answer' or to see Cutters on a catalogue record that 'don't make sense', but you should be reassured that the problem is not with you. A more immediate difficulty for the beginner is that making up answers for exercises has no context and you can only guess at an appropriate number. In a real library situation you would be fitting your Cutter into an existing sequence, and see more clearly how this adjustment of numbers works.

Although Cutter numbers are primarily used to provide an 'author' arrangement, difficulties arise when there is no personal author. Nowadays Cutters are linked to main entry, so if the main entry were to be something other than an author (the title, a corporate body or a named conference, for instance) you should make the Cutter for that instead. Editors can never be the main entry point, so you will never need to make a Cutter for an editor's name. If the state of your cataloguing knowledge makes deciding on main entry a bit of a challenge, it is safest to make the Cutter for title when there is no personal author.

You add the Cutter to the classmark after an intervening full stop (period).

Examples

```
Sacred and the feminine : toward a theology of housework
/ Kathryn Allen Rabuzzi. - New York : Seabury Press, 1982

LCC Classmark: BL458
Cutter for Rabuzzi:    R33
Call-mark:             BL458.R28


Who's who in barbed wire. - [Texline, Tex. : Rabbit Ear
Pub. Co.], 1970

LCC Classmark:          TS271
Cutter for Who's who…:  W5
Call-mark:              TS271.W5
```

Exercise 15.3

Create classmarks with appropriate Cutter numbers for the following books:

1 Extinct land mammals and those in danger of extinction / Philip Steele. - New York : Franklin Watts, 1991
2 Belgium: a view from the sky / [photography] Wim Robberechts. - Brugge : Van de Wiele, 1997
3 Cucumber growing / R.T. Spencer. - [Sydney] : N.S.W. Dept. of Agriculture, 1969

Continued on next page

Exercise 15.3 *Continued*

4 Underwater explosions / R.H. Cole. - New York : Dover, 1965

5 Better than beauty: a guide to charm / Helen Valentine, Alice Thompson. - San Francisco : Chronicle Books, 2002

6 Yodelling in Switzerland / Hans Curjel. - Zurich : Pro Helvetia, 1970

7 Gluing and clamping: techniques for better woodworking / Nick Engler. - Emmaus, Pa. : Rodale Press, 1993

8 Business ethics: critical perspectives on business and management / [edited with an introduction by] Alan Malachowski. - London : Routledge, 2001

9 First aid for dogs: what to do when emergencies happen / Bruce Fogle. - London : Pelham, 1995

10 New dictionary of liturgy & worship / edited by J.G. Davies. - London : SCM Press, 1986

In addition to the author Cutters, LCC also uses Cuttering as the basis of alphabetical subject arrangement. If you look at the alphabetical list of subjects in poetry you can see the Cutters added to the basic classmark.

PR1195.M2	Madrigals
PR1195.M22	Magic
PR1195.M24	Manners and customs
PR1195.M33	Medicine
PR1195.M53	Mice
	Military aeronautics see PR1195.A37
PR1195.M6	Monsters
PR1195.M63	Mothers
PR1195.M65	Mountains

In theory you can add any other 'Poetry by subject' to the list by making an appropriate Cutter. But LCC has not always applied the Cutter chart consistently in creating these lists of subjects. You can probably also see where the Cutters are not derived from the Cutter chart, and where difficulties could arise. How, for instance, would you deal with books of poetry about macaroni or moles? Nevertheless this use of the Cutter number is widespread throughout the scheme, so you must make the best of it.

Cutters are also used for A/Z geographical arrangement, another very common situation. In a situation where you have a subject or geographical Cutter, this precedes the author Cutter, and the two are separated by a space.

Examples

```
Step-by-step book about stick insects / David Alderton.
- Neptune City, N.J. : T.F.H. Publications, 1992
```

```
LCC Classmark:                          SF459
Cutter for subject (Stick insects):S75
Cutter for author (Alderton):           A43
```

```
Call-mark:                              SF459.S75 A43
```

```
Antwerp in the age of Reformation : underground
Protestantism in a commercial metropolis, 1550-1577 /
Guido Marnef. - Baltimore ; London : Johns Hopkins
University Press, 1996
```

```
LCC Classmark:                BR828
Cutter for place (Antwerp):   A58
Cutter for author (Marnef):   M37
```

```
Call-mark:                    BR828.A58 M37
```

Normally no more than two Cutters are used in a call-mark. If it happens that there are two subject/geographical Cutters (perhaps because an A/Z subject arrangement is further subdivided by A/Z geographical arrangement), the author Cutter is left out. This is because the point is to create a unique number (rather than provide information about the author) and two Cutters are likely to achieve this.

The Library of Congress completes the call-mark by adding the date of publication.

Example

```
Picture your dog in needlework / B. Borssuck, Ann
Jackson. - New York : Arco, 1980
```

```
Classmark:            TT778.C3
Author Cutter         B67
Date of publication:  1980
```

```
Call-mark             TT778.C3 B67 1980
```

Again this is aimed at producing a unique book number, and it's not very likely that libraries other than the Library of Congress will want to follow the practice, although in a large library it is a useful device for breaking up long runs of books at the same number.

Exercise 15.4

Construct a complete LCC call-mark for the following titles:

1 Biowarrior: inside the Soviet/Russian biological war machine / by Igor V. Domaradskij. - Amherst, N.Y. : Prometheus Books, 2003

2 Birdwatching on inland fresh waters / M.A. Ogilvie. - London : Severn House, 1981

3 Building an igloo / text and photographs by Ulli Steltzer. - New York : H. Holt, 1995

4 Contemporary architecture of Washington, D.C. / Claudia D. Kousoulas, George W. Kousoulas. - Washington, D.C. : Preservation Press, 1994

5 Cultivated plants of Southern Africa: botanical names, common names, origins, literature / H.F. Glen. - Johannesburg : Jacana in association with the National Botanical Institute, 2002

6 Cycling past 50 / Joe Friel. - Champaign, Ill. : Human Kinetics, 1998

7 Greek insects / Malcolm Davies & Jeyaraney Kathirithamby. - New York : Oxford University Press, 1986

8 Horizon book of great cathedrals / by the editors of Horizon magazine; editor in charge, Jay Jacobs. - New York : American Heritage Pub. Co., 1984

9 Macramé gnomes and puppets: creative patterns and ideas / by Dona Z. Meilach. - New York : Crown, 1980

10 Thermodynamics of pizza / Harold J. Morowitz. - New Brunswick : Rutgers University Press, 1991

Answers to exercises
Exercise 15.1

1 HD4844
2 GV775
3 HF5387
4 HE6183.A5
5 TR729.B5
6 TX819.V5
7 TX724.5.C5
8 ND623.L5
9 BV173
10 PQ6059

Exercise 15.2

1 D53
2 S53
3 M67
4 B76
5 B48
6 I84
7 F69
8 S74
9 E45
10 Q55

Exercise 15.3

1 QL707.S74
2 DH424.R63
3 SB337.S64
4 QC151.C65
5 RA778.V35 (Cutter for the first author only)
6 ML3721.C87
7 TT185.E54
8 HF5387.B87 (Cutter for title in an edited work)
9 SF991.F64
10 DV173.N49 (Cutter for title in an edited work)

Exercise 15.4

1 UG447.8 .D66 2003
2 QL690.G7 O35 1981 (Table doesn't allow for the author Cutter here, and it would need to be fitted into the existing sequence)
3 E99.E7 S74 1995
4 NA735.W3 K68 1994
5 QK394 .G59 2002 (another 'invented' Cutter where the table doesn't make provision)
6 GV1043.7 .F75 1998
7 QL482.G9 D38 1986
8 NA4830 .H67 1984 (Cutter for title here)
9 TT840 .M45 1980
10 QH505 .M67 1991

16 Library of Congress Classification 2: use of tables

As we saw in the previous chapter, it's very straightforward to construct LCC call-marks. In most cases, the subject part of the call-mark is lifted from the schedule without any alteration. The only real intellectual work for the classifier is the creation of the Cutter number, deciding whether it should be for the author or for another aspect of the work, and contriving a number that will fit in with the existing sequence. Very often, even this isn't required, as LCC is so fond of lists that it offers thousands of ready-made subject Cutters.

There are, however, some areas where more detail can be achieved by a limited sort of number building, and you normally do this by using tables.

Tables in LCC

LCC is quite unlike any other classification in its use of tables. In most schemes you would expect to find commonly occurring concepts, such as place, time or form, provided for in a general table to be used throughout the system. This is what happens in DDC and UDC, and of course has its equivalent in LCSH in the free-floating subdivisions.

In LCC every table is special to the place where it is applied. Even where a table is used frequently in a particular main class (as happens in Class H, Social sciences) it can still be used only where the instructions permit. For example, in the part of the schedule shown in Figure 16.1, Table 21 can be used to expand the classes for Bisons (sic), Edible caterpillars, Edible snails and Kangaroos, but Table 23 must be used for Goats. You can't use a table to expand Rabbits since there is no instruction to do so.

This means that adding notation from tables is a laborious business since there is no single consistently used table for common concepts, nor is there any mnemonic value in the notation, since it hardly ever remains the same in two different classmarks.

In the online version of LCC the tables are very easy to use: when you click on the link to a table it pops up and inserts itself into the schedule.

HD	
	Agricultural industries
	Animal industry
9438.B57-B574	Bisons. American buffaloes (Table H21)
	Caterpillars, Edible, see HD9438.E32
9438.E32-E324	Edible caterpillars (Table H21)
9438.E34-E344	Edible snails (Table H21)
9438.G63-G632	Goats (Table H23)
9438.K35-K354	Kangaroos (Table H21)
	Rabbits
9438.R3	General works
9438.R4A-Z	By region or country, A-Z

Figure 16.1 LCC schedule showing where tables may be applied

The print version is slightly more complicated, and since it involves some basic arithmetic, we shall concentrate on this method for the benefit of those who have access only to paper copy.

Content of tables

You can use tables to improve subject description, i.e. to obtain some further subject subdivision, in a number of different ways. Tables exist for a range of purposes, and we'll look at several different types. The following are the main areas covered:

- geographical subdivision: although Cutter numbers are the usual means of geographical arrangement, in some parts of the classification tables are used instead
- form and common subject subdivisions: these are probably the commonest type of table, allowing for the addition of such concepts as statistics, societies, periodicals, dictionaries, biography, period and place
- subdivision special to a particular topic: class H contains a number of tables of this type, providing additional detail for topics such as taxation, real property, insurance, societies and so on
- arrangement of 'works': tables for the arrangement of works of individual authors are common in the schedules for literature; they provide a means of organizing individual works, collections and selections of works, different editions, translations and so on.

In this chapter we'll concentrate mainly on the tables in Class H, since they include most of the common kinds of number building through tables.

How tables work

Part of the difficulty of using the tables is the lack of instructions in the schedule. This situation has improved in recent revisions, but generally the classifier is expected to understand what is required without much assistance from the published scheme. Unfortunately the application of tables isn't as intuitive as the editors imagine and beginners can easily get confused. I'll endeavour to dispel that confusion here, and give you some practical rules for using the tables.

The basic principle underlying the tables is the idea of substitution. The notation from the table is not attached to the base classmark as in most classification schemes. Instead a notational gap is left in the schedule into which the table is slotted. For example, in the class HC, Economic history and conditions, we find:

HC	Economic history and conditions
	By region
161-70	South America
167.A-Z	Regions, A-Z
171-80	Argentina (Table H15)
181-85	Bolivia (Table H16)
186-90	Brazil

If we turn to table H16, we find that it consists of five numbers (with some decimal and alphabetical subdivision to allow for A–Z arrangement), as in Figure 16.2:

H16	TABLE FOR ECONOMIC HISTORY AND CONDITIONS BY COUNTRY (5 NOS.)
	Documents
1.A1-A3	Serial documents
1.A4-A42	Separate documents
1.A5-Z	Periodicals. Societies. Serials
	Biography
1.5.A2	Collective
1.5.A3-Z	Individual A-Z
2	General works
2.5	Natural resources
3.A-Z	Local, A-Z
4	Colonies
5.A-Z	Special topics A-Z

Figure 16.2 Table H16

The table has to be inserted into the notational 'gap' provided for it at the location for Bolivia at HC 181-85. The five numbers in the table must be 'mapped' to the five numbers allocated within the class. Hence, the first number in the table is equivalent to the first number in the schedule. In this example, 1 in the table becomes 181 in the schedule, 2 in the table becomes 182, and so on. Any decimal or alphabetical subdivisions are also attached e.g. 2.5 becomes 182.5, and 5.A-Z becomes 185.A-Z, as in Figure 16.3:

HC	
181-185	Bolivia
181.A1-A3	Serial documents
181.A4-A42	Separate documents
181.A5-Z	Periodicals. Societies. Serials
	Biography
181.5.A2	Collective
181.5.A3-Z	Individual A-Z
182	General works
182.5	Natural resources
183.A-Z	Local, A-Z
184	Colonies
185.A-Z	Special topics A-Z

Figure 16.3 Table H16 applied to the notation classes for Bolivia

In this particular example (and it's quite typical) a country is allocated a range of numbers according to its importance in the field of economic history. Individual countries may have 1, 4.5, 5, 9.5 or 10 numbers, and there are two tables each for the 1 and 5 number countries with slightly different distributions of classes.

If you examine the tables you'll see that a concept such as Natural resources can occupy position 3.5, 2.5 or .Z65 in the tables, according to the number of numbers allocated. In any event the notation would not be consistent even if there were only one table, since the notation isn't 'tacked onto' a classmark as it is in the other general schemes.

Example

```
Industrialization in Indonesia : developments and
perspectives / Peter McCawley. - Canberra : Development
Studies Centre, A.N.U., 1979

Concept analysis: Economic conditions - Indonesia
```

```
Classmark for Indonesia HC 446-450 (Table H16)

In Table H16 General works are represented by 2, so
the second number from the range is chosen i.e. HC447

Final classmark:         HC447

Cutter for McCawley:     M33 (note that this Cutter
                         has been made for a general
                         'Mac/Mc' filing sequence)

Complete callmark:       HC447.M33 1979
```

Now let's look at some examples of how different concepts are expressed using this table method.

Geographical subdivision

Although Cutter numbers are often used for geographical subdivision, the use of tables has some advantages that Cutter numbers don't offer. Firstly, there can't be any further subject subdivision after a geographical Cutter, but the use of the table generates a 'normal' classmark, or set of classmarks that don't have this limitation, so that form subdivisions can be 'added' on. (This is a little more complicated than the normal table number building, and we'll look at some examples later.) Secondly, because the table method allows a spread of numbers to be used, the classmarks are a bit shorter than otherwise they would be.

Let's look at some places where tables are used to create classmarks for countries. Class HB has several such sections, for example:

HB

Demography. Population. Vital events

3501-3697   By region or country (Table H2)

Table H2 has 197 numbers to represent the regions and countries of the world. If you look at the table you'll see that New England is 7, Nicaragua 41 and Scandinavia 109. Just as in the example above, these numbers are mapped onto the 'notational space' at HB3501-3697. So the demography of New England is the 7th number (HB3507), the demography of Nicaragua the 41st (HB3541) and the demography of Scandinavia the 109th (HB3609).

You might spot that a quick way to work these numbers out is to add the table number to the starting classmark *minus* one. Things would be much easier if the schedule told us to do this, but unfortunately it doesn't, so you must work it out for yourself. Always remember to take one away to get the base number.

Example

The evolution of demography in the Americas / Gérard-François Dumont. - Nice, France : Académie de Nice ; Paris, France : Université de Paris-Sorbonne, Institut de démographie politique, [1997]

Base number for demography by country: HB 3501
Table H2 number for the Americas: 1

Classmark: HB3501
Call number: HB3501.D86 1997

Exercise 16.1
Use table H2 to create classmarks for the following titles:

1   *La population française au XXe siècle* [the population of France in the twentieth century]
2   *Case studies in population policy: Kuwait*
3   *Japan's changing population structure*
4   *American demographics* [this is about the USA]

If you had the full bibliographic details here, you would add the Cutter for main entry and date to give the complete call number.

Form subdivisions

Although there isn't any systematic way to create form subdivisions, many of the tables can be used to express a limited number of forms. The commonest are periodicals and directories, and form subdivisions for history are also quite often included. The tables for the subdivision of statistics are a good instance of this, and include provision for serials, abstracting services and censuses.

Example

```
Annual abstract of statistics / Office for National
Statistics. - London : HMSO, 1997-

Base number for Statistics-Great Britain:
                        HA 1121-1139 (Table 11)

Table H11 number for Statistical abstracts:   2

Classmark:              HA1122

Complete call number: HA1122.A55
Cutter for the title, and because this is a serial
publication, there's no date to add.)
```

Exercise 16.2

Create classmarks for the following titles using Tables 11/12:

1   1991 census: key statistics for local authorities /
    Office of Population Censuses and Survey. - London :
    HMSO, 1994
2   Demographic review. London : HMSO, 1977-

Subject subdivision

A small number of tables exist to provide subdivisions for specific topics. This is usually, but not exclusively, where something peculiar to the subject is required. One such example is the provision for subdividing national and local railways, which allows you to specify 'timetables', 'government policy' and named railway companies as well as the usual form and history.

Example

```
History and development of railways in India / Aruna
Awasthi. - New Delhi : Deep & Deep, 1994

Base no. for Indian railways:        HE3291-3300(Table H37)
Table 37 number for History:         8
Classmark:                           HE3298

Complete call number:                HE3298.A93 1994
```

Exercise 16.3

Use the appropriate tables to create classmarks for the following titles. You can add main entry Cutters and dates to give the complete call number if you wish.

1   Indian railways, the final frontier: genesis and growth of the North-East Frontier Railway / Arup Kumar Dutta. - Guwahati : Northeast Frontier Railway, 2002

2   Working the rough stone: freemasonry and society in eighteenth-century Russia / Douglas Smith. - DeKalb, Ill. : Northern Illinois University Press, 1999

3   Investment plan 1994-2003 for Swedish trunk railways: summary of background and contents. - Borlange, Sweden : Banverket, 1994

4   Boston. Police Department. Rules and regulations. - Boston 1950-

5   Days pleasant and unpleasant in the Order Sons of Italy in America: the problems of races and racial societies in the United States / Robert Ferrari. - Clifton, N.J. : A.M. Kelley, 1974

Tables for classes using Cutter numbers

Tables of the same sort, mixing mainly form subdivisions with history, local arrangement and provision for specifying companies, are very common in parts of the schedule dealing with industry sectors and manufacturing, particularly for named products. There isn't very much in the way of structure in these schedules, and they consist mainly of long alphabetical lists; the tables are a limited way of providing more specificity. Looking at the catalogue of the Library of Congress suggests that much of the literature here is rather old, but nevertheless these tables illustrate the working of the system rather well.

Most of the 'subjects' here are arranged by Cutter numbers, and the tables are inserted into a range of three or four of these. These tables are rather differently set out from the ones we've seen already. They use an *x* to represent the Cutter number in the classmark, so you simply need to substitute the first Cutter number from the schedule for the *x* in whatever part of the table you need. The new Cutter numbers that are created by doing this correspond to the range given in the schedule.

Example

```
Yeast: the elixir of life / Cedric Axelsen. -
Rushcutter's Bay, N.S.W. : Halsted Press, 2001

Base number for yeast:       HD9330.Y4-43 (table 22)
Table 22 number for general works: .x2

Classmark:                   HD9330.Y42
Complete call number:        HD9330.Y42 A94 2001
```

Exercise 16.4
Create classmarks for the following titles using tables H20/23 and H50

1 The international soup market. – New York : Packaged
  Facts, [1996]

2 Buffalo producer's guide to management & marketing. –
  Ft. Pierre, SD : National Buffalo Association, 1990

3 Year book of the British paper box industry. – London :
  Verstone, [n.d.]

4 The button, buckle and fastener industry / prepared in
  the General Manufactures Section, Industry and
  Merchandising Division, Dominion Bureau of Statistics. –
  [Ottawa] : The Bureau, [1951]-1971

5 Water bed dealers directory. – Omaha, Ne : American
  Business Directories [this is a serial]

6 Christmas year round: a guide to America's Christmas
  shops / James R. Heintze. – Michigan : Harmonie Park
  Press, 1991

7 Boiler makers on the prairies / Robert M. MacIntosh. –
  [Canada] : International Brotherhood of Boilermakers,
  1979

8 Market opportunities in broccoli / Market Opportunity
  Identification Project. – [Victoria, B.C.] : Ministry of
  Agriculture, 1979

9 Window washer: at work above the clouds / Keith
  Greenberg. – Woodbridge, Conn. : Blackbirch Press, 1995

10 Nuremberg thimblemakers / Helmut Greif. – [Des Moines,
   Iowa] : Thimble Collectors International, 1986

Tables embedded in the schedules

As LCC has developed there have been some changes in the way tables are presented. Nowadays many tables are embedded in the schedules: that is to say, they're printed fully where you need to apply them (or at the first place where they're to be used).

Mainly these are very small tables, with few subdivisions. Lots of them appear in the criminology schedules, and they are mainly attached to countries. Figure 16.4 shows a typical example:

HV	Social pathology. Criminology
	Homicide. Murder, etc.
	By region or country
	United States
6535.A-Z	Other regions or countries, A-Z
	Under each country
.x	*General works*
.x2A-Z	*By region, state or province, A-Z*
.x3A-Z	*By city, A-Z*

Figure 16.4 Embedded schedule in Class HV

Clearly it is a lot more convenient to have the table in front of you when classifying like this, and it uses much the same method of *Classweb* with its pop-up tables. By now you should have the idea of how it will work, but here's an example for demonstration.

Example

```
Clarence : was he Jack the Ripper? / Michael Harrison. -
New York : Drake, 1974

Murder by region or country  HV6535.A-Z
Murder in Great Britain       HV6535.G7
Murder in London              HV6535.G73 L66

Complete call number:         HV6535.G73 L66 1974

(No author Cutter as there are two geographical Cutters)
```

Tables used in combination

The embedded table in the last example is a very small and simple one, but they are often more substantial than this. An additional complication is when you must apply another table before you arrive at the point of using the embedded one. This is normally because a 'geographical' table is needed to provide the starting numbers for the embedded table. The schedule for 'protection of animals by country' is very typical of how this works in practice: see Figure 16.5.

HV	SOCIAL PATHOLOGY... ...
	Protection, assistance and relief
	Protection of animals
	Animal rights
4761-4890.8	(By region or country) (Table H5)
	Add country number in table to HV4760
	Apply Table HV4761/1 for 4 number countries
	Apply Table HV4761/2 for 1 number countries
	Apply Table HV4761/3 for 1 number regions
	Under each:
	TABLE HV4761/1
	Table for animals rights by country (4 numbers)
	1 Societies. Association
	2 General works, history, etc.
	3.A-Z By region or state A-Z
	4 .A-Z By city A-Z

Figure 16.5 Tables embedded in a schedule

This sort of arrangement is very common in the sociology and social welfare part of Class H. You can see how the two tables are being used in tandem here: first of all you apply Table 5 to get the base numbers for animal protection in a particular country or region, then you use Tables HV4761/1-3 to provide further detail. Let's look at a real example:

Example

```
Story of the Battersea Dogs' Home / Gloria Cottesloe. -
Newton Abbott : David & Charles, 1979

Animal welfare by country:   HV4761-4890.9 (Table H5)
    In England and Wales:   HV4806 (46 from Table H5)
    Using Table HV4761/2:   .A6-Z for city (London L66)
    By institution A-Z:   B38 for Battersea

Classmark:   HV4806.L66 B38 1979

(No author Cutter again as there are two geographical
Cutters)
```

I hope you will agree that these tables aren't too difficult to use once you understand the conventions used. It's annoying that LCC doesn't provide clearer instructions, but if you keep your head and take them one step at a time they're fairly straightforward.

One outcome is that the classmarks are quite brief. The disadvantage of course is that they're completely non-expressive. As a classifier you can never hope to remember the notation, but have to work it out every time you come across a table in the schedules. The end-user will also suffer from this when it comes to searching, but the expectation is that users will use LCSH for subject retrieval, rather than the classification, which is there only as a device for shelf ordering.

Remember too that if you check your answers against the Library of Congress catalogue you may find that sometimes the Congress numbers are difficult to understand. Cutter numbers will probably be different from those you work out yourself from the chart in Chapter 15 (for reasons explained there) but you might also come across some variations in the way the tables are applied. Most of these differences arise for historical reasons: either the tables have been expanded or modified over time, but old LCC numbers are retained, or there has been some local adjustment to fit in with existing classmarks.

Answers to exercises
Exercise 16.1
1 HB3593
2 HB3636
3 HB3651
4 HB3505

Exercise 16.2
1 HA1124
2 HA1123

Exercise 16.3
1 HE3295.D88 2002 Table H37 – General work
2 HS624.S68 1999 Table HS557/1 – History
3 HE3186.I58 1994 Table H37 – Management. Cutter for title
4 HV7578.K3 1950 Table H69 – Regulations
5 HS1848.O6 F47 1974 Table H48 – General societies in the US, A-Z

Exercise 16.4

1 HD9330.S622 I58 1996 General work. Cutter for title
2 HD9438.B572 B84 1990 General work. Cutter for title
3 HD9839.P33 G74 Regional. Cutter for place
4 HAD 9969.B9 C26 Regional. Cutter for place (note the schedule has changed since this title was catalogued)
5 HD9971.5.W383 U55 Regional. Cutter for place
6 HD9999.C423 U55 1991 Regional. Cutter for place
7 HD8039.B62 C26 1979 Regional. Cutter for place
8 HD9235.B762 C26 1979 Regional. Cutter for place
9 HD8039.W492 U55 1995 Regional. Cutter for place
10. HD8039.T522 G47 1986 Regional. Cutter for place

17 Dewey Decimal Classification

The Decimal Classification, devised by Melvil Dewey, is the oldest of the classification schemes still in common use, and by far the most widely used. It is the scheme that most non-librarians are familiar with, and indeed few of them will be aware of any other library classification.

Although it is the oldest scheme, I have chosen to place it after the Library of Congress Classification, since the latter is a somewhat simpler scheme to apply and doesn't show the complexity of operation that DDC now does. DDC is an enumerative scheme with analytico-synthetic features and as such sits quite neatly between LCC and UDC.

DDC is used all over the world and in all types of libraries, although most British readers will think of it as the 'public library' classification, since there is only one British public library which doesn't use it. It's also the predominant classification in school libraries. As it becomes more detailed and with more facilities for number building, it has increased in popularity as a scheme for academic libraries. Despite the fact that its publishers claim it to be used by 20% of special libraries in the US, it's probably not sufficiently specific for many special libraries or those with a great deal of technical material.

DDC is quite exceptionally well supported institutionally, and this is undoubtedly one of the reasons for its tremendous success. DDC classmarks appear on all Library of Congress catalogue records, and its editorial office is located there, which enables close monitoring of trends in documentation and the emergence of new topics. It has for several decades been the classification used in the *British National Bibliography*, and it was adopted by the British Library for the organization of the Reading Room collections at the new library when it opened.

OCLC, the Online Computer Library Center, a not-for-profit organization, publishes the classification, and maintains *WorldCat*, a 54 million item database of records with DDC data. OCLC also undertakes research and has a number of interesting projects in the area of vocabulary management and automatic indexing, some of which are concerned with developing new roles and applications for the classification.

Formal maintenance and revision of the classification is undertaken by the editor and assistant editors under the guidance of the Editorial Policy Committee. The EPC includes representatives from OCLC, the Library of Congress, the American Library Association and the UK Chartered Institute of Library and Information Professionals, but it also has members representing the many different types of libraries which use DDC.

The DDC is updated about every seven years, and is now in its 22nd edition. The full edition is in four volumes, the first volume containing the introduction and auxiliary tables, and volume four, the index; volumes two and three contain the schedules. Nowadays an abridged edition is produced for each full edition about a year after it's published. Minor revisions, amendments and corrections in between new editions are published in *Dewey Decimal Classification: Additions, Notes and Decisions*. DDC has been available in electronic format since 1993. The CD version, *Dewey for Windows*, has now been replaced by *WebDewey*, the online equivalent. The electronic products including *WebDewey* have been developed over a number of years to ensure that the potential of the new format is fully exploited. *WebDewey* is more than an electronic version of the text, and is possibly the best of the online classifications in terms of functionality.

History of the Dewey Decimal Classification

The Decimal Classification was devised by Melvil Dewey in 1876, when he was still a student at Amherst College, Massachusetts, and he was actively involved with its development until his death in 1931. It was only after this that its name officially became the Dewey Decimal Classification (despite the long existence of the Universal Decimal Classification), but now it is popularly known the world over as 'Dewey'.

It would be silly to pretend that Dewey was a marvellous theorist or that any great philosophic principles of classification underlay the original scheme – it was just a sensible, pragmatic arrangement for books, suitable for a general library. It shows an indication of some of the principles of classification theory that were rationalized later on (such as the principle of general-before-special and an implicit sense of inversion) but these are mainly based on common sense (of which Dewey had a good deal), and suggestions that there is a philosophical basis to the scheme have been largely superimposed retrospectively.

The great innovation was the notation. Prior to this most libraries used a scheme of **fixed location**, with the classmarks corresponding to the part of the library where the books were shelved; as the collection grew and books had to be moved, they also had to be re-classed to indicate their new position. Dewey's notation permitted the **relative location** of books. Because his classmarks indicated the subject of the book (rather than a shelf where that subject was placed) there was no need to re-label books, or shelves, when books were moved. There was one single sequence which remained constant; books could be removed, or new ones inserted, but the overall order wasn't affected, and a book once classified could retain its classmark for the whole of its life.

The use of nothing but arabic numerals was also quite unusual at the time. Most schemes of arrangement used a combination of arabic numerals, letters and roman numerals, with the type of character being changed at each step of division of the classification, or to indicate the bookcase, shelf and position of the book (and often these were closely related). Dewey's notation with its single character set, its decimal points and its single uninterrupted numerical sequence must have looked strikingly modern and scientific. There have been suggestions that Dewey copied the idea of the decimal notation, perhaps from the scheme in use at the Boston Public Library, but although that scheme was based on the use of divisions of ten, it was still a fixed location system and the notation looked nothing at all like the Decimal Classification. Dewey's ideas appear to have been entirely his own.

Great theorist he may not have been, but Dewey was one of the most energetic, forceful and innovative men of his generation. In addition to his work on the classification, he was one of the founders of the American Library Association, a pioneer of library education and a champion of women in the profession. He was an advocate of spelling reform, and the early editions of DDC were written in Dewey's own spelling system; the original introduction, with improved spelling, was reproduced in every edition, up to and including the 18th. He was also a veritable goldmine of common-sense ideas about practical classification, and the introductions to the early editions are worth reading for these alone.

The structure of the classification
The main classes
Like all the classifications considered in this book, DDC is an aspect

classification. That is to say, it is a knowledge-based classification, consisting of a series of main classes which correspond to traditional disciplines or areas of study. A particular topic, rabbits for example, might occur several times in the classification, depending on the aspect which is studied. DDC does tend to replicate topics rather more than its offspring the UDC. The relative index is vital in allowing the classifier to identify the different locations and make a choice between them.

There is nothing particularly innovative or unusual about the broad structure of DDC, and Dewey doesn't seem to have given a great deal of thought to the order of his main classes. What we think of as the humanities (philosophy, theology, language and literature, history and so on) are all over the place, language and literature are widely separated, and all the mathematical, physical and biological sciences are squashed into one class, as are medicine, engineering, agriculture, management, technology and manufacturing industry. Although achieving a satisfactory order of main classes is notoriously difficult, there seems hardly to be a single classification that hasn't done better than Dewey.

Nevertheless, this is probably the most familiar main class order, and it has affected the way most librarians (and possibly library users) think about the disposition of subjects. There are, naturally enough, ten main classes: see Figure 17.1.

0	Generalities
1	Philosophy, including psychology
2	Religion
3	Social sciences
4	Language
5	Mathematics and natural sciences
6	Applied sciences, technology
7	The arts
8	Literature
9	Geography, history, and auxiliary subjects

Figure 17.1 Main classes in DDC

The hierarchical structure

These ten classes are then subdivided into a hundred sub-classes (see Figure 17.2), and the hundred further subdivided into a thousand (see Figure 17.3) and so on. In order to make the notation easier to understand, three digits are always used to represent these first thousand classes, and noughts are put in where necessary to fill any spaces.

700	The arts
710	Civic and landscape arts
720	Architecture
730	Sculpture and the plastic arts
740	Drawing and decorative arts
750	Painting
760	Graphic arts
770	Photography
780	Music
790	Recreation, sport and performing arts

Figure 17.2 First hundred subdivisions - the 700s

780	Music
781	General principles
782	Vocal music
783	Music for single voices
784	Instruments and instrumental ensembles
785	Ensembles with one instrument per part
786	Keyboard and other instruments
787	Stringed instruments
788	Wind instruments
789	(Optional number)

Figure 17.3 First thousand subdivisions – the 780s

After the first three digits, the decimal point is inserted, and then the subdivision carries on in this fashion for as long as is necessary. Except for the first thousand classes (which all have three digits), this regular subdivision into more and more specific classes is represented both in the notation and in the schedule display. At every level of subdivision another digit is added to the classmark, and each new subordinate class is indented to the right underneath its containing class. You can see how this happens in the (abbreviated) section of the 200s shown in Figure 17.4.

284	Protestant denominations of Continental origin
.1	Lutheran churches
.131	Specific denominations in the United States
.131	The American Lutheran Church
.131 2	The Evangelical Lutheran Church
.131 3	United Evangelical Lutheran Church
.131 4	Lutheran Free Church
.133	The Lutheran Church in America
.133 2	American Evangelical Lutheran Church

Figure 17.4 Notation and hierarchy in DDC

Note that in the published schedules DDC doesn't repeat the first three digits, and that a space is put in after each set of three digits following the decimal point. This space is just there to rest the eye and to make the notation easier to read, and it's not usually reproduced on catalogue records or spine labels, or in classified lists.

Notation
Numerical notation
The notation, as has already been stated, is one of the most distinctive features of DDC. The use of the pure numerical notation has certainly not hindered the spread of DDC internationally, since arabic numerals are understood throughout the world. The natural filing order of the notation, without any odd characters or symbols, is also to the scheme's advantage, and most users understand this without instruction. The only major disadvantage is that, because of the small number of characters in a numerical notation, the numbers are longer than they would be in a mixed character notation.

Expressiveness of notation
The second feature of the notation is that it is usually expressive of the hierarchy. In other words, the number of characters in the classmark for a subject corresponds directly to the position of the subject in the hierarchy. You can easily see this relationship between structure and notation in Figure 17.4. As with any expressive notation, it leads to very long numbers for subjects which are located deep in the hierarchy. This is a frequent criticism of DDC, particularly in areas such as computer science or electronic engineering, which have developed out of all expectation since Dewey's time. Numbers such as 005.74068 Database management or 621.3815483 Oscilloscopes are not uncommon, but there is nothing really to be done about this. Expressiveness in notation is a useful feature, since it supports machine retrieval (numbers can be shortened, or the truncation facility used, to broaden or narrow a search), and users seem instinctively to understand an expressive notation of this sort.

Compound subjects and number building
DDC was initially an enumerative scheme; the tables were introduced much later in its history, as were other means of creating numbers for compound subjects. Because of this it has no general mechanisms for handling

compound subjects, but only 'local' provision in some classes. For example, under the law of social welfare at 344.032 notation from the social welfare class in 362 can be added to create numbers for the law relating to particular social welfare problems:

344.032 04–.032 8 Specific social welfare problems and services

> Add to base number 344.032 numbers following 362 in
> 362.04 – 362.8

Following this rule will create new classes in social service law, such as:

344.0327   Law of child welfare problems and services
          (from 362.7 Problems of and services to young people)

Unfortunately you can't add numbers from anywhere else in the scheme to this number, however useful that might be. The standard subdivisions in Table 1 are the only parts of the scheme that can be compounded without specific instruction. The result is that some parts of the system can achieve high levels of specificity and subject description, while other parts can provide only a broad level classification.

Citation order and preference order

You'll remember from earlier chapters that wherever there is any provision for building numbers you need to be clear about the order in which you combine concepts, i.e. the citation order. While some schemes, like UDC, CC and BC2, have general rules for this, DDC, because compounding is only sometimes allowed, makes it clear at the place where the number building happens exactly what you are to do.

In some cases this will be the same as standard citation order, but in others it won't conform. For example, in class 590, zoology, it's possible to subdivide the classes for individual animals by various aspects of zoological science, such as behaviour, ecology, genetics, evolution and so on.

Example

```
Reindeer on South Georgia: the ecology of an introduced
population / N. Leader Williams. - Cambridge, England :
Cambridge University Press, 1988

DDC number for reindeer:    599.658
```

```
Number for animal ecology:     591.7

Reindeer ecology:              599.65817
```

In this example the citation order is 'animal – ecology' or 'thing – process', which conforms with standard citation order.

Example

```
Trends in European forest tree physiology research /
Satu Huttunen ... [et al.]. – Dordrecht ; Boston :
Kluwer Academic, 2001.

DDC number for plant physiology:   571.2
DDC number for trees:              582.16

Physiology of trees:               571.2216
```

Here the number for plant physiology is divided by the kind of plant (in fact this is a built number adding the notation for tree to the base number for plant physiology). The citation order is therefore 'process – thing', the reverse of the previous example, and of standard citation order. We can see, therefore, that DDC acknowledges the idea of citation order, but there isn't always a consistent order applied.

Much of the time it isn't possible to combine two concepts, and in that case a sort of implicit or unofficial citation order comes into operation determining which of the two concepts is the more important. In DDC this is called **preference order**, and it tells you which aspect of a compound subject to express. An example from zoology again is shown in Figure 17.5. In this part of the classification it isn't possible to combine notation (as you can when dealing with particular sorts of animals). If you have a document that has two aspects of zoology, you need to decide which of them you should select as the subject of the book. You use the preference order to do this. When applying this preference order you should choose the aspect of the subject that appears first in the list. So, if you have a document about the behaviour of animals in a particular country, you should class it with animal behaviour rather than with the animals of the country. Notice that the preference order isn't related to the schedule order in any way.

When we look at number building in the next section we'll try several

591	Specific topics in natural history of animals	
	Unless other instructions are given, observe the following table of preference, e.g. social behavior of beneficial animals 591.56 (*not* 591.63)	
	Behavior	591.5
	Miscellaneous nontaxonomic kinds of animals	591.6
	Physical adaptation	591.4
	Genetics, evolution, young animals	591.3
	Animal ecology, animals characteristic of specific environments	591.7
	Treatment of animals by specific continents, countries, localities	591.9

Figure 17.5 Preference order

different styles and methods of combining notation. The most important thing to remember with DDC is to follow the instructions in the schedule, and not to look for general rules.

Summary
- DDC is the oldest and most widely used library classification scheme in the world.
- It is an enumerative classification with analytico-synthetic features.
- Its most distinctive feature is its pure numeral notation.
- It has a hierarchical structure with expressive notation.
- It has some facilities for number building.
- It uses the idea of citation order, but this isn't always the same as standard citation order.
- Preference order tells you which parts of a compound subject should have priority.

Practical classification with DDC

DDC is probably the most complicated of the general schemes to apply, but the editors provide a good deal of help to the classifier in the way of notes and instructions. Figure 17.6 shows a typical page of DDC schedule.

| 686 | *Manufacture of products for specific uses* | 686 |

SUMMARY

686.1	Invention of printing
.2	Printing
.3	Bookbinding
.4	Photocopying (Photoduplication)

.1   Invention of printing

.2   Printing

Class here printing in the Latin alphabet

Class works on desktop publishing that emphasize typography in 686.22; class comprehensive works on printing and publishing in 070.5; class interdisciplinary works on print media in 302.232

See also 070.593 for self-publishing

.209   Historical, geographic, persons treatment

Class invention of printing in 686.1

.21   Printing in non-Latin alphabets and characters

Standard subdivisions are added for either or both topics in heading

Class here typefounding, typecasting, typefaces for non-Latin alphabets and characters

For other specific aspects of printing in non-Latin alphabets and characters, see the aspect, e.g. letterpress printing 686.2312

.218   Greek alphabet

.219   Other non-Latin alphabets and characters

Add to base number 686.219 the numbers following —9 in notation 91–99 from Table 6, e.g. Cyrillic alphabet 686.21918

Figure 17.6 DDC schedule display

You can see how many explanations and instructions are included. Of course not every page is as 'dense' with extra text as this one, but it provides a good opportunity to examine these different rules and regulations. Although we've considered these in a general way in Chapter 14, it's necessary to see specifically how DDC uses them.

You can divide these instructions into two sorts:

- instructions about what to put in the class
- instructions about how to build numbers.

Notes and instructions in DDC

Of all the schemes DDC is the clearest in defining the content of classes. In this section of the schedule you can see three aspects of class definition: scope notes, or 'class here' instructions, which define narrowly the content of the class, 'see also' references which direct you to related classes, and finally instructions about what to do with compound classes which you might feel tempted to put here but which DDC prefers to locate somewhere else. You can see this in the note beginning 'For other specific aspects of printing in non-Latin characters'. Notes such as these control any implicit citation or preference order in DDC.

There is also a number-building instruction at 686.219, telling you to add notation from Table 6 to a base number, and giving an example. DDC is particularly good at illustrating number building with practical examples. There are several different ways of number building which we'll look at in more detail below.

It's important that you pay attention to all these instructions. Because DDC has evolved over a long period the scheme isn't always consistent in the way it does things, and it's impossible to provide generally applicable rules. Therefore you must take very careful note of the rules at any given place, and not try to impose rules of your own. DDC is always very clear about what can and can't be done and you should follow the guidelines. Otherwise the potential for confusion is great and you'll end up with numbers that conflict with numbers for other subjects, or that don't mean anything at all.

Choosing basic numbers

You should remember all the things from the chapters on content analysis and try to make an independent assessment of the document's subject before you turn to the DDC schedule. But, much of the time, if the subjects of your documents are simple and straightforward, you won't need more than a basic DDC number taken directly from the schedule.

It's important in any bibliographic classification that you use the index, since different aspects of a subject might be found in several places in the classification, and you need to be aware of all your options before you make a decision.

Here's the DDC index entry for the term Gold:

Gold	669.22
chemical engineering	661.065 6
chemistry	546.656
economic geology	553.41
materials science	620.189 22
metallography	669.952 2
metallurgy	669.22
metalworking	673.22
mining	622.342 2
monetary law	343.032
physical metallurgy	669.962 2
production economics	338.272 1
prospecting	622.184 1
see also Chemicals; Metals	
Gold coins	332.404 2
investment economics	332.63
monetary economics	332.404 2
numismatics	737.43
Gold movements	332.042
Gold standard	332.422 2
foreign exchange	332.452

The indented headings indicate the classes where various aspects of gold are to be found. It's quite likely that you might not think of all these possible locations for gold if the index didn't bring them to your attention, so it's a very necessary prerequisite to examining the schedules. British users need to remember that American spelling is used. Although there aren't any examples in this section, you will find some entries with a T number and a dash preceding the numbers:

Egypt	962
	T2—62
ancient	932
	T2—32

These are notations from the tables in volume 1; they are used only in number building (which we'll look at below) and can't be used on their own.

Remember not to rely on the index alone: it is essential to look at the schedules to establish that you have found the correct place in the hierarchy, and that there aren't more suitable classes for your document. You must also examine the notes and instructions attached to classes, so it's really impossible to classify directly from the index, even if you try.

DDC provides frequent summaries of the schedules, at the head of each class, and also preceding major sections of the class. This is a useful alternative means of finding your way into the classification once you've gained an idea of the broad structure. I usually prefer this method since it provides you with a sense of the overall structure and order of the class to which you're assigning your book. It also helps you to become acquainted with the classification rather more quickly than you might otherwise. Remember too, to look at the scope notes and instructions for each class to make doubly sure that the subject of your document fits properly.

With all this in mind let's find some straightforward 'simple' DDC numbers:

Example

```
Abuse of elderly people : a handbook for professionals /
Jacki Pritchard. - London : J. Kingsley, 1992
```

This general book on abuse of the elderly can be classed at 362.6. There are some notes there on where to locate other aspects of the subject, such as elder abuse as a crime, or abuse specifically of parents, but the general class will be sufficient for our needs. Here are some other examples of books for you to try.

Exercise 17.1

Find main class numbers for the following titles:

1 British Museum book of cats
2 Brussels sprout facts
3 Business ethics: critical perspectives on business and management
4 Christmas cooking
5 Great cathedrals of the world
6 Incredible secrets of vinegar

Continued on next page

> **Exercise 17.1** *Continued*
>
> **7** *The secret life of wombats*
> **8** *Teach yourself alcoholism*
> **9** *There is a life without snoring*
> **10** *The art and industry of sandcastles*

These numbers are very straightforward. You'll notice that one at least – *Christmas cooking* – has a compound subject, combining an activity (cooking) and a time (Christmas). Although not on the same scale as LCC, DDC has some elements of pre-coordination in its schedules.

Compound subjects

Sometimes the subject of a book doesn't exactly match the scope or range of a class in the scheme; you can usually be very sure about this in DDC because it is so precise as to what should be included in a class. Normally the problem arises because the subject of the document is a compound one. There are various ways to deal with this through number building, but often this happens because the subject is a compound one the parts of which can't all be expressed through number building.

You'll remember that we discussed this back in Chapters 8 and 9 on content analysis, where we looked at the problems of multi-disciplinary and interdisciplinary works, and where to place such documents. DDC has two rules for dealing with such situations: the first-of-two rule and the rule of three.

The first-of-two rule is designed for the document that consists of two intersecting subjects but where you can't build a number expressing both parts.

Example

    The portable pet: how to travel anywhere with your dog
    or cat / Barbara Nicholas. - Harvard, Mass. : Harvard
    Common Press, 1983

The first-of-two rule says that in this situation you should class the book at the first of the two subjects to appear in the schedule, i.e. at the lower of the two numbers. Dogs are classed at 636.7 and cats at 636.8, and, since there isn't any way we can link these two numbers notationally, the book goes at the first location, 636.7.

The rule of three tells us that if three or more topics are represented we should use a broader class that contains all of them.

Example

```
Raising turkeys, ducks, geese, pigeons and guineas /
Cynthia Haynes. - Blue Ridge Summit, PA : Tab Books, 1987
```

Here, although all these different birds are listed in the DDC schedules (at 636.592/.598), rather than opting for the first of these classes, we choose the broader class 636.59, other poultry.

Exercise 17.2
Find DDC numbers for the following titles:

1 *Horse, tapir and rhinoceros*
2 *Another look at population and global warming*
3 *Gardens for birds*
4 *Bush walking and camping*
5 *Gibson banjos, guitars, mandolins, ukuleles*
6 *Television and radio announcing*

Approximation to the whole

In many cases we are able to deal with these more complicated subjects by building a number that expresses the different parts of the subject. But before we begin to build any numbers we need to understand an important DDC concept, that of approximation to the whole. The idea behind approximation to the whole is that of the match between the main subject of a document (ignoring any elements such as time, place, persons, etc.) and the definition of the class in which you as classifier intend to place it. A subject is said to approximate to the whole if it is more or less equivalent to the class. Sometimes DDC helps you decide this by telling you to class certain subjects in the class under discussion. For example:

> 333.917   Lands adjoining bodies of water
>
> > Class here coasts, seashores, shorelands

These 'class here' instructions are very common, but on some occasions you'll have to decide for yourself whether the subject of your document 'approximates to the whole'. Suppose you have a book about pony trekking, that is, cross-country riding, often in hilly or otherwise difficult terrain. There seems to be no particular class for pony trekking in DDC, but there is a class for riding generally at 798.23. We can say that pony trekking doesn't approximate to the whole of riding; it isn't the same thing as riding, nor is it more or less the same. It's a particular kind of riding, and a book about it will only cover part of what riding is.

Sometimes the relationship is made clear by what are known as 'including notes'. These tell you for certain that a subject is only part of the bigger class. Staying with the horsy theme we see further down the schedule:

798.24   Riding exhibitions and competitions
                       Including three-day events

This including note tells you that 'three-day events' is only a smaller part of the class 'Riding exhibitions and competitions', and doesn't have enough literature to warrant having a class (with notation) of its own. It is said to have 'standing room' in the broader class, because there's always the possibility that such a subject may become more important and be given its own notation.

From the point of view of number building, a subject that doesn't approximate to the whole, or is in an including note, shouldn't have any further notation added to it. No matter how complex a subject may be, if the main topic doesn't have class status, you shouldn't attempt to express any other elements of the content.

Summary
- DDC provides a large number of notes and instructions to aid classifiers, and you should always read these carefully.
- Class definition in DDC is usually very explicit.
- It's important to use the Relative Index to identify all the places where a concept occurs in the schedules.
- You should also use the summaries and scan the schedules themselves to make sure you have the appropriate location for a topic.

Continued on next page

Summary *Continued*
- When the parts of a compound subject can't be combined notationally, the first-of-two rule and the rule of three help you to decide where to locate it.
- Class definition in DDC is usually quite explicit and precise.
- The notion of approximation to the whole establishes whether a subject can be further extended by synthesis.

Number building

Number building in DDC normally takes one of three forms:

- adding from the tables in volume 1
- adding from special tables in the schedules
- adding notation from other classes in the scheme

You should remember when you're building classmarks that, however the classmark is constructed, there is only ever one decimal point. Decimal points in any added notation are dropped. You'll see some examples of this below.

Number building from auxiliary tables

The tables in volume 1 of DDC contain concepts that occur frequently in number building. They are an alternative (and more economical) way of providing for these common concepts than repeated enumeration of them in combination with main class numbers. The tables cover the following:

- standard subdivisions (Table 1)
- places, periods and persons (Table 2)
- subdivisions for arts and literature (Table 3)
- subdivisions for individual languages (Table 4)
- ethnic and national groups (Table 5)
- languages (Table 6).

Tables 3 and 4 are for use in classes 4, 7 and 8, but the other tables can all be used throughout the classification. Only Table 1, the standard subdivisions, may be applied without specific instruction.

Standard subdivisions (Table 1)

The standard subdivisions encompass a variety of concepts, all of which occur very commonly in document description. We met many of them in the chapters on content analysis. They include form (both inner and outer), persons, historical and geographical treatment, and also a range of common subject subdivisions such as philosophy and theory, research, management, organizations and so on.

The notations for these subdivisions all begin with a zero, and they can be attached directly to the classmark for any topic. The zero is sometimes described as a facet indicator, and although it isn't precisely that (since it doesn't introduce a specific facet), it certainly alerts the user to the fact that some further subdivision of a topic is now happening.

The dash in front of the Table 1 notations shows that they can't be used on their own. A number from the main schedules must be inserted in place of the dash to create a valid DDC classmark.

Remember when you're building numbers that the decimal point comes after the third digit, but that there is no other spacing or punctuation in a DDC number, however long it may be. If you add a notation containing a decimal point to a base number, that decimal point must be dropped when the number is built.

Example

```
Coins and currency : an historical encyclopaedia / Mary
Ellen Snodgrass. - Jefferson, N.C. : McFarland, 2003

Classmark for Coins:              737.4

Table 1 notation Encyclopedia:    -03

Built number:                     737.403
```

Although in the vast majority of cases the Table 1 notation is added directly to the classmark, a complication occurs if the classmark already ends in a zero. In that event, the zero (or zeros) are disregarded, and the Table 1 notation added directly to the significant part of the classmark. The decimal point is put in after the third digit wherever the zeros happen to be.

630   Agriculture
630.5   A periodical in agriculture
            = 63 + —05

780   Music
780.79   Music competitions
            = 78 + —079

500   Science
503   A dictionary of science
            = 5 + —03

There are a number of exceptions to this rule, so until you know the schedules really well you need to check the instructions for any departure from the normal procedure.

Exercise 17.3

Build numbers for the following titles using concepts from Table 1:

1 *Career opportunities in advertising and public relations*
2 *Handbook of pottery and porcelain marks*
3 *Do stars have points? Questions and answers about stars and planets*
4 *On concepts and classifications of musical instruments*
5 *American photographic patents*
6 *Encyclopedia of origami*
7 *Marketing of quality graded potatoes*
8 *The clockwork of the heavens: an exhibition of astronomical clocks*
9 *Fotofest 98: the seventh international festival of photography*
10 *How to open and operate a restaurant: step-by-step guide to financial success*

Subdivisions for place and time

Probably the commonest use of Table 1 is to introduce geographical and historical concepts. These can always be added to the classmark for any subject by using the —09 divisions of the table, which provide for geographical, historical and biographical aspects. Geographical subdivisions are introduced by —091 for general concepts of place, and by —093 to 099 for specific places, such as countries, cities and named regions.

The details of these places are to be found in Table 2, and the notation from the two tables is used in conjunction when concepts are being added as standard subdivisions. (Sometimes notation from Table 2 can be added directly to a main number, but you'll always be instructed when you can do this.) You must therefore be careful always to put in the —09 part of the number.

I've inserted some spaces into the notations in Figure 17.7 to try to make clearer what's happening; these need to be removed in the finished class-mark. You'll probably spot that you just need to put —09 in front of the table 2 notations to use them as standard subdivisions.

Tropical areas	—09 to introduce general place from Table 1
+	—13 for tropics from Table 2
=	—0913
Oceans & seas	—09 to introduce general place from Table 1
+	—162 for oceans and seas from Table 2
=	—09162
Scotland	—093–099 for specific places from Table 1
+	—411 for Scotland from Table 2
=	—09 411

Figure 17.7 Combining Table 1 and Table 2 notations to create standard subdivisions for place

Examples

```
Australian freshwater turtles / John Cann. - Singapore :
Beaumont, 1998

Concept analysis: Turtles - Australia
                  597.92    —09 + —94

Classmark:     597.920994


Beehives of the ancient world / Eva Crane and A.J.
Graham. - Gerrards Cross : International Bee Research
Association, 1985

Concept analysis: Beehives - ancient world
                  638.14          —093

Classmark:     638.14093
```

Exercise 17.4

Create classmarks for the following titles, using Tables 1 and 2 together:

1   *Bogs of the Northeast [United States]*
2   *Cultivated plants of Southern Africa*
3   *Flights of fancy: early aviation in Battersea and Wandsworth*
4   *Fun with the family in Illinois: hundreds of ideas for day trips with kids*
5   *Greek insects*
6   *Hydrology in mountainous regions*
7   *Marsupials in New Zealand*

The —09 subdivisions of Table 1 also contain provision for qualifying subjects by historical period. The periods are not very specific, being mainly centuries, with the 20th and 21st century divided into decades. Notation is added in the same way as the form and subject subdivisions of Table 1.

Example

```
Trombone in the Middle Ages and the Renaissance / G.B.
Lane. - Bloomington : Indiana University Press, 1982

Concept analysis:     trombone - Middle Ages
                      788.93      —0902

Classmark: 788.930902
```

Exercise 17.5

Create classmarks for the following titles using Table 1:

1   *Images in ivory: precious objects of the Gothic age*
2   *Porcelain of the Nineteenth Century*
3   *We'll eat again: a collection of recipes from the war years*
4   *Thirty greatest tennis matches of the twentieth century*
5   *Advent Christians and the Bible: theological discussion and confessional change in the early 1960s*
6   *100 years of popular music: [19]20s*
7   *World of fashion, 1837–1922*
8   *From the ballroom to hell: grace and folly in nineteenth century dance*

If you look at the beginning of the sections for historical and geographical subdivision in Table 1, you'll see that it's possible to add some further
subdivisions for form and subject, using a table 'embedded' in the schedule. These subdivisions are not as extensive as the whole of Table 1, but
they are nevertheless useful where you have a complicated document.
Note that only the time subdivisions marked with an asterisk can be further qualified in this way, but that all the specific places are eligible.

Examples

```
Encyclopedia of twentieth-century technology / Colin
Hempstead. – New York : Fitzroy Dearborn, 2005


Concept analysis:      Technology – 20thC – encyclopedia
                          600        –0904          03


Classmark: 609.0403


Beast in the boudoir: pet keeping in nineteenth-century
Paris / Kathleen Kete. – Berkeley ; London : University
of California Press, 1994


Concept analysis:      Pets – Paris – 19th century
                   636.0087 –944361     –09034
Classmark: 636.0087094436109034
```

You can see in the above example how the 09s act as 'facet' indicators, sig-
nalling the introduction of another part of the complex subject. Fortunately
not all built numbers are as complicated as this one.

Persons subdivisions

Another very important part of Table 1 is that dealing with different
kinds of persons, at —08. This includes persons by age and gender, by family relationships, and by social characteristics, occupations, religion, and
ethnic and national groups. The notation is added to main numbers in just
the same way as the geographical and historical notation, and there is the
same provision for form, etc., in an embedded table.

Examples

```
Cycling past 50 / Joe Friel. - Champaign, Ill. : Human
Kinetics, 1998

Concept analysis:      Cycling - persons in late adulthood
                       796.6                    -0846


Classmark:     796.60846


Victorian murderesses : a true history of thirteen
respectable French and English women accused of
unspeakable crimes / Mary S. Hartman. - London : Robson
Books, 1977.

Concept analysis:      Murder - women - 19thC.
                       364.1523    -082   -09034

Classmark: 364.152308209034
```

It would be possible to locate the second book with other characteristics of the women – English, French, middle-class – and DDC appears to prefer that treatment. Nevertheless, I feel that the emphasis of this book is on women rather than nationalities or social status and exercise my judgement in making that the focus.

More detailed notation for nationality and ethnic groups can be obtained by adding numbers from Table 5 to —089, e.g. —08968 Spanish Americans, –08994541 Finns.

Exercise 17.6

Create classmarks for the following titles, using the persons subdivisions of Table 1:

1   *Women with alcoholic husbands*
2   *Chess for children*
3   *50 easy to play children's favourite hymns and songs*
4   *Disabled people in refugee and asylum seeking communities*
5   *Innovator's situation: upper middle class conservatism in agricultural communities*
6   *Refugee women and their mental health*

Adding the tables directly to class numbers

Although the commonest use of the Table 2 numbers is to attach them to the —09 notation from Table 1 and apply them as standard subdivisions, sometimes you are instructed to add them directly to a class number. In such cases no intermediary notation is needed.

Example

```
Muldoon : a true Chicago ghost story : tales of a
forgotten rectory / Rocco A. Facchini, Daniel J.
Facchini. - Chicago, Ill. : Lake Claremont Press, 2003

Concept analysis:     Haunting - Chicago
```

The class for haunted places is:

> 133.129   Specific haunted places
>
> > Add to base number 133.129 notation 3-9 from Table 2 . . .

The notation in Table 2 for Chicago is —773 11 and this can be added directly to the base number to give 133.12977311.

The other tables in Volume 1 are frequently used in the same way.

Exercise 17.7

Construct classmarks for the following titles using direct addition from the tables:

1 *The Irish constitution*
2 *A concise dictionary of New Zealand sign language*
3 *Disease in the history of Latin America: from malaria to AIDS*
4 *Minimus secundus: moving on in Latin. Teacher's resource book*
5 *Month-by-month Spanish write and read books: 15 reproducible predictable books that your students help write*
6 *Housing options for older adults*
7 *Educating homeless students: promising practices*
8 *Arabic proverbs*
9 *Modern Icelandic syntax*

Tables within schedules

So far all the numbers we have built have used notation from the auxiliary tables in Volume 1, but sometimes DDC provides tables that are 'special' to certain parts of the scheme, and are inserted in that part of the classification to which they apply. These tables function rather in the same way as the tables in LCC, and the special auxiliaries in UDC.

The 'embedded' table of additional subdivisions for geographical subdivisions we looked at on page 197 is an example of such a 'special' table. Here is another (slightly abridged) one:

636.1–636.8 Specific kinds of domestic animals

Except for modifications shown under specific entries, add to each subdivision identified by * as follows:

01	Philosophy and theory
02–06	Standard subdivisions
07	Education, research, related topics
079	Competition, festivals, awards, financial support
08–09	Standard subdivisions
1	Showing
	Class here judging
2	Breeding
22	Breeding records
	Class here origin of the breed or breeds; herdbooks, pedigrees, studbooks
3	Care, feeding, training
35	Training
39	Veterinary care

At 636.182 we find *Donkeys, and see from the asterisk that the special table can be applied to subdivide donkeys.

Example

```
Training mules and donkeys: a logical approach to
longears. Donkey training / Meredith Hodges. - Loveland,
Colo. : Lucky Three Ranch, 1999

Concept analysis:    Donkeys - training
```

The use of the special table means that we can take 35 (for training) from the table and add it directly to the number for donkeys to create a new number 636.18235, training of donkeys.

Building numbers in other ways
Adding whole class numbers

Sometimes extra specificity within a subject is achieved by adding notation from other parts of the classification, i.e. from other main classes rather than from tables. Sometimes the whole number from another class is used. This often happens when it is necessary to divide a subject 'by the whole classification'. A typical example is the class at:

> 016   **Bibliographies and catalogs of works on specific subjects or in specific disciplines**
>
> Add to base number 016 notation 001–999

This tells us that we can add any number from the whole classification to the number for bibliographies and catalogs, 016. Although the instruction says 001-999, this is shorthand for 'any DDC number', and doesn't mean that only three digits are to be used. You can take this to be the case wherever you're told to add 001-999.

Example

```
International proverb scholarship, an annotated
bibliography. Supplement / Wolfgang Mieder. - New York :
Garland, 1990-

Concept analysis:      Bibliography - proverbs
```

Here we can take the notation for Proverbs, 398.9, and add it directly to the notation for Bibliographies, to give the new classmark 016.3989. Note that the decimal point is dropped from 398.9 when it's added to the 016 notation. You can only ever have one decimal point in a DDC classmark (after the third digit).

Exercise 17.8

Construct classmarks for the following titles:

1 *Capital punishment: a bibliography with indexes*
2 *Forty years in science and religion*
3 *Saunders textbook of medical office management*

Continued on next page

Exercise 17.8 *Continued*

4 *The problem of war in the Old Testament*
5 *Dinosaurs and the Bible*
6 *An annotated bibliography of Canadian ornithology*
7 *Real sports reporting*

Adding partial notations

At other times only part of a number will be added. This is normally where there is some parallel structure in two subjects, and the second 'borrows' the notation from the first subject, rather than repeating it.

In earlier editions of DDC this operation was introduced by a 'Divide like' instruction rather than the 'Add' instruction we have currently, because the division of the two classes was exactly the same. This practice is also known as **parallel subdivision**, again because the two sequences run in parallel. Not only is this borrowing an economical way to schedule (because it saves repetition), it also ensures consistency of order and structure in the classification.

In this situation you will be instructed to 'add to' a base number, the numbers x-y following the source number. This will create the parallel sequences in the two different classes.

Example

```
Culture and children's intelligence: cross-cultural
analysis of the WISC-III / edited by James Georgas. -
Amsterdam ; Boston : Academic Press, 2003

Concept analysis:      Intelligence tests - children

Classmark: 155.41393
```

The class for Child psychology is 155.4, and intelligence 155.413. Here we see the instruction:

Add to base number 155.413 the numbers following 153 in 153.1–153.9

The number for intelligence tests in 153, Mental processes and intelligence, is 153.93, so we take the 93 and add it to our base number to give 155.41393:

$155.413 + 93$ (from 153.93) $= 155.41393$

Thus the order of classes in 155.413, Mental processes and intelligence in child psychology, will exactly mirror the order in the general class Mental processes and intelligence in 153.

Exercise 17.9
Construct classmarks for the following titles, by adding partial notations to a base number:

1   *The horse in myth and magic*
2   *Chicken: over 130 inspirational step-by-step recipes*
3   *The flooring handbook: the complete guide to choosing and installing floors*
4   *Drawing dogs*
5   *The curious morel: mushroom hunters' recipes, lore and advice*
6   *Mangrove management and conservation*
7   *An economic analysis of bird damage in vineyards*
8   *The mink trapper's guide*
9   *Buddhist art and architecture*

Summary
*   Standard subdivisions from Table 1 can be added to any number without instructions.
*   Subdivisions for place can be added to any number using —09 from Table 1 with detailed notation from Table 2.
*   Persons and periods are also always applicable using Table 1 subdivisions.
*   Otherwise you may build numbers only when instructed.
*   'Special' tables within schedules allow for extension of numbers within particular parts of the classification.
*   You can also construct classmarks by adding main numbers, or parts of numbers, to base numbers as instructed.

Answers to exercises
Exercise 17.1

1 636.8
2 635.36
3 174.4
4 641.5686
5 726.6
6 664.55
7 599.24
8 616.861
9 616.209
10 736.96

Exercise 17.2

1 599.72
2 363.7874
3 635.9
4 796.52
5 787.8
6 791.443

Exercise 17.3

1 659.023
2 738.0278
3 523.076
4 784.19012
5 770.272
6 736.98203
7 635.210688
8 681.113074
9 770.79
10 647.95068

Exercise 17.4

1 Bogs 577.687 and Northeast United States —0974: 577.6870974
2 Garden crops 635 and South Africa —0968: 635.0968
3 Aviation 387.7 and London Borough of Wandsworth —0942166:

387.70942166

4   Recreational activities for families 790.191 and Illinois —09773: 790.19109773

5   Insects 595.7 and Greece —0945:   595.70945

6   Hydrology 551.048 and Mountains —09143:   551.04809143

7   Marsupials 599.2 and New Zealand —0993:   599.20993

Exercise 17.5

1   Carvings in ivory 736.6 and 6th to 15th centuries —0902: 736.60902

2   Porcelain 738.2 and 19th century —09034:   738.209034

3   Food 641.5 and Period of World War II —09044:   641.509044

4   Tennis 796.3 and 20th century —0904:   796.30904

5   Christianity 230 and 1960s —09046:   230.09046 (Note that standard subdivisions at 230 are modifications of Table 1.)

6   Popular music 781.64 and 1920s —09042:   781.6409042

7   Costume and personal appearance 391 and 19th century —09034: 391.09034 (19th century is the nearest that DDC can come to the date involved.)

8   Ballroom dancing 793.33 and 19th century —09034: 793.3309034

Exercise 17.6

1   Alcoholism 362.292 and Married persons —08655:   362.29208655

2   Chess 794.1 and Children —083:   794.1083

3   Songs 784.42 and Children —083:   784.42083

4   Refugees 305.906914 and Disabled persons —087:   305.906914087

5   Rural communities 307.72 and Middle classes —08622: 307.7208622

6   Mental health 362.2 and Refugees —086914:   362.2086914 (Note that women and refugees cannot both be expressed, and the later occurring concept, i.e. refugees, is the one used.)

Exercise 17.7

Each classmark here is preceded by a 'deconstructed' version where a solidus (oblique stroke) has been inserted to show you where the base number ends and the notation from the table begins.

1   342./41502 = 342.41502

2   419/.93/03 = 419.9303
3   614.42/8 = 614.428
4   372.65/71044 = 372.6571044
5   372.65/61 = 372.6561
6   363.59/46 = 363.5946
7   371.826/942 = 371.826942
8   398.9/927 = 398.9927
9   439.69/5 = 439.695

Exercise 17.8

Again, a solidus is used to show how the number is constructed.

1   016./36466 =016.36466
2   201.6/5 = 201.65
3   651.9/61 = 651.961
4   220.8/35502 = 220.835502
5   220.8/5679 = 220.85679
6   016.598/0971 = 016.5980971
7   070.449/796 = 070.449796

Exercise 17.9

The solidus is again used to demonstrate the structure of the classmark.

1   398.369/96655 = 398.36996655
2   641.36/5 = 641.365
3   690.1/6 = 690.16
4   743.6/9772 = 743.69772
5   641.3/58 = 641.358
6   634.9/73763 = 634.973763
7   634.8/268 = 634.8268
8   639.11/74447 = 639.1174447
9   704.9489/43 = 704.948943

18 Universal Decimal Classification 1: general properties and basic number building

The Universal Decimal Classification (UDC) was devised in the early 20th century by two Belgians, Paul Otlet and Henri La Fontaine. Otlet and La Fontaine had conceived the idea of making a bibliography of all works published since the invention of printing – a project that was just about feasible a hundred years ago – and they wanted a system for the subject organization of their bibliography.

At that time there were several bibliographic classification schemes available to them, but the one that impressed them the most was Dewey's Decimal Classification, then in its fifth edition. They did not find in the DDC exactly what they wanted, and so they made some amendments and additions of their own to create what was the first edition of the Universal Decimal Classification, published between 1905 and 1907.

UDC is thus unique among the well-known schemes in that it wasn't originally intended to arrange a physical collection of documents, but rather to organize a card catalogue. As a consequence, the decisions that were made about its structure and function at that time placed the main emphasis on its use as a tool for retrieval. Great importance was attached to its ability to provide very detailed subject description, particularly for complex topics, and this was achieved at the expense of simplicity in the notation. This has continued to be an important characteristic of UDC, which means it is favoured in situations where retrieval is more important than browsing.

General characteristics of UDC

The scheme is very much more flexible that the enumerative schemes we've considered in previous chapters, and it can be used to create very detailed classmarks for documents with complicated subject content. As a result it has been a popular choice for use in scientific and technical libraries, and those that deal with large amounts of technical literature and reports. In the UK it can be found in a number of research establishments such as the Polar Research Institute, in government libraries at the Ministry of

Defence and DEFRA, and in large academic scientific collections, such as the library at Imperial College. In recent years it has been much favoured for the organization of digital collections, and is probably the most frequently encountered of the traditional classification schemes on the world wide web (although often the notation isn't displayed to the end user).

In continental Europe UDC is very widely used in academic libraries as well as special libraries, and in Eastern Europe in particular it is also used in public libraries. In some parts of the classification there is evident European bias (comparable with the American bias seen in LCC); for example, the religion class has a vocabulary strongly inclined towards Roman Catholicism, and the schedules for social welfare reflect the arrangements of many European countries. The scheme was also used by the Dutch Patent Office, and for many years edited by a member of staff there; this resulted in enormous detail in the technology classes, with specification for many bizarre objects, such as the coin-operated typewriter.

In terms of the range of cultures, nations and languages in which it is used, as well as the variety of types of library, UDC can certainly challenge the Dewey Decimal Classification as the most widely used scheme, although of course it can't compete with the sheer number of libraries worldwide that use DDC.

Management of UDC

UDC is owned and managed by the UDC Consortium, a body which consists of those who publish the scheme in various different languages. The publisher of the English edition is the British Standards Institution. The headquarters of UDC is at the Royal Library in The Hague from where the administration of the scheme is carried out.

UDC exists in several different formats. The authoritative version of the classification is held on a database in The Hague, which is known as the Master Reference File (MRF). It contains about 65,000 classes. This is the basis of the translations published by members of the Consortium, and appears in English as the Standard Edition. Since 2002 the English edition has been available by subscription online and it is intended that this should replace the print version. BSI also publishes an abridged version known as the Pocket Edition, which has about 4,000 classes. During the mid-20th century, a more detailed version of the scheme (known as the Full Edition) was published in English, French and German, although not all of the scheme appeared in all three languages. The English Full Edition was published by BSI in the form of separate fascicles or pamphlets for individual classes and sub-classes. Many of the special libraries that use UDC use this version, despite the fact that it is no longer being maintained.

Most of the examples in this chapter and the next have been worked using the UDC Pocket Edition. Where this doesn't have enough detail, the Standard Edition is used.

Amendments to the scheme and new schedules are published annually in UDC's bulletin *Extensions and corrections to the UDC*. More information about UDC can be found on the official website at www.udcc.org.

The structure of UDC
UDC as an aspect classification
Like the other general schemes UDC is an **aspect classification**. That is to say, the first division of the classification is into **main classes**, which reflect traditional **disciplines**.

UDC as a hierarchical classification
Like DDC, UDC is also a **hierarchical** classification, with its structure closely tied into, and expressive of, the decimal notation. The first division into main classes largely reflects that of its parent, the Dewey Decimal Classification:

Class	0	Generalities
	1	Philosophy (including Psychology)
	2	Religion
	3	Social sciences
	4	[currently empty after relocation of languages]
	5	Science
	6	Technology
	7	Arts (including recreation and sport)
	8	Language and literature
	9	Geography, history, biography

The major departure from DDC order is the bringing together of language and literature in Class 8, leaving Class 4 empty. (Class 4 may be occupied in the future by Medicine, a very large class, which is currently being extensively revised.)

Each main class is then subdivided into ten constituent sub-classes, and those classes are further subdivided, and so on. The result is a hierarchy of classes, reflecting the successive decimal subdivision. For example:

First level of subdivision:

3	Social sciences
31	Demography. Sociology. Statistics
32	Politics
33	Economics
34	Law
35	Administration
36	Social work. Social aid
37	Education
39	Ethnography

Second level of subdivision:

3	Social sciences	
34	Law	
341		International law
342		Public law
343		Criminal law
344		Military and naval law
346		Economic law
347		Civil law
348		Canon law. Ecclesiastical law
349		Special branches of law

Third level of subdivision:

3	Social sciences	
34	Law	
341		International law
342		Public law
343		Criminal law
343.1		Criminal investigation
343.2		Criminal law proper
343.3		Offences against public order

343.4	Offences against human rights
343.5	Offences against decency
343.6	Offences against the person
343.7	Offences against property
343.8	Punishment and crime prevention
343.9	Criminology
344	Military and naval law
346	Economic law
347	Civil law
348	Canon law. Ecclesiastical law
349	Special branches of law

The structure and notation of UDC corresponds quite closely to DDC, certainly at the three-digit level, and in many cases beyond.

UDC as an analytico-synthetic classification

UDC is an excellent example of that type of scheme known as an **analytico-synthetic** classification; that is, a scheme in which a complex subject can be broken down (or analysed) into its constituent parts, and a classmark built up (or synthesized) from the notational codes for those separate parts.

Unlike an **enumerative classification** (in which only the classmarks that are listed are valid), the analytico-synthetic scheme allows new classes to be created by the classifier. The number of potential classes is therefore very much greater than those listed in the printed schedules.

In UDC this number building is achieved in two ways:

- by linking numbers from the main classes together
- by adding numbers from a series of auxiliary tables.

The way in which this is done is considered in detail in the sections on practical classification later in the chapter.

UDC notation

The notation used in UDC is the arabic numeral system, linked together by various other symbols. You'll remember from an earlier chapter that using numbers has several advantages:

- They are almost universally recognized and can be used in cultures where the roman alphabet is not familiar.
- They have a clear filing order.

• Although classmarks using numeral notations tend to be longer than corresponding letter notations, users appear to find them more memorable (perhaps because they can be articulated – for example 347 as 'three hundred and forty-seven' – in a way that letters cannot).

Filing value of notation

UDC notation functions slightly differently from DDC notation, and if you are familiar with that scheme you may find UDC a little confusing at first. UDC classmarks file decimally: that is, as if they have an invisible nought and a decimal point at the beginning of each number.

A sequence of numbers such as

1, 02, 16, 35, 76, 114, 347, 347.2, 757, 767,

arranged here in order of their numerical value, is known as an ordinal sequence. In order to achieve the correct filing order in UDC, you will need to mentally rewrite them as:

0.1, 0.02, 0.16, 0.35, 0.76, 0.114, 0.347, 0.347.2, 0.757, 0.767.

The filing order now becomes:

0.02, 0.1, 0.114, 0.16, 0.347, 0.347.2, 0.35, 0.757, 0.75, 0.767.

This is sometimes called decimal filing (as opposed to the ordinal filing above). You can see this more clearly if we represent it vertically:

'Imaginary' decimal fractions	UDC numbers
0.02	02
0.1	1
0.114	114
0.16	16
0.347	347
0.347.2	347.2
0.35	35
0.757	757
0.76	76
0.767	767

In theory these decimal fractions can be of any length, but because very long numbers are confusing to the eye (and consequently difficult to remember), the number is broken down by putting in a decimal point after every third digit. For example:

004.738.52   The Worldwide Web
599.735.5   Wildebeest
687.517   False beards and moustaches
681.817.81   Hurdy-gurdies
784.011.26   Pop songs

When new numbers are created by joining pieces of notation together it will sometimes happen that the decimal points don't occur every three places:

687.53.05   Hairdressing equipment
7.038.5   Body art
72.052.4   Vestibules in architecture

We'll look at how and why this happens when considering number building below.

Symbols in UDC notation
UDC uses a number of other symbols in building up more complicated classmarks. The filing order of these symbols is as follows:

+
/
Simple number with no symbols
:
=
(0...)
(1/9)
(=...)
"..."
A/Z
−0
−1/9
.0
,

UDC is often criticized because of its notation. The principal objections are that:

- the classmarks are very long and can be hard to remember
- there is no natural filing order for the non-numerical symbols, and so filing and shelving order has to be learned by both staff and users
- the symbols may cause difficulties in some computerized library management systems.

These are all valid criticisms, but they arise directly out of UDC's greater capacity to express the full subject content of documents; a simpler notation wouldn't be able to achieve this objective, and for UDC collections the balance falls in favour of the complicated, but precise, classmarks.

Expressiveness of notation

In UDC the structure of the classification is mirrored very closely in the notation. As one goes deeper into the hierarchy of classes, so the notation lengthens; for each new level of hierarchy an extra character is added to the classmark, and the classmark is said to be expressive of the structure. For example:

3	Social science
34	Law
343	Criminal law
343.6	Offences against the person
681	Precision mechanisms and instruments
681.8	Technical acoustics
681.81	Musical instruments
681.816	Keyboard instruments
681.816.8	Accordion

In UDC this principle is adhered to very rigorously. It is particularly important because, unlike the other schemes that we've considered, the layout of schedules in the published classification doesn't show the structure of the classification. In the case of the law schedule shown above, the classes are displayed in a way that suggests they are all of equal, or co-ordinate, status:

3	Social sciences
34	Law
341	International law
342	Public law
343	Criminal law
343.1	Criminal investigation
343.2	Criminal law proper
343.3	Offences against public order
343.4	Offences against human rights
343.5	Offences against decency
343.6	Offences against the person
343.7	Offences against property
343.8	Punishment and crime prevention
343.9	Criminology
344	Military and naval law
346	Economic law

Although different fonts and typefaces are used to indicate different levels in the hierarchy, the notation bears most of the burden of communicating to the user the relationship of classes within the classification.

The UDC notation is also expressive in that, unlike DDC, the numbers are not altered in any way when building classmarks for compound subjects. This means that the notation for a topic can be searched for wherever it appears within a built number.

Summary

- UDC is an analytico-synthetic scheme.
- It was originally designed for use in a card catalogue, rather than as a tool for shelf arrangement.
- It is based on DDC but has more synthetic facilities, and is capable of great precision in classification.
- It is widely used in technical and special libraries.
- It is an aspect classification.
- It is hierarchical in structure.
- The notation is expressive and uses numerals and many other symbols..

Practical classification using UDC
Schedule layout and display

We have already noted above that UDC doesn't employ the usual indentation of classes that most other schemes use. It's therefore doubly important to scan the schedules for broader and narrower classes, and to use the notation to check whether classes are subordinate or co-ordinate, and so on. UDC uses quite a lot of 'shorthand' instructions or symbols as to what to do. You can see some of these in Figure 18.1:

636.085	**Feedstuffs, fodder in general**
636.085.1	Composition of feedstuffs
636.085.5	Individual kinds of feedstuffs
636.085.51	Green fodder in general
	→ *636.086*
636.085.6	Preparation of fodder for consumption
636.086	Specific vegetable feedstuffs
	→ *636.085.51, 664.78*
	636.086.1/.4 ≅ *633.1/.4*
636.086.5	Sprouted grain
636.086.7	Other vegetable feedstuffs
636.086.74	Fruit bearing plants
	636.086.741/.747 ≅ *634.1/.7*
636.086.75	Market garden plants
	636.086.751/.756 ≅ *635.1/.6*
636.086.8	Chemically treated cellulose foodstuffs
636.087	Industrial by-products as feedstuffs

Figure 18.1 Schedule layout of UDC

- → acts as a *See also* reference, pointing to other related class numbers. Until you're very familiar with the scheme you should always look at the cross-references in case they might fit your topic better than the number you first thought of.

- the congruent sign which looks like an equals sign with a tilde over it, ≅, means that you should divide your number in the same way as the set of numbers that are referred to. This is sometimes called **parallel subdivision**.

In Figure 18.1, for example,

636.086   Specific vegetable feedstuffs
→ *636.085.51, 664.78*
636.086.1/.4 ≅ *633.1/.4*

Earlier in the schedule, under 633 Field crops, we find:

633.1   Cereals. Grain crops
633.2   Forage grasses
633.3   Forage plants except grasses
633.4   Edible roots and tubers. Root crops

If we want to create a number for root crops as feedstuffs, we take the .4 from 633.4 and add it to 636.086, to give 636.086.4.

Usually UDC is more helpful than this, and gives you what is called an 'example of combination': see Figure 18.2. This shows how the number building is meant to work by practical demonstration; it is also useful to the compilers because it allows them to include numbers for topics that classifiers need but which would otherwise not appear.

In the Pocket Edition of UDC you can identify the examples of combination by the small diamond shape in the left hand margin. Don't worry if you don't understand how these examples of combination are constructed. When we've been through the whole process of number building this will be quite clear.

636.2	**Large ruminants. Cattle. Oxen**
	Example(s) of combination:
	636.2.053 Young oxen. Calves
636.3	**Small ruminants. Sheep. Goats**
636.32	**British sheep breeds**
636.33	**Dutch and German sheep breeds**
636.34	**French and Flemish sheep breed**
636.37	**Other European sheep breeds**
	Example(s) of combination:
	636.37(48) Scandinavian sheep breeds
636.38	**Non-European sheep breeds**
	Example(s) of combination:
	636.38(5) Asiatic sheep breeds

Figure 18.2 Examples of combination in UDC

The main tables

The Standard Edition of UDC in English is in two volumes: an index volume and a volume called *Systematic Tables*. This contains the main classes of the classification, sometimes known as **main tables**, and a large number of **auxiliary tables**. We'll look at using the main tables first.

In many cases UDC won't be any different in use to the enumerative schemes. If the subject of a document is simple in nature, numbers can be taken directly from the main tables. You should remember to use the index to discover the possible locations for a topic, and then to refer to the schedules to see whether the context is appropriate, and to consult the various notes, explanations and instructions there. When you look at the index you'll find lots of 'examples of combination' included there; this is precisely because the compilers need to put into the index the sort of topics that classifiers look for, even if they have to be artificially constructed.

Let's start with something appropriate to the Belgian origins of UDC.

Example

```
Brussels sprout facts / National Vegetable Research
Station. - 3rd ed. - Warwick : NVRS, 1984

UDC number:    635.36
```

The example here is just a general book about Brussels sprouts. We can class it at the number for Brussels sprouts, 635.36. Let's try another title.

Example

```
Incredible secrets of vinegar / Marie Nadine Antol. -
Garden City Park, N.Y. : Avery Pub. Group, 2000

UDC number:    641.882
```

Here is another 'simple' book, this time about vinegar, and the number for this, 641.882, can also be found in the main tables.

In cases like these, where the subject of the document is straightforward and can be represented by a number found in the main tables, you need do nothing else.

Exercise 18.1

Find appropriate main table numbers for:

1	Boot-making	6	Raffia work
2	Gender studies	7	Sea shanties
3	Hypnotism	8	Sick pay
4	Moon rats	9	Weightlifting
5	The Pope	10	Whisk ferns

Building numbers in UDC

We have already said that the principal features of UDC include its analytico-synthetic nature and its facilities for number building. In the next few pages we'll look at the basic methods of number building that UDC uses.

Joining together main table numbers 1: the colon

Very often the subject of a document is a compound consisting of two or more concepts that can be located in the main tables of UDC. Look at Figure 18.3, *Collect mammals on stamps*. This is a book about stamp collecting, but it's also about mammals. There are two elements to the subject, which ideally both need to be expressed in the document description. These sorts of compound subjects are quite common as pre-coordinated classes in the enumerative schemes, where they can be taken directly from the

Figure 18.3 *Collect mammals on stamps*

schedules. For example:

> Smoking and heart disease
> Fashion photography
> Judaism and Christianity
> Political cartoons
> Respiratory diseases of the horse

However, if the compound isn't included in an enumerative scheme, then only one part of the subject can be specified. In UDC the compound subject can always be specified. It has first to be analysed into its constituent parts, and then the classmark is synthesized from the notation for the different parts – hence the analytico-synthetic label given to the scheme.

Sometimes the two topics to be joined will be in the same main class:

Example

```
Teaching mathematics in primary schools : a handbook of
lesson plans, knowledge and teaching methods / Sue
Jennings and Richard Dunne. - London : Letts
Educational, 1998
```

In other cases the two subjects can come from different main classes:

Examples

```
The history and social influence of the potato /
Redcliffe N. Salaman ; with a chapter on industrial uses
by W.G. Burton. - Rev. impression / edited by J.G.
Hawkes. - Cambridge : Cambridge University Press, 1985

The kangaroo in the decorative arts / [catalogue
prepared and written by Terence Lane]. - Melbourne :
National Gallery of Victoria, [1980]
```

In the first of these examples the potato comes from plant science, and the social influence from sociology; in the second there is a combination of animal science and the fine arts.

In UDC you can create classmarks for these compound subjects by joining together the main table numbers for their constituent concepts. It doesn't matter whether the topics are in the same class or not; the same procedure is followed.

The principal means of joining together main table numbers in this way is the **colon** :. The colon is placed between the two classmarks, and indicates that there is some general relationship between the two subjects. It may occur to you that there are different sorts of relationships between the concepts in the examples on p. 220: i.e. the *influence* of smoking on heart disease, the *application* of photography to fashion, the *comparison* of Judaism and Christianity. Such relations are known as **phase relations**. Some indexing schemes do allow you to specify these different kinds of relationship, but UDC doesn't.

When building the classmark there is no alteration of either number, which means that the second number can still be searched for on the catalogue, since it doesn't change by dropping characters, or in any other way.

So, in the examples above, we have:

Examples

```
Teaching mathematics in primary schools : a handbook of
lesson plans, knowledge and teaching methods

Concept analysis:      Primary school  -  Maths teaching
UDC numbers                 373.3                 372.47
UDC classmark        373.3:372.47


The history and social influence of the potato

Concept analysis:      Potato - Sociology
UDC numbers          635.21      316
UDC classmark        635.21:316


The kangaroo in the decorative arts

Concept analysis:      Kangaroo - Decorative arts
UDC numbers:           599.224             74
UDC classmark        599.224:74
```

UDC rules tell us that, all other things being equal, the numbers should be combined in the order in which they appear in the schedule, i.e. in ascending numerical order. However, the classifier is allowed to vary the order of the concepts to show a particular emphasis, or to meet the needs of different users. For example, a book on 'Information skills in the curriculum' might be usefully classified as 372:025 in a collection for teachers, but in a library and information studies collection the users might prefer to find it at 025:372.

Therefore, when using the colon, you can put the numbers to be joined in any order, depending on which you think is the most important in terms of placing the document. If you would rather put the book about the kangaroo with other books on decorative arts you can reverse the order to make it 74:599.224 instead. If you have no strong feelings, or can't make up your mind, use the ascending order rule. In that case the kangaroo book would be located with other books on kangaroos.

Exercise 18.2
Construct UDC classmarks for the following titles

1 *Abortion in Judaism*
2 *Another look at population and global warming*
3 *Degrees of difference: influences on the development of tourism as a subject in UK higher education*
4 *Essential guide to bird photography*
5 *Impact of internet trading on the UK antiquarian and second-hand bookselling Industry*
6 *Picture your dog in needlework*
7 *Sacred and the feminine: toward a theology of housework*
8 *Smoking and disease*

If required, any number of main table numbers can be joined together with colons:

Examples

```
Giraffe in history and art / by Berthold Laufer. –
Chicago : Field Museum of Natural History, 1928

UDC numbers:    Giraffe     599.735.4
                Art         7
                History     94
Classmark:      599.735.4:7:94
```

```
Opera, liberalism and anti-Semitism in nineteenth century
France : the politics of Halévy's La juive / Diane R.
Hallman. - Cambridge : Cambridge University Press, 2002

UDC numbers:     Opera         792.54
                 Liberalism    329.12
                 Anti-Semitism 296.2
Classmark:       296.2:329.12:792.54
```

In the last example we could also add notation to express the concepts of France and the 19th century, and we'll return to this title when we've learned how to do that.

Joining together main table numbers 2: the plus sign

The plus sign + has the same meaning in a UDC number as it does in mathematics, and it indicates that the document contains two distinct subjects. You should use the plus sign in preference to the colon when two subjects are treated equally in the same document.

Example

```
Tail-ends : of bells and bell-ringing / by Joan M.
Foxon. - [Hinckley : J. Baxter, 1982]

UDC numbers:        Bells        673.5
                    Bell ringing 789.5
UDC classmark:  673.5+789.5
```

UDC beginners have a tendency to use the plus sign much more often than it normally warrants. The colon is by far the more usual of the two linking devices, and there is a distinct difference between the two.

The plus sign indicates a subject that is broader than the individual parts, whereas the colon indicates a subject that is narrower than either of them. The plus sign *extends* the subject, whereas the colon *restricts* or *limits* it.

Examples

```
Islam, Hinduism, Sikhism resource pack. - [London] : BBC
Educational, 1998
```

```
UDC classes:    Hinduism      294.5
                Sikhism       294.55
                Islam  297
UDC classmark:  294.5+294.55+297


Sikh rebellion and the Hindu concept of order / by
Cynthia Mahmood. - [S.l., 1989]

UDC classmark:  294.5:294.55
```

In the first case the subject is broader than either Hinduism or Sikhism or Islam alone; the document deals with all three religions, and thus it extends the subject of Hinduism. In the second example the subject is narrower than Hinduism: the document deals with the relationship between Hinduism and Sikhism, and thus restricts Hinduism to that aspect. When in doubt use the colon.

As with the colon, the classifier has the freedom to put either part of the classmark in the lead position according to the most useful position for the document. It might be more appropriate to locate *Tail-ends* with books on Campanology at 789.5 rather than with Bells and bell-founding as the number above would do.

Exercise 18.3
Create UDC classmarks for the following subjects, using the plus sign:

1 *Australasian marsupials and monotremes*
2 *Bookbinding and the care of books*
3 *Castles and cathedrals*
4 *Ground-water hydrology and hydraulics*
5 *Mining and metallurgy*
6 *Painting and drawing: a step-by-step guide to art techniques*
7 *The best of sewing and embroidery*
8 *The book of tea and coffee*
9 *The Oxford first companion to singing and dancing*

Exercise 18.4

Decide whether the following need a colon or a plus sign, and make appropriate classmarks:

1   *Algebra and geometry*
2   *Drugs and athletic performance*
3   *Homework literacy: spelling, grammar and handwriting*
4   *Poverty and health: a sociological analysis*
5   *Teaching and learning styles: how they affect truancy*
6   *Vocal and instrumental music*

Joining together main table numbers 3: the oblique stroke

When the plus sign is used to join consecutive numbers, the oblique stroke / or slash (or solidus, which is its correct name) can be used between the first and last numbers.

This, which is also known as a range number, is often used to represent a broad subject. Examples of range numbers regularly occur in the UDC schedules. For example, in pre-2000 editions of Class 2, there is no single class number to represent the Christian Church, the different parts of which occupy classes 26, 27 and 28. If the classifier needs to express the concept of the Christian Church then he or she must use 26+27+28 or (with the oblique stroke) 26/28. In the case of the oblique stroke the numbers must be put in ascending order, or they will appear nonsensical.

Example

```
Horse, tapir and rhinoceros / Michael Brambell. - London
: Bodley Head, 1976

UDC numbers:    Tapirs        599.721
                Rhinoceroses  599.722
                Horses        599.723
UDC classmark:  599.721+599.722+599.723

or              599.721/.723
```

Notice that if the range number has a decimal point in it, you need repeat only that part of the number from (and including) the decimal point.

Range numbers are useful for expressing a broad subject, but, if you're searching by classmark, the ones in the middle of the range are lost as far as the catalogue is concerned. For example you would not find this book if you were searching for rhinoceroses using the classmark 599.722. For this reason many technical and special libraries prefer not to use range numbers in classifying.

It isn't good practice to use a large number of plus signs for consecutive classes. In the rhinoceros example an alternative approach would be to locate the book in the broader class 599.72 Perissodactyla. This is a better solution if the number of pluses exceeds three.

Exercise 18.5
Make classmarks for the following titles using the oblique stroke:

1 *Anatomy and physiology : the basic principles*
2 *Grass and forage breeding*
3 *Hunting and shooting: from earliest times to the present day*
4 *Pets and how to keep them*
5 *The life sciences*

Summary
- Numbers from UDC main tables can be joined together to make classmarks for compound subjects.
- The colon is the main method of joining two numbers, and it denotes a general relationship between them.
- The numbers can be put in any order to suit the needs of the collection and its users.
- The plus sign is used where subjects are treated independently in the same document; it extends rather than restricts each element of the subject.
- Where plus signs join adjacent classes, the oblique stroke can be used instead.
- The colon is the commonest linking device in UDC.

Answers to exercises
Exercise 18.1

1 685.34
2 305
3 159.962
4 599.365
5 262.13
6 746.6
7 784.4
8 331.216
9 796.8
10 561.391

Exercise 18.2

1	Judaism	296	Abortion	618.39
	Classmark:	296:618.39		
2	Population	314	Global warming	551.588.7
	Classmark:	314:551.588.7		
3	Tourism	379.85	Higher education	378
	Classmark:	379.85:378		
4	Birds	598.2	Photography	77
	Classmark:	598.2:77		
5	Bookselling	665.425	The Internet	004.738.5
	Classmark:	665.425:004.738.5		
6	Dogs	636.7	Needlework	746
	Classmark:	636.7:746		
7	Theology	2	Housekeeping	648.5
	Classmark:	2:648.5		
8	Smoking	178.7	Pathology	616
	Classmark:	178.7:616		

Exercise 18.3

1 599.11+599.22
2 686.1+025.85
3 726.6+728.81
4 626+556.3
5 622+669
6 741+75

7 746.3+746.4
8 663.93+663.95
9 784.9+793.3

Exercise 18.4

1 512+514
2 796.015.8:615.2
3 81'35+81'36+003.053 (the index entries for 'spelling' and 'grammar' will lead you to these classmarks containing apostrophes in the main table for linguistics. The use of the apostrophe in number building will be explained in the next chapter.)
4 364.22:613
5 371.3:371.52
6 784+785

Exercise 18.5

1 611/612
2 633.2/.3
3 799.2/.3
4 636.6/.9
5 57/59

19 Universal Decimal Classification 2: auxiliary tables

Auxiliary tables in the UDC

One of the principal features of Otlet's original scheme was the introduction of **auxiliary tables**. These auxiliary tables provide an economical way of scheduling the sort of terms that occur over and over again in the subjects of documents. When we looked at LCC we saw that concepts such as periodicals or geographical treatment were repeated very many times in the schedules, and that this repetition leads to very lengthy schedules. In UDC such terms are listed only once, in a series of special tables which can be used to qualify classes in the main tables. Although other schemes do make use of auxiliaries, UDC is unusual in the number of tables that it provides.

The auxiliaries in UDC greatly increase the specificity that you can achieve in subject description, and they are one way in which very detailed and expressive classmarks can be built.

The tables which can be applied to any classmark throughout the scheme are known as **systematic auxiliary tables**. Other auxiliaries exist which are used only in particular subjects, and they are called **special auxiliary tables**.

Systematic auxiliaries

The systematic auxiliaries provide for:

- concepts that relate to the form of documents
- very commonly encountered subject concepts.

There are three tables concerned with form, and they cover:

- the language of the document
- the physical form of the document
- the form of presentation.

You will notice that these are concepts that don't tell us anything about the *content* of a document, but they are nevertheless useful to express since readers may look for them.

The rest of the systematic auxiliaries deal with subject-related concepts. You'll remember some of these concepts from the chapters on content analysis. The common subject concepts include:

- places
- periods
- ethnicity and nationality
- persons
- materials
- properties

Each of these auxiliaries is introduced by its own particular symbol, and we'll look at each in turn. Generally, you can add a systematic auxiliary directly to the main table number which it qualifies. Because each auxiliary has a distinctive symbol to introduce it you don't need to alter either the main table number or the auxiliary when you're adding them together.

Auxiliary tables can be used in combination. Because of UDC's flexibility you can vary the order of combination of auxiliaries to suit your own purpose (although once you've decided on such a variation, you should remember to apply it consistently). UDC does give a preferred order of combination, which is the reverse of the order in which the auxiliaries are printed in the tables. In other words, the auxiliaries for persons and materials are the first to be added to the main table number, followed by time, ethnic properties, place, form and language in that order.

Auxiliaries can also stand alone, or be used as the first element in a built classmark. This might happen if you want, for example, to file all the journals or non-book material together, or to arrange material by language.

Language of the document: Table 1c

The language in which it is written is usually considered the least important aspect of a document from the classification point of view. It isn't really part of the subject, or intellectual content, of the document, but nevertheless many schemes make some provision to indicate language. It can be useful to indicate in the catalogue record that a document is in a specific language, particularly if it's uncommon. Sometimes it's helpful to be able to arrange material by language (for example in a subject where there may be versions of the same text in several different languages, as in literature).

Be careful to distinguish between language used in this sense and language as the *subject* of the book. A book *about* the German language is not the same as a book *in* the German language, which might have tapirs or extreme ironing or anything else as its subject.

Language is represented in Table 1c, and the equals sign = is its particular symbol.

Example

```
Domus Anguli Puensis / librum exornavit E.H. Shepard ;
liber alter de Urso Puo de anglico sermone in Latinum
conversus auctore Briano Staplesio. - Londinii :
sumptibus Methuen, [1997]
```

If you're not sure what this is, Figure 19.1 may give you a clue as to this Latin translation of a popular children's book. This is a slightly difficult title, because it is also a work of fiction, so a classmark has to be developed using the methods we discussed in Chapter 9. You probably won't understand the whole classmark at this stage (it contains auxiliaries), so just concentrate on the language part.

Example

```
Concept analysis: English - fiction - in Latin
UDC classes:       English fiction   821.111-3
                   Latin             =124
Classmark:         821.111-3=124
```

Figure 19.1 *Domus Anguli Puensis*

In many cases it is not especially helpful to express the language of the document; in a library in the UK or USA it serves no useful purpose to say that a book is in English, as that can be assumed unless otherwise stated.

Exercise 19.1

Create classmarks for the following titles, using the systematic auxiliary of language:

1 The Bible in Welsh
2 Les papillons [Butterflies]
3 Moral und Politik [Ethics and politics]
4 Das Kapital: Kritik der politischen Ökonomie [Capital: a study of political economy]
5 L'Égyptologie

Note that there are some classes at the beginning of the systematic auxiliary for language that allow you to further qualify the language by its stage of development, or to express notions such as dialects. These classes, which are introduced by an apostrophe, can be added directly onto the language notation. For example:

Hebrew	=411.16
Classical Hebrew	=411.16'02
English	=111
English dialects	=111'282

The subdivisions for translations are also very useful, particularly if you have technical literature in a range of languages. The code for a translation is =03. If you want to specify the original language of the document, use =03. and add the language notation. So a translation of the Vulgate (a Latin version of the Bible) will be:

Bible	22
Vulgate	22=124
A translation of the Vulgate	22=03.124

The target language can now be added to this in the normal way, so that a translation of the Vulgate into English will become:

22=03.124=111

In its amazingly flexible way UDC allows you to juggle this if you would rather keep all your English versions of the Bible together (rather than group all the translations). The classmark could then be written as:

22=111=03.124

Usually, when more than one language is involved, the rule of ascending order applies, and the languages are placed in numerical order.

Example

```
Ein Garten Eden : Meisterwerke der botanischen
Illustration = Garden Eden : masterpieces of botanical
illustration = Un jardin d'Eden : chefs-d'oeuvre de
l'illustration botanique / H. Walter Lack . - Köln :
Taschen, 2001

At head of title: Botanical illustrations in the
collection of the Österreichische Nationalbibliothek
Includes bibliography and index
Text in German, English and French
        75.043=111=112.2=133.1
```

Form of the document: Table 1d

The form of the document can be of two kinds:

- the 'physical' form of the document, i.e. whether it is a text, an image, a computer file, a three-dimensional object, and so on; this is also sometimes referred to as **outer form**
- the form of presentation of the document, i.e. a dictionary, a letter, a history; this is sometimes referred to as **inner form**.

It's not uncommon for a document to have a distinctive inner *and* outer form, for example, an online encyclopaedia or a journal on microfilm. As in the case of language, we don't bother to indicate the default form; so, in a conventional library you would not include the concept of 'book' in the classmark.

Another similarity to the language table is the need to distinguish between form as a property and form as a subject. If you have a book *about* encyclopedias or dictionaries, such as *The meaning of everything*, Simon Winchester's history of the *Oxford English dictionary*, this goes into the main table at 030. The auxiliary table is for the expression of the form of presentation as in a dictionary of chemistry or an encyclopaedia of the social sciences.

Forms in UDC are found in Table 1d and are expressed by brackets containing a number beginning with zero (0...).

Examples

```
Third International Hedgehog Workshop of the European
Hedgehog Research Group 29-30 January 1999 / edited by
Nigel Reeve. - London : Roehampton Institute London,
1999

Concept analysis: Hedgehogs - conference proceedings
UDC classes:      599.365     (063)
Classmark:        599.365(063)


Encyclopædia of curtains : the complete curtain maker /
Catherine Merrick and Rebecca Day ; edited by Phoebe
Phillips. - Gainsborough : Merrick & Day, 1996

Concept analysis: Curtains - encyclopedia
UDC classes:      645.312     (031)
UDC classmark:    645.312(031)
```

Remember that two or more concepts from the form auxiliary can be added together just as they could in the language table. So, a form auxiliary for an illustrated catalogue can be constructed from the notation for catalogues (083.82) and that for illustrations (084.1) to give (083.82)(084.1).

Exercise 19.2

Construct classmarks for the following titles using the systematic auxiliary table for form:

1   *Concise encyclopedia of Hinduism*
2   *Introduction to subject indexing: a programmed text*
3   *British Standard 1722: specification for fences*
4   *Bees without frontiers: proceedings of the Sixth European Bee Conference*

Continued on next page

Exercise 19.2 *Continued*

Construct classmarks for the following titles using the systematic auxiliary table for form:

5 *Encyclopaedia of religion and ethics*
6 *Astronomically speaking: a dictionary of quotations on astronomy and physics*
7 *Business glossary : English–Dutch/Dutch–English*
8 *[Odhams encyclopaedia of knitting.] Die Afrikaanse brei-ensiklopedie*
9 *Snakes, marsupials and birds: a book of anecdotes*

Place auxiliaries: Table 1e

The idea of location or place is very commonly encountered in the subjects of documents. In some subjects it occupies a prominent position and may be enumerated in the main tables; obvious examples are history and geography, where place is the most significant aspect, and is usually the primary means of arrangement. In such cases UDC uses notation that is consistent with the notation to be found in the auxiliary table for place. This table is used where there is a need to combine the concept of a place with any other subject.

Place is represented by the numbers 2/9 enclosed in brackets: (2/9). It includes not only political places (such as Germany, Brazil and Zimbabwe), but other spatial concepts such as physiographic areas (mountains, deserts, rivers, tropics), orientation (east, north) and relative position (home country, abroad, international).

Just as with the auxiliaries we've already seen, the place notation is added directly to the main table number. The same questions of whether the auxiliary table or a main table number is required also apply, so keep in mind whether the place is the principal subject and should be classified in history or geography, or whether it is secondary to another subject and should appear as an auxiliary.

Examples

```
Fun with the family in Illinois : hundreds of ideas for
day trips with the kids / by Lori Meek Schuldt. - 3rd
ed. - Guilford, Conn. : Globe Pequot Press, 2001

Concept analysis: Leisure activities - Illinois
UDC notation:     379.8              (773)
Classmark:        379.8(773)
```

```
Wild flowers of Britain and Europe / text by Bob Press,
Barry Tebbs, Nick Turland. - London : New Holland, 1993

Concept analysis: Flowers - Britain - Europe
UDC notation:    582.5    (41)        (4)
Classmark:       582.5(4+41)
```

In the last example you can see the plus sign used in just the same way as it is used to join main table numbers. The colon, plus sign and oblique stroke can all be used with the auxiliaries where needed. This number is also interesting because one wouldn't normally express a subordinate class (Britain) where the containing class (Europe) is already notated; in this particular case a user might well be looking for British wild plants and so the notation for Britain is retained.

There are lots of concepts for place that don't refer to modern places, or indeed to what we call 'political' or administrative place at all. General concepts of place come in at (1) and (2), and a useful part of the table is that for the ancient world at (3).

Examples

```
Fairy tales from many lands / illustrated by Arthur
Rackham. - London : Piccolo, 1978

Concept analysis: Fairy tales - international
UDC notation:    398.2           (100)
Classmark:       398.2(100)


Ancient Roman jobs / Brian Williams. - Chicago, Ill. :
Heinemann Library, 2003

Concept analysis: Occupations - ancient Rome
UDC notation:    331.54          (37)
Classmark:       331.54(37)
```

As with the previous auxiliaries, combinations of two place concepts often happen. Here are some examples; mostly the place concepts will just be added one after the other, but the plus sign could be used if it were appropriate.

Examples

```
Encyclopaedia of underwater and maritime archaeology /
edited by James P. Delgado. - London : British Museum
Press, 2001
```

```
Concept analysis: Archeology - underwater - seas -
                  encyclopaedia
UDC notation:     902             (204.1)        (26)
                  (031)
Classmark:        902(204.1+26)(031)
```

```
Mountain flowers of Scandinavia / Olav Gjærevoll, Reidar
Jørgensen ; illustrations by Dagny Tande Lid. -
Trondheim : Bruns, 1963
```

```
Concept analysis: Flowers - mountains - Scandinavia
UDC notation:     582.5    (23)         (48)
Classmark: 582.5(23)(48)
```

Exercise 19.3

Construct classmarks for the following titles using the auxiliary schedule for place:

1 *South African merchant ships*
2 *Hydrology in mountainous regions*
3 *Climates of polar regions*
4 *Outdoor games for brownies in built-up areas*
5 *Urban education in America: problems and prospects*
6 *Beekeeping in rural development*
7 *Archaeology in the lowland American tropics*
8 *Encyclopaedia of fairs and festivals in India*
9 *Marsupials in New Zealand: first symposium*
10 *Encyclopaedia of the umbelliferae (carrot/parsley family) of the British Isles*

Auxiliaries of race, ethnic grouping and nationality: Table 1f

This table deals with the hard to distinguish concepts of race, culture and nationality. It takes most of its detail from the auxiliaries of language (for ethnic groups) and place (for nationality). There are also some classes that deal with race and ethnicity that can't be derived from the language table.

The symbol that introduces this auxiliary is (=) and you will need to take care that you don't confuse it with the symbol for language =.

The early part of the table deals with general ethnic concepts, such as mixed race and native. The notation (=1.2/.9) is subdivided by the place table to give the notion of nationality. For example:

Place table 1e	*Ethnicity table 1f*
Europe (4)	Europeans (=1.4)
Spain (460)	Spaniards (=1.460)
Bangladesh (549.3)	Bangladeshis (=1.549.3)
Canada (71)	Canadians (=1.71)

The latter part of the table (=11/=8) is subdivided like the language table, to give the idea of race or culture. For example:

Language table 1c	*Ethnicity table 1f*
Classical Greek =14'02	Ancient Greeks (=14'02)
Romany =214.58	Romanies. Gypsies (=214.58)
Basque =361	Basques (=361)
French =133.1	French speakers (=133.1)

Table 1f gives a number of examples of combination, but you can expand this table (on the pattern of the examples above) to create numbers for any nationalities or ethnic groups that you need.

Examples

```
Shadows from the singing house : Eskimo folk tales /
retold by Helen Caswell. - Rutland, Vt. : Tuttle, 1968

Concept analysis: Folk tales - Eskimo
UDC notation:     398.2          (=562)
Classmark:        398.2(=562)


Anthropometric measurement of Brazilian feet / by Delfina
Faco and Mario D. D'Angelo. - Manchester : Manchester
Metropolitan University, Institute of Advanced Studies,
1993
```

Concept analysis:	Anthropometry	–	feet	–	Brazilian
UDC notation:	572.087		611.986		(=1.81)
Classmark:	572.087:611.986(=1.81)				

Note that in the first example the idea of ethnicity is applied to a cultural entity (folk tales) rather than a person. Nationality can't be applied in this way, and it would always be better to use the place table to specify, for example, British architecture – giving 72(410) – but there seems no reason why ethnic artefacts or cultural activities cannot be specified using Table 1f.

Exercise 19.4

Construct classmarks for the following titles using Table 1f:

1 *Arabic bread production*
2 *Black American music past and present*
3 *Gypsy politics and social change*
4 *Belgians in Canada*
5 *Mixed feelings: the complex lives of mixed race Britons*
6 *Jewish folk art*
7 *Secrets of romany astrology and palmistry*
8 *Colonial migrants and racism: Algerians in France*
9 *On Eskimo music in Greenland*

Auxiliaries of time: Table 1g

The common auxiliary of time (it is hard to resist calling it the timetable) is probably the most complex of the auxiliary tables. It's very logical in its application but it does demand careful thought on the part of the classifier to ensure that mistakes don't happen.

UDC expresses time by actually putting down the date itself. Let's start with dates of the Common Era, or CE dates. (If you're not familiar with this expression, the terms Common Era (CE) and Before Common Era (BCE) are widely used for the date system of the modern world to avoid the Christian associations of AD and BC.)

The special symbol for time is to enclose it in double quotation marks "...". So, if we want to express a specific day, say, 18 January 2004, or 25 December 2003, we write (starting with the year, then month, then day):

"2004.01.18" or "2003.12.25"

This method can be extended to include hours and minutes or even beyond. If I want to denote 4.25 in the afternoon of 17 September 1999, I can write it as "1999.09.17.16.25".

Figures can also be removed from the date to convey the idea of months, years, decades and centuries, right down to millennia. At all times the actual date is used, and you must be careful with centuries, remembering them as, say, 1600s rather than 17th century. A year is always regarded as a four-figure number, so you must also note where zeros need to be put in to keep matters straight; for instance, 195 CE must be written as "0195" and not "195", which means the 1950s. The following table is a quick guide to how to do it.

Date	UDC notation
1984 CE	"1984"
The 1960s	"196"
11 November 1918	"1918.11.11"
21st century	"20"
70 CE	"0070"
5th century BCE	"-04"
The first millennium	"0"

The oblique stroke is used in the same way that it is in the main tables to indicate a range or span of time, i.e. from a start date to a finish date.

Examples

```
Censorship in Ireland, 1939-1945 : neutrality, politics
and society / Donal O Drisceoil. - [Cork] : Cork
University Press, 1996

Concept analysis: Censorship  -  1939-1945  -  Ireland
UDC notation:     351.751.5      "1939/1945"    (417)
Classmark:        351.751.5"1939/1945"(417)


The dictionary of picture postcards in Britain, 1894-1939
/ A.W. Coysh. - Woodbridge : Antique Collectors' Club,
1984

Concept analysis: Postcards  -  1894-1939  -  Britain  -
                      dictionary
```

```
UDC notation:      676.813        "1894/1939"    (410)
                   (038)
Classmark:         676.813"1894/1939"(410)(038)
```

As the place auxiliary contains non-political place concepts, so the time auxiliary contains a number of more general temporal terms alongside those for historical periods. There is provision for times of the day, days of the week, seasons, and geological and archaeological periods.

Examples

```
Wheat management for the autumn / Home Grown Cereals
Authority. - London : Home Grown Cereals Authority, 2001

Concept analysis: Wheat - autumn
UDC notation:     633.1    "323"
Classmark:        633.1"323"


Temporary habitats / edited by Rosemary J. Mackay. -
[U.S.] : North American Benthological Society, 1995

Concept analysis: Habitats - temporary
UDC notation:     574.2       "742"
Classmark:        574.2"742"
```

Exercise 19.5

Construct classmarks for the following titles using the auxiliary table for time:

1 *Aspects of costume: the nineteenth century*
2 *Meissen porcelain dogs, 1875–1925*
3 *The beast in the boudoir: pet-keeping in nineteenth-century France*
4 *Pioneers of Soviet architecture: the search for new solutions in the 1920s and 1930s*
5 *The function of theatre entertainment in the First World War*
6 *Water resources in the twenty-first century*
7 *Looms and textiles of the Copts: first millennium Egyptian textiles*
8 *Agriculture in Iron Age Israel*

Continued on next page

Exercise 19.5 *Continued*
 9 *Stone Age tattoos*
 10 *Vasantotsava: the spring festivals of India*
 11 *Nocturnal birds of Australia*
 12 *The Jurassic flora*

Auxiliaries of general characteristics: Table 1k

These auxiliaries of general characteristics were introduced to accommodate a number of concepts that were listed in the main tables, but occurred with some regularity. These have been edited out of the main tables and brought together in a series of auxiliaries which are introduced by the notation –0.

The two auxiliary tables published in the Pocket Edition of UDC are for materials, –03, and persons, –05. They have now been joined by two new auxiliaries for common properties, –02, and common processes, –04. We'll consider only the Pocket Edition auxiliaries here, as most of you won't have access to the online UDC.

Common auxiliaries of materials, –03

Although concepts relating to materials are not very widely distributed, they occur sufficiently often (in the fine and applied arts, in construction and in manufacturing) to make it worthwhile to have a single table for them. They range from chemicals and minerals to organic materials, and to manufactured materials such as plastics and textiles. They can of course be used in combination with any number from the main tables, and are simply added onto the number. Unlike the other auxiliaries, they can't be used alone or brought to the front of a compound number; they must always be attached to a main table number.

Examples

```
History of the concrete roofing tile : its origin and
development in Germany / by Charles Dobson ; with
technical notes by F.L. Brady. - London : Batsford, 1959

Concept analysis: Roofing materials - concrete - Germany
UDC notation:     692.415          -033.3     (430)
Classmark:        692.415-033.3(430)
```

```
Knitting with dog hair : a woof-to-warp guide to making
hats, sweaters, mittens, and much more / Kendall Crolius
and Anne Black Montgomery. – New York : St. Martin's
Press, 1994
```

Concept analysis:	Knitting	–	hair	–	dogs
UDC notation:	746:677.025		–035.55		636.7
Classmark:	746:677.025-035.55:636.7				

Notice that in the last example the main table number for dogs must be introduced by a colon in order to separate it from the –03 auxiliary, which doesn't having a 'closing' symbol like the other auxiliary tables.

Common auxiliaries of persons, –05

The auxiliaries for persons are very widely used indeed in UDC. In recent years great efforts have been made to remove all the compound classes involving persons from the main tables, so that such compounds should be built using the auxiliary table. The auxiliary comes into play whenever any aspect of persons occurs in a document, and it includes provision for persons by age, gender, kinship, social status, occupation and other traits, and for persons as 'doers' and persons as recipients of the 'doing'.

The notation –051 is used to turn an activity into the people who perform it; for example, 63 Agriculture gives us 63–051 Farmers, and 669 Metallurgy is used to construct the number 669–051 Metallurgists.

The –05 auxiliaries are used in just the same way as the –03 concepts; they can't stand on their own or come first in a compound number, but must always be attached to a main table number.

Example

```
Surrealist women : an international anthology / edited
with introductions by Penelope Rosemont. – London :
Athlone Press, 1998
```

Concept analysis:	Surrealism	–	women	–	anthology
UDC notation:	7.037.5		–055.2		(082)
Classmark:	7.037.5-055.2(082)				

More than one concept from the auxiliary can be used in combination, as in the following example.

Examples

```
Abuse of elderly people : a handbook for professionals /
Jacki Pritchard. - London : J. Kingsley, 1992

Concept analysis: Aggression - recipients - elderly
UDC notation:      364.271       -052          -053.9
Classmark:         364.271-052-053.9


Victorian murderesses : a true history of thirteen
respectable French and English women accused of
unspeakable crimes / Mary S. Hartman. - London : Robson
Books, 1977

Concept analysis: Murder - 'doers' - women  - middle class
                       - French  - English - 19th century
UDC notation: 343.61-051-055.2-058.13(=1.111+1.133.1)"18"
```

A useful application of the persons auxiliary is in combination with a class from the form auxiliary (0.05), Documents for particular kinds of user. Notation from the –05 auxiliary can be used to expand (0.05) through parallel subdivision, as the following table demonstrates:

–05 Aux.	(0.05) expanded	Class name
–053.2	(0.053.2)	[a book] for children
–053.9	(0.053.9)	for old persons
–055.1	(0.055.1)	for men
–055.2	(0.055.2)	for women
–056.262	(0.056.262)	for blind persons.

Example

```
Etiquette for men : a book of modern manners and customs
/ by G.R.M. Devereux. - London : C. Arthur Pearson, 1919

Concept analysis: Etiquette - for men
UDC notation:      395          (0.055.1)
Classmark:         395(0.055.1)
```

It's not very clear whether the persons auxiliary can be applied to animals, or whether it is only for characteristics of human beings. The English

Medium Edition does contain some examples of combination using this auxiliary with animals. I think that if these concepts are helpful they may be used, as in the following delightful book about the care of your female dog:

Example

```
The book of the bitch : a complete guide to
understanding and caring for bitches / J.M. Evans and
Kay White. - Lydney, Gloucestershire : Ringpress, 1997

Concept analysis: Dogs  - female
UDC notation:     636.7   -055.2
Classmark:        636.7-055.2
```

Exercise 19.6

Construct classmarks for the following titles using the –03 and –05 auxiliaries:

1 *Rubber floors*
2 *Wooden furniture in Herculaneum*
3 *Prehistoric origami: dinosaurs and other creatures*
4 *Ivory carvings of early mediaeval England*
5 *Grandparents' rights*
6 *Left-handed calligraphy*
7 *Refugee women and their mental health*
8 *Scots law for journalists*
9 *Scientists and the media*
10 *Black American women in Olympic track and field*
11 *Victims of bullying*
12 *Women who made the news: female journalists in Canada, 1880–1945*

UDC also allows you to 'borrow' notation from another established system of classification where it helps to give greater detail. If the borrowed notation consists of numbers it should be introduced by # or some other symbol to avoid confusion with UDC notation. In a compound classmark such notation would be cited between the time auxiliary and the –0 auxiliaries.

Examples

```
Dynamics of the spiral galaxy M81 / Hermanus Visser. -
Groningen : Rijkuniversiteit te Groningen, 1978

UDC number for spiral galaxies:  524.726
Classmark for spiral galaxy M81: 524.726M81
```

In exactly the same way you can use alphabetical extensions if you want to introduce names, abbreviations or acronyms. In this case you don't need to use a distinguishing symbol because there won't be any confusion with UDC notation.

Example

```
Period piece : a Cambridge childhood / by Gwen Raverat.
- London : Faber and Faber, 1952

Concept analysis: Biography - Raverat
Classmark:        929RAV
```

Used in combination the common auxiliaries can help you to express very considerable detail in document description; the example of Victorian murderesses above demonstrates this nicely. It's also useful to be able to exercise some choice in the citation order to meet local needs.

Two auxiliaries (the language auxiliary and the –0 auxiliary) have no distinctive symbol to close the notation; if, as a result of number building, they appear before a main table number, a colon must be used to introduce the main table number. Otherwise, it won't be clear where the auxiliary finishes and the main number begins. As we've progressed through the different auxiliaries the titles have been getting gradually more difficult and involving more than one auxiliary table. Let's finish this section on the auxiliaries with some particularly complicated titles that you can really get your teeth into.

Exercise 19.7

Construct classmarks for the following titles using the whole range of auxiliary tables:

1 Arabic historical writing, 1973: an annotated bibliography of books
2 Dictionary of proverbs in England in the sixteenth and seventeenth century
3 Effects of nocturnal shift work on student nurses
4 Lexicon of Arabic horse terminology
5 Linguistic analysis of music and dance terms from three sixteenth-century dictionaries of Mexican Indian languages
6 Pathological evidence in newborn children from the sixteenth century in Huelva (Spain)
7 Reaching our children through song: an approach to the development of communication with deaf pre-schoolers
8 Sexual life of the Belgians, 1950–1978 [Video recording of UK television programme – in Flemish with English subtitles]
9 Metal weapons of the early and middle Bronze ages in Syria-Palestine
10 Dictionary of scientific terms: covering mathematics, astronomy, physics, chemistry, geology, zoology, and botany, with definitions in Persian, and equivalents in Persian, English & French

Summary

- The common auxiliaries can be added to any numbers from the UDC main tables.
- Auxiliaries can be added without altering either the main table number or the auxiliary number.
- Each auxiliary has a distinct notational symbol to introduce it.
- Auxiliaries should be combined in the reverse of the order in which they appear in the tables i.e. beginning with the –0 auxiliaries and ending with the language auxiliary.
- This order can be varied to suit local needs.
- The –0 auxiliaries can only be added directly to a main table number.
- Alphabetical extensions and notations from other systems can be inserted where they are useful.

Special auxiliaries

In addition to the common auxiliaries, which may be attached to any number from the main tables, UDC contains a number of special auxiliaries which are applied only in parts of the classification.

The special auxiliaries stand at the top of the class to which they apply, and in the Pocket Edition you can recognize them by the heavy black line to the left of the number (side-lining).

The subdivisions of an auxiliary table can be attached to any *enumerated* subdivisions of the class where the auxiliary is given. Let's look at a very small special auxiliary to see how this works:

64	HOME ECONOMICS. DOMESTIC SCIENCE. HOUSEKEEPING
|64.03	Money management in the household. Buying. Consumer interests, policy and research
|64.04	Housekeeping services, jobs, tasks
|64.06	Household appliances and machines. Labour-saving devices in the home
|64.08	Moving house. Removals

The side-line here tells us that this is a special auxiliary, and that the side-lined subdivisions of the class 64 can be added to any other decimal subdivision of that class, i.e. any number that begins with 64. This is more difficult to explain in words than it is to demonstrate in practice, so let's consider an example:

64	HOME ECONOMICS
|64.03	Money management in the household. Buying
|64.04	Housekeeping services, jobs, tasks
|64.06	Household appliances and machines
641.1	Foodstuffs
641.1.03	Buying foodstuffs
648.1	Laundry and laundries in general
648.1.04	Laundry services
648.1.06	Laundry appliances. Washing machines

The numbers 641.1.03, 648.1.04 and 648.1.06 have been built by taking the special auxiliary subdivisions of 64 (.03, .04 and .06) and adding them to subdivisions of 64, i.e. 641.1 and 648.1. These subdivisions can be attached to any numbers that begin with 64, but not to any other classes. They are auxiliaries special to 64.

Special auxiliaries in Class 8, Language and literature

Although special auxiliaries are important in other classes, particularly class 6, the language and literature class makes particularly extensive use of them. Because of this the class occupies very little space, but its capacity to express linguistic and literary classes is very great. The common auxiliaries also come into play in this class, which is the most 'faceted' in UDC. Only simple concepts are enumerated, and the classifier has considerable freedom in the way in which these can be put together.

The main table numbers for particular languages and their literatures are built from the notation of the common auxiliary for language. The numbers following the equals sign in the auxiliary are added to 811. and 821. for language and literature respectively, in the following way:

Table 1c		81			82	
=111	English	811.111	English language	82 1.111	English literature
=124	Latin	811.124	Latin language	821.124	Latin literature
=134.2	Spanish	811.134.2	Spanish language	821.134.2	Spanish literature
=211	Sanskrit	811.211	Sanskrit language	821.211	Sanskrit literature
=412	Coptic	811.412	Coptic language	821.412	Coptic literature
=573	Tamil	811.573	Tamil language	821.573	Tamil literature

Exercise 19.8

Build the classmarks for the following subjects, using Table 1c:

1 French language
2 Chinese literature
3 Swedish literature
4 Italian language
5 Caucasian languages
6 Modern Hebrew literature
7 Maltese language
8 Pali literature

To these base numbers for language and literature you can then add any of the side-lined numbers in Class 8. There are quite a number of examples of combination given in the tables to show you how this is done. You can express other concepts such as period and place using the common auxiliaries if necessary.

Example

```
Selected themes and icons from medieval Spanish
literature : of beards, shoes, cucumbers, and leprosy /
by John R. Burt. - Madrid : José Porrúa Turanzas, 1982

Concept analysis: Spanish literature - mediaeval -
                  criticism
UDC notation:     821.134.2              "04/14"
                  82.09
Classmark:        821.134.2"04/14".09
```

Summary
- The special auxiliaries in UDC apply only to certain parts of the classification.
- They are placed at the head of the section to which they apply.
- In the Pocket Edition, special auxiliary notation is side-lined in the left-hand margin.
- Special auxiliaries can be added to any decimal subdivision of the class where they first appear.
- Special auxiliaries are especially important in the language and literature class.

Answers to exercises
Exercise 19.1
1   Bible 22   Welsh =153.1
    Classmark: 22=153.1
2   Butterflies 595.78   French =133.1
    Classmark: 595.78=133.1
3   Ethics 17   Politics 32   German =112.2
    Classmark: 17:32=112.2
4   Economic theory 330.1   German =112.2
    Classmark: 330.1=112.2

5   Egyptology 94(32)   French =133.1
    Classmark: 94(32)=133.1

Exercise 19.2

1   Hinduism 294.5   Encyclopedias (031)
    Classmark: 294.5(031)
2   Subject indexing 025.4   Programmed text (076.6)
    Classmark: 025.4(076.6)
3   Fences 692.88   Standards (083.7)
    Classmark: 692.88(083.7)
4   Bees 638.1 (or 595.799)   Conference proceedings (063)
    Classmark: 638.1(063) or 595.799(063)
5   Religion and ethics 2+17   Encyclopedias (031)
    Classmark: 2+17(031)
6   Astronomy & physics 52+53   Dictionaries (038)
    Quotations (082.22)
    Classmark: 52+53(038)(082.22)
7   Business management 658   Dictionaries (038)
    English =111   Dutch =112.5
    Classmark: 658(038)=111=112.5
8   Knitting 746:677.025   Encyclopedias (031)   Afrikaans =112.6
    Classmark: 746:677.025(031)=112.6
9   Snakes 598.115   Marsupials 599.2   Birds 598.2   Anecdotes (089.3)
    Classmark: 598.115+598.2+599.2(089.3)

Exercise 19.3

1   Merchant ships 656.612   South Africa (680)
    Classmark: 656.612(680)
2   Hydrology 556   Mountainous areas (23)
    Classmark: 556(23)
3   Climatology 551.58   Polar regions (211)
    Classmark: 551.58(211)
4   Outdoor games 796.1   Built-up areas (257)
    Classmark: 796.1(257)
5   Education 37   United States (73)   Urban areas (257)
    Classmark: 37(257)(73)
6   Beekeeping 638.1   Rural areas (254)
    Classmark: 638.1(254)

7 Archaeology 902 America (7) Lowland (25) Tropics (213.5)
  Classmark: 902(213.5)(25)(7)
8 Festivals 394.2 India (540) Encyclopedias (031)
  Classmark: 394.2(540)(031)
9 Marsupials 599.2 New Zealand (931)
  Conference proceedings (063)
  Classmark: 599.2(931)(063)
10 Umbelliferae 582.794 British Isles (41) Encyclopedias (031)
  Classmark: 582.794(41)(031)

Exercise 19.4

1 Bakery 664.6 Arabic (=411.21)
  Classmark: 664.6(=411.21)
2 Music 78 Black people (=414) USA (73)
  Classmark: 78(=414)(73)
3 Social change 316.4 Politics 32 Gypsies (=214.58)
  Classmark: 316.4:32(=214.58)
4 Belgians (=1.493) Canada (71)
  Classmark: (=1.493)(71)
5 Social psychology 316.6 Mixed race (=088) Britain (41)
  Classmark: 316.6(=088)(41)
6 Folk art 7.011.26 Jewish (=411.16)
  Classmark: 7.011.26(=411.16)
7 Astrology 133.52 Palmistry 133.6 Romany (=214.58)
  Classmark: 133.52+133.6(=214.58)
8 Racism 323.1 Algerians (=1.65) France(44)
  Classmark: 323.1(=1.65)(44)
9 Music 78 Eskimo (=562) Greenland (988)
  Classmark: 78(=562)(988)

Exercise 19.5

1 Costume 391 19th century "18"
  Classmark: 391"18"
2 Porcelain 666.5 Dogs 636.7 1875-1925 "1875/1925"
  Classmark: 666.5:636.7"1875/1925"
3 Pets 636.6/.9 19th century "18" France (44)
  Classmark: 636.6/.9"18"(44)

4 Architecture 72   1920s and 1930s "192/193"   Soviet Russia (47+57)
   Classmark: 72"192/193"(47+57)

5 Theatre 792   First World War "1914/1918"
   Classmark: 792"1914/1918"

6 Water management 556.1   21st century "20"
   Classmark: 556.1"20"

7 Textiles 677.074   First millennium "0"   Egypt (620)
   Classmark: 677.074"0"(620)

8 Agriculture 63   Iron age "638"   Israel (569.4)
   Classmark: 63"638"(569.4)

9 Tattoos 391.91   Stone age "631/634"
   Classmark: 391.91"631/634"

10 Festivals 394.2   Spring "321"   India (540)
    Classmark: 394.2"321"(540)

11 Birds 598.2   Night "345"   Australia (94)
    Classmark: 598.2"345"(94)

12 Flowers 582.5/.9   Jurassic "6152"
    Classmark: 582.5/.9"6152"

Exercise 19.6

1 Concept analysis: Floors – rubber
   UDC notation: 645.1   –036.4
   Classmark: 645.1–036.4

2 Concept analysis: Furniture – wooden – Herculaneum
   UDC notation: 645.4   –035.3   (37)
   Classmark: 645.4–035.3(37)

3 Concept analysis: Dinosaurs – paper
   UDC notation: 568.19   –035.4
   Classmark: 568.19–035.4

4 Concept analysis: Carvings – ivory – medieval – England
   UDC notation: 736   –035.56   "4/14"   (410.1)
   Classmark: 736–035.56"4/14"(410.1)

5 Concept analysis: Rights – grandparents
   UDC notation: 342.7   –055.53
   Classmark: 342.7–055.53

6 Concept analysis: Calligraphy – left handed persons
  UDC notation: 003.077   –056.173
  Classmark: 003.077–056.173

7 Concept analysis: Mental health – refugees – women
  UDC notation: 616.89   –054.7   –055.2
  Classmark: 616.89–054.7–055.2

8 Concept analysis: Law – Scotland – journalism – persons
  UDC notation: 34   (410.5)   070   –051
  Classmark: 34(410.5):070–051

9 Concept analysis: Broadcasting – science – persons
  UDC notation: 621.39   5   –051
  Classmark: 621.39:5–051

10 Concept analysis: Olympic games – athletics – women – black –
   American
   UDC notation: 796.03   796.4   –055.2   (=414)
                   (73)
   Classmark: 796.03:796.4–055.2(=414)(73)

11 Concept analysis: Bullying – victims
   UDC notation: 364.271   –058.6
   Classmark: 364.271–058.6

12 Concept analysis: Journalism – persons – women – "1880-1945"
   – Canada
   UDC notation: 070   –051   –055.2   "1880/1945"
                   (71)
   Classmark: 070–051–055.2"1880/1945"(71)

Exercise 19.7

Note that there are usually several ways to construct the numbers for the titles in this exercise. This will sometimes allow you to make a choice of main classes by making one element a main table number and the others auxiliaries.

1 Concept analysis: History – in Arabic – a bibliography
  UDC notation: 94   (=411.21)   (048)
  Classmark: 94(=411.21)(048)

2 Concept analysis: English language – Proverbs – 16/17th centuries

                         – dictionaries
UDC notation: 821.111   –84   "15/16"   (038)
Classmark: 821.111–84"15/16"(038)

3   Concept analysis: Shift work – Night time – Medical staff
    UDC notation: 331.31   "345"   616-051
    Classmark: 331.31"345"616-051

4   Concept analysis: Horses   – Lexicon – Arabic – English
    UDC notation: 636.1   (038)   =411.21   =111
    Classmark: 636.1(038)=111=411.21
    This might alternatively be put under Arabic language, with the
    horse number coloned on: 811.411.21:636.1(038)

5   Concept analysis: Music – 16th century – Dictionaries –
                       Mexican languages
    UDC notation: 78   "15"   (038)
                    =822
    Classmark: 78 "15"(038)=822
    Another example that might be put in the language class

6   Concept analysis: Pathology – 16th century – Spain – newborn
    UDC notation: 616   "15"   (460)   –053.2
    Classmark: 616"15"(460)–053.2

7   Concept analysis: Song   –   deaf   –   children
    UDC notation: 784   –056.26   –053.2
    Classmark: 784–056.26–053.2

8   Concept analysis: Sexual customs – Belgians – Video –
                       English – Flemish
    UDC notation: 392.4   (=1.493)   (086.8)
                    =111   =112.5
    Classmark: 392.4(=1.493)(086.8)=111=112.5

9   Concept analysis: Weapons – metal – Bronze Age – Palestine
    UDC notation: 903.22   –034   "637"   (394)
    Classmark: 903.22–034"637"(394)

10 Concept analysis: Science – Dictionaries – English – French –
                       Persian
    UDC notation: 5   (038)   =111   =133.1
                    =222.1
    Classmark: 5(038)=111=133.1=222.1

Exercise 19.8

1   811.133.1
2   821.581
3   821.113.6
4   811.131.1
5   811.35
6   821.411.16'08
7   811.411.216
8   821.212

20 Faceted classification

Even in the 21st century you won't encounter many libraries organized by a faceted classification, yet faceted classification is probably the most important development in classification theory of the last hundred years.

Facet analysis has influenced the structure and development of all the general classification schemes, and today there are few classifications that don't show some evidence of that influence. The identification of precise relationships between classes, the use of synthetic notations, and ideas such as facet indicators, the consistent application of citation order, and schedule inversion all come from faceted classifications, and all are to be found in the more recent revisions of (originally) non-faceted classifications.

Because the methodology of faceted classification (what we shall call facet analysis) provides very clear principles for the organization of concepts, first into categories and then into a linear sequence, it produces very predictable and robust structures. These structures are particularly good at accommodating compound subjects at any level of complexity, and their internal logic makes them very suitable for use in automated systems. The much better structure of a faceted scheme explains why the general systems of classification have been keen to import these methods into their own revision processes.

The nature of faceted classification
Before we go further with the discussion of faceted classification, let's deal with some common misapprehensions about it.

Firstly, although there are classification schemes that are faceted, faceted classification itself is not a particular scheme or system, but rather a method for making a classification. You can see elements of faceted structure in schemes that are not themselves completely faceted. UDC in particular has some completely faceted main classes now, and some of the recent revisions of DDC have sections that are plainly based on facet analysis. As we look at the various aspects of facet analysis, we'll see illustrations from a range of schemes, not just the fully faceted ones.

There is also quite a widespread belief that any scheme with analytico-synthetic features is a faceted scheme. This is particularly the case among computer scientists who've become interested in classification, and is also sometimes encountered in the US literature. Most schemes allow some measure of classmark building, but this doesn't make them faceted schemes. The faceted scheme is a system in which *all* of the concepts have been analysed and sorted, and in which they can *all* be combined into classmarks. S. R. Ranganathan, when he was describing faceted classification in the early days, likened it to a popular construction toy of the time called Meccano: this consisted of a lot of metal pieces, plates, rods and wheels, which you could use to build cranes and bridges and vehicles and so on. The modern equivalent is Lego and the analogy is clear: the faceted scheme is composed of all these little bricks and building blocks which must be put together to achieve the end result. A scheme in which most of the building blocks are already put together in unchangeable structures isn't a faceted scheme.

A third misconception, based on the appearance of the early faceted schemes, is that, because of the analysis into little building blocks, faceted schemes are very simple in structure, and the schedules relatively brief in length. This was true of faceted schemes produced in the 1950s and 1960s, but today's schemes are much more complex with a more sophisticated use of citation order. BC2 in particular incorporates many examples of built classmarks in its schedules, and has a very intricate (although entirely logical) structure.

Summary
- Facet analysis is a method of constructing classifications, rather than a particular classification scheme; elements of faceted structure can be seen in most modern schemes.
- Being able to build some classmarks doesn't make a scheme faceted.
- Modern faceted schemes can be quite complicated in structure, with lots of examples of compound classes.

The history of facet analysis

Facet analysis began formally with the theories of the Indian librarian S. R. Ranganathan in the 1920s and 1930s. Ranganathan, who was a mathematician by training, attended the library school at University College London in 1924, and was taught classification by Charles Berwick Sayers. The latter was a fine theorist and one of the leading lights of the profession at that time, but classification was still largely a practical art, and Ranganathan was puzzled by much of what he learned. Back home in India he began to work on the theoretical nature of classification and came up with the idea of fundamental categories (PMEST) for the analysis of concepts. We'll look at these categories in more detail shortly.

Of course, Ranganathan was not the first to notice the repetitive nature of many classification schedules and suggest an analytico-synthetic approach to commonly occurring concepts. Otlet and La Fontaine had made UDC highly synthetic with their broad sweep of auxiliary tables some thirty years before, and Bliss's embryonic BC, to be published in 1935, also had both common and special auxiliaries. Perhaps more significantly, Kaiser had used the categories of concretes, processes and place as the basis of the subject indexing system which he wrote about in 1911.

Ranganathan's contribution was the expansion of the fundamental categories, so that the analysis could be carried out for all the concepts in a discipline, rather than just the commonly occurring ones. He also addressed the problems of citation and schedule order, and formalized his ideas in a number of theoretical publications, and in the Colon Classification itself, first published in 1933. Work on the development of the Colon Classification, and research into classification theory, continues today at the Documentation Research and Training Centre, Bangalore.

There was much work on faceted classification in the UK and in mainland Europe from the 1950s onward. The European work tended to concentrate on an analysis of the relationships *between* concepts, with the creation of indexing schemes using relaters, or symbols representing the relationships, to link terms. Research in the UK followed more closely the style of the Colon Classification, with the relationships implicit in the citation order.

Members of the Classification Research Group, founded in 1952, carried out most work on the creation of schemes, and in the process they established a substantial body of theory. This was published in works by Brian Vickery, Eric Coates, Douglas Foskett, Jack Mills, Derek Austin and a number of others, both practising librarians and academics.

Many of the classifications constructed at that time were special classifications, including one for the library of the (then) Library Association and another for the Institute of Education in London. The CRG work also influenced the way in which thesauri were constructed, and generated a major system of subject indexing, PRECIS, which was used in the *British National Bibliography* for many years. The CRG's efforts culminated in the revision of Bliss's Bibliographic Classification, begun in the 1960s and still in progress. This second edition of BC (known as BC2) was a testing ground for the full application of CRG theory, and will be used extensively to illustrate this chapter.

Summary
- Facet analysis was invented by the Indian librarian S. R. Ranganathan.
- It had been preceded by ideas of analytico-synthesis in the work of Otlet, Kaiser, Bliss and others.
- Work on the further development of facet analysis was carried out in Europe during the 20th century.
- The UK Classification Research Group built on the Ranganathan tradition and developed an expanded set of fundamental categories.
- The culmination of their work can be seen in the revised edition of Bliss's Bibliographic Classification (BC2).

How faceted classifications are constructed

We've already had a brief look at the structure of faceted classifications in Chapter 6, but now we'll examine the process of facet analysis in more detail.

The building blocks of classification

If you examine a traditional classification scheme, particularly in an edition from before 1970, you'll notice that within a specific subject, all of the terms associated with that topic tend to be grouped together, but this is often in a rather unstructured and inconsistent way. This example from Brown's Subject Classification, first published in 1906, shows a fine mixture of products, activities, equipment, persons and abstract concepts.

I 060	Dairy Farming
061	Milk
062	Milk Products
063	Cream. Separators
064	Clotted Cream
065	Condensed Milk
066	Butter
067	Churns
068	Cheese
069	Koumiss
070	Dairy and Milk Trade
075	Farmers and Agriculturalists
080	Farm Servants and Labourers
081	Housing (Bothies)
090	Agricultural Depression and Distress

The Subject Classification is quite well structured by the standards of its age, although Brown himself claimed only that it was fairly logical. At that time there were no established methods for ordering terms, other than just clustering them together and applying pragmatic methods. As facet analysis was developed it provided a detailed methodology for constructing classifications, with very specific processes for organizing and ordering terms.

Faceted classification simplified

Many introductory books on classification present faceted classification in a simplified but rather limited manner by using an example based on the attributes of entities. We can try to create a classification for such an entity – let's say 'the sock'.

Suppose that we have a large number of socks to organize; perhaps we're in a sock shop, or we just happen personally to have rather a lot of socks. There are obvious features of socks that we might use as the basis for sorting them all out. Firstly we probably have socks in different colours and in different patterns; there will be socks made of different materials, and socks for different occasions; we might also have socks of different lengths. We could create a spreadsheet or database for our socks with different fields in it for these attributes: see Figure 20.1.

Colour	Pattern	Yarn	Purpose	Length
Black	Plain	Wool	Work	Ankle
Grey	Striped	Polyester	Evening	Calf
Brown	Spotted	Cotton	Football	Knee
Green	Chequered	Silk	Hiking	
Blue	Novelty			
White				

Figure 20.1 Sock classification

We can select terms from this table to define our socks: we could have 'plain black silk evening socks' or 'blue and white striped polyester football socks' or 'grey wool hiking socks'. We can build up these descriptions without having to have boxes specifically labelled 'grey wool hiking socks', and if we attach the terms in a consistent order we can create a systematic classification of socks, just using the table. In outline the classification would have the following classes:

Black
Grey
Brown
Green
Blue
White

Plain
Striped
Spotted
Chequered
Novelty

Wool
Polyester
Cotton
Silk

Work
Evening
Football
Hiking

Ankle
Calf
Knee

If we begin to fill this out with some examples of socks it could begin to look like this:

Black socks
    Black wool socks
    Black polyester socks
    Black cotton socks
Grey socks
    Grey wool socks
        Grey wool work socks
        Grey wool hiking socks
            Grey wool ankle socks for hiking
            Grey wool knee socks for hiking
Blue socks
    Blue wool socks
    Blue polyester socks
        Striped blue polyester football socks

Of course, if you didn't want to arrange the socks by colour, you could use a different order of combination, or citation order, so that the socks were grouped into, say, work socks, evening socks, and sports socks.

Such an arrangement is often presented as an example of a faceted classification, and it does give quite a good sense of how a faceted classification is structured. It is, however, just a classification of entities, and it uses the same classificatory principles, based on attributes of things, that Aristotle used to create a taxonomy in the fourth century BCE. Remember Chapter 4 on scientific classifications and aspect classifications, where we looked at the difference between classifications of objects and classifications of information.

A faceted bibliographic classification has to do a great deal more than this. A set of terms as in Figure 20.1 is very useful for sorting out your sock drawer, but you could not use it to classify documents about sock design or manufacture, the history of socks or the sock trade in general. In a faceted classification for those subjects, the terms above would all be in a single facet – the personality or entity or sock facet. A proper faceted classification will have many more facets, covering a much wider range of terminology.

We'll now make a closer examination of the complete spectrum of the categories on which facets are based.

Fundamental categories

At the beginning of the 20th century UDC, with its systematic auxiliary schedules, had created tables for place, time and form (including the language of the document), and race, and a table for 'point-of-view', which has now been superseded, to accommodate concepts which regularly recurred in the subjects of documents. Ranganathan agreed that place and time were common attributes in all subjects, but he then made a tremendous leap forward in the business of organizing concepts. He noticed that (apart from these commonly occurring terms) there was no great repetition of actual concepts in different subjects, but within a subject the concepts did always seem to consist of just a few *types* of term.

Firstly, in every subject there is a group of concepts that represent what the subject is essentially about: that is, the object of study. For example, if we happen to be ornithologists we're studying *birds*, chemists are concerned with *chemical compounds*, linguists examine *languages*, and so on. In each of these disciplines we can easily identify and list the concepts that form the main focus. Ranganathan called concepts of this sort 'personality', because they are the essence of the discipline, and he considered them to be the most important group of concepts in the discipline. In many cases the terms in the personality facet are entities or objects of some sort, but this is not invariably so, as we can see from the examples of languages above.

Ranganathan also observed that terms related to matter occurred in several different disciplines, and in the Colon Classification there are terms such as oil, fat, stone, clay, plastic, cotton, canvas, bone, hair, metal and glass, in classes as diverse as technology, chemistry, geology, medicine, useful arts, architecture and fine arts.

Ranganathan's third big group was of terms that are actions or activities of some sort, which he called energy terms. As in the case of personality, most of these terms aren't generally applicable; each subject has its own set of energy terms. So, in construction you might have energy terms such

Ranganathan		Later developments
Personality	=	Thing Kind Part Property
Matter	=	Material
Energy	=	Process Operation
		Patient Product By-product Agent
Space	=	Space
Time	=	Time

Figure 20.2 Comparison of Ranganathan's and CRG categories

as bricklaying, plastering, glazing or tiling; performing arts would include singing, acting, dancing and juggling, and chemistry's energy facet might contain analysing, filtering, centrifuging or dissolving.

Adding to these three the common facets of space and time gave Ranganathan his famous facet formula: PMEST. These five categories can handle the vocabulary of most subjects, but they don't allow you to make fine distinctions within the categories. For example, you can't distinguish between internal activities or processes (such as growth, change and decay) and external actions (such as manufacturing, testing and categorizing). The great range of terms that must go in the P facet without further subdivision includes not only the entities themselves, but also their parts and properties and their different varieties. Those who came after Ranganathan, and who developed a larger set of categories, made the task of analysis much easier.

This was a major contribution of the CRG. During the 1960s members working on special classification schemes reached a consensus on a set of categories parallel to, but more numerous than, Ranganathan's. These can be set out as shown in Figure 20.2. These fundamental groupings, known as categories, form the basis of facet analysis.

When you set out to create a faceted classification scheme the first task is to take all the concepts or terms from the subject and sort them into categories. The standard set of categories given above serves very well for the majority of subjects, although in some disciplines (notably in the humanities) the standard categories are less applicable, and it's sometimes necessary to introduce other categories. 'Form' and 'genre' are essential to categorize concepts in the creative arts, for example. At this stage we'll look at a straightforward case: for example, in BC2 Class H, Medicine, terms are allocated to categories as follows:

(Thing)	Human beings
(Kind)	Women, children, old people, etc.
(Part)	Head, legs, muscles, bones, heart, brain, lungs, etc.
(Process)	Respiration, digestion, reproduction, disease, etc.
(Operation)	Surgery, drug therapy, physiotherapy, etc.
(Agent)	Doctors, nurses, equipment, buildings, etc.

The terms within each category now constitute a facet of the subject. Here, in medicine, all the terms in the category of 'Part' become the 'anatomy' or 'parts–organs–systems' facet, and the terms in the category of 'Operation' become the 'treatment' or 'therapy' facet.

Space and time facets are not included here because the concepts in those two facets don't usually change from one subject to another. In nearly all schemes they are provided for by auxiliary schedules applicable to the whole classification.

Summary
- Ranganathan first thought of the idea of fundamental categories.
- He identified five categories: personality, matter, energy, space and time.
- The CRG expanded these categories to give: thing, kind, part, property, material, process, operation, patient, product, by-product, agent, space and time.
- Sorting concepts into categories is the first stage in facet analysis.
- The complete set of terms in a category in a particular subject is known as a facet of that subject.
- The facets of space and time are common to all subjects and are usually provided for by auxiliary schedules.

In an average academic discipline there are hundreds or even thousands of terms; sorting them into a dozen categories won't give us very much in the way of a detailed order, so we must find some means of further organizing these big groups.

Arrays

Now we can use the methods of the sock taxonomy to sort our terms into groups on the basis of their attributes. These groups within the facet we call **arrays**. Note that some people call an array a **sub-facet**.

Each array will be defined by some specific property or attribute, which is called the **characteristic of division** or **principle of division**. If we go back to our sock classification we can see five arrays, with the principles of division: socks by colour, socks by pattern, socks by material, socks by purpose, socks by length. It's common practice to place these principles of division in brackets (parentheses) since they aren't themselves classes.

An important thing to notice about the members of an array is that they are all **mutually exclusive classes**. That is to say, an entity can only be in one class. If we look at our array (socks by length) we can see that a sock cannot be both an ankle sock and a knee sock; the classes of ankle socks and knee socks are mutually exclusive. If you have a set of classes that are not mutually exclusive then they don't constitute a proper array. For example a set of classes named (Types of socks) and containing the concepts brown, patterned, green, white, striped, blue, is not a proper array because some socks could go in more than one class; the terms need further separation and organization into two distinct arrays. Muddles of this kind are found in lots of schemes that are not properly faceted.

The list of games from Colon Class M, Useful arts, shown in Figure 20.3. is a classic example of organization into arrays, with the principles of division clearly stated (purists might want to disagree with some of these definitions).

UDC contains a nice example of organization into arrays in its Table 1e for common auxiliaries of place (see Figure 20.4). Although UDC doesn't display any labels for characteristics of division, in this edited version from

```
MY21       Ball games
MY211      Thrown by hand
MY2115     Basket ball
MY2116     Volley ball
MY212      Driven by foot
MY2121     Football
MY2122     Rugby
MY213      Thrown with rackets
MY2131     Tennis
MY2132     Badminton
MY214      Driven by bats
MY2141     Cricket
MY2142     Baseball
MY2143     Hockey
MY2144     Croquet
MY2145     Golf
MY2146     Polo
```

Figure 20.3 Arrays in Colon Class M

(20)	Ecosphere
(203)	In the air. Aerial
(204)	In the water. Hydrosphere
(205)	Earth's mantle. Lithosphere
(207)	Sphere of nature. Biosphere
(211/213)	Climatic zones
(211)	Cold regions
(212)	Temperate zones
(213)	Subtropical and tropical zones
(215)	Hemispheres
(215-11)	Eastern hemisphere
(215-17)	Northern hemisphere
(23)	Mountains
(24)	Subterranean
(25)	Flat ground
(251)	Steppes. Prairies
(253)	Virgin woods and forests
(254)	Arable land

Figure 20.4 Arrays in UDC Table 1e

the Pocket Edition you can clearly see the structure of the schedule and the organization of terms into arrays. You can see that there are several arrays here (even though I haven't included every term). Their principles of division are (levels of ecosphere), (places by temperature), (places by compass orientation), (places by elevation) and (places by vegetation), and within each group the classes are plainly mutually exclusive.

The naming of arrays can be quite problematic. Sometimes the principle of division is easily named, as in the above examples, but often, although it's clear what the principle is, the label can't be constructed very tidily. In the BC2 classification of physics there are labels such as (Nuclear reactions by incident and emitted radiation/particle combined) or (Types of changes in solids, by states involved – to and from plasmas), which do not exactly trip off the tongue. This clumsiness needn't concern the classifier, but it is a problem for the editor of the scheme, who has to think how to get such expressions into the index in a helpful way.

Order of and within arrays

Having put the terms into facets and then into arrays, there is still a need firstly to put the terms within arrays into order, and then to order the arrays themselves. Several different ordering principles can be used, all based on general rules of ordering, and common sense. Usually the terms themselves suggest an appropriate order. Although it's not strictly an array, the

		Commerce		
		Europe		
		Great Britain		
		General works		
		History		
HF	3505.15	Medieval		
	3505.2	Modern		
	3505.4	17th century		
	3505.6	18th century		

1	Town planning
11	Village
13	Town
15	City
17	Metropolis

Figure 20.5   Chronological order in LCC Class H

Figure 20.6   Order by size in CC Class N

sequence of terms from LCC Class H shown in Figure 20.5 could hardly be in any other order. Chronological order, as here, is a very common method of ordering, as is geographical proximity, size and developmental order.

Figure 20.6 shows an array from the third level personality facet in Colon Class N, Fine arts, which uses size as the ordering principle, whereas the list of prisons from BC2 Class Q shown in Figure 20.7 uses the degree of security as the basis of arrangement.

QQS K	(Types of prisons)
QQS M	Maximum security
N	Medium security
P	Minimum security, open prisons
R	With semi-liberty (living in institution, working outside)
S	With restricted liberty (living at home, working at institution)

Figure 20.7 Order by degree of security in BC2 Class Q

The order of arrays within the facet can be more problematical since there is often no clear principle by which to proceed. If we look again at the example of games in Colon Class M (Figure 20.3), we can see that the order of arrays is 'thrown by hand', 'driven by foot', 'thrown with rackets', 'driven by bats'. There's clearly an unmentioned initial subdivision into 'propelled by parts of the body' and 'propelled by equipment', subdivided by 'thrown' and 'driven'. This could just as well have been the other way about, giving a sequence of 'thrown by hand', 'thrown by rackets', 'driven by foot', 'driven by bats'. The choice of order in a case like this is completely arbitrary. Sometimes a general order of increasing concreteness can be applied: we can see that, in the UDC arrays in Figure 20.4, orientation and temperature are more abstract notions than the terrain and vegetation, but it is hard to say which way round each pair should be listed. Usually the final decision is made on a practical basis: which will give the most useful order of combination, for that is the next thing to consider.

Summary

- Concepts within the facet are arranged in smaller groups known as arrays or sub-facets.
- Arrays are labelled with the principle or characteristic of division.
- The order of classes within the array can be based on various principles, such as chronological order, size, stage of development, etc.
- The order of arrays within the facet is also decided on a practical basis, depending on how compounds would be best located.

Relationships between terms

So far we have a fair degree of order imposed on the concepts in our subject. We've sorted all the terms into facets, and we've organized the facets into arrays; within each facet the arrays have been put into order using a variety of principles, as have the terms within the arrays.

Now we have to think about the relationships between terms, both the *intra*-facet relationships (semantic relationships) and the *inter*-facet relationships (syntactic relationships). Let's look first at the relationships within the facet – what I've called the intra-facet relationships.

Because all the terms within a facet come into the same category (they're all 'things' or 'parts' or 'processes'), the relationships between them will be those of hierarchy, or broader, narrower and co-ordinate terms. They are the semantic relationships which we talked about in Chapter 5, and which we find in all types of bibliographic classification. In a faceted scheme they're equally likely to be found in the operations and processes facets as they are in those facets dealing with entities or objects, as Figure 20.8, an example from BC2 Class Q, shows.

Where a faceted classification differs most significantly from an enumerative classification is in its potential to combine terms from different facets, and it is here that the compiler has to think most carefully about

QP		Police work, law enforcement
QPD		Police work narrowly
QPD	O	Communications
QPD	P	Patrol and surveillance
	Q	Patrolling, beat
	R	Stopping and questioning
	S	Search and seizure
	T	Surveillance
	U	Pursuit and apprehension
	V	Pursuit
	W	Apprehension, arrest and charge
QPE		Criminal investigation, detection

Figure 20.8   Hierarchy in an operations facet in BC2

the relationships between facets, and between terms from different facets – the inter-facet relationships.

Any system of rules for combining terms in a language is called syntax. The system syntax for an indexing language is just the same as the syntax for a natural language, such as Swahili or Russian. It tells you how terms are to be put together (either as sentences or index descriptions); how you indicate what the status of a word is (a noun, a verb, an adjective, or an entity, a process, an agent); and what the order of combination (word order in the sentence, or citation order in the index description) is to be.

We've already sorted out the status of our words, or terms; now we need to look at syntax, that is the rules for combination or citation order.

Citation order

Citation order controls several aspects of the classification and the classified order:

- it gives you rules for the order of combination of terms when you're classifying
- it determines which aspects of a subject are brought together and which are distributed
- it affects the logical structure of the system, the predictability of locating compound subjects and the effectiveness of retrieval.

Any system that allows combination will have a citation order. Citation order need mean no more than the order of combination of terms. In this sense even pre-coordinated systems such as LCC and LCSH have citation order. We know, for example, that when using the tables in Class HD of

LCC an industry will be cited before a regional location. For example, a document on the manufacture of chemistry sets will be classed at HD9993.C48; manufacturing chemistry sets in Paraguay goes at HD9993.C484 P37 (using Table 21). The citation order, or order of combination, is Chemistry sets – Paraguay, or Industry – Place, and this will be true of any combination of industry and place in Class HD.

Similarly in LCSH, a free-floating subdivision or geographical subdivision is suffixed to a heading like this:

Beetles as pets– –Bolivia
Dangerous plants– –Wales– –Catalogs

The order of combination, or citation order, here is Subject – Place – Form.

You, as classifier, don't even have to be building classmarks (or headings) yourself in order for a citation order to be in operation. Even where there are no explicit rules for dealing with compound subjects (as in an enumerated classification), an implicit citation order can be seen. Look at this example of kinds of voice from the music schedules in DDC:

782

.6	**Women's voices**	
.66	Soprano voices (Treble voices)	
.67	Mezzo-soprano voices	
.68	Contralto voices (Alto voices)	
.7	**Children's voices**	
.76	Soprano voices (Treble voices)	
.77	Mezzo-soprano voices	
.78	Contralto voices (Alto voices)	
.79	Changing voices	
.8	**Men's voices**	
.86	Treble and alto voices	
.87	Tenor voices	
.88	Baritone voices	
.89	Bass voices	

Here the age or gender of the singer is subdivided by the pitch of the voice, and this subdivision of the one to the other is carried out absolutely consistently and predictably. Although there is no number building here, and the numbers are not arrived at synthetically, the citation order is very evidently 'age/gender – pitch' and it is applied without exception. Simple 'faceted' structures of this type are very common in DDC and in LCC although we don't usually think of them as faceted schemes in any theoretical sense. The beginning of most LCC schedules contain an enumeration comibining forms (periodicals, societies, congresses, dictionaries) with language or place in a similar regular, repetitive pattern. The combinations of terms are all enumerated, but the pattern of the enumeration shows the clear application of citation order, as one would expect in a synthetic classification.

Citation order in the faceted scheme is more complicated because there are a great many more facets to enter into the equation. Rather than make a decision about citation order at every potential place of compounding, the faceted scheme has a general rule for citation order based on the fundamental categories. This states that in the majority of cases the order of combination will be that of the categories as we've listed them so far in this book, i.e.:

thing – kind – part – property – material – process – operation – patient – product – by-product – agent – space – time.

This means that, given a document about respiration in the frog, the order of combination will be 'frog – respiration', or 'thing – process'. Hence the different processes affecting frogs (digestion, locomotion, sensory perception, etc.) will all be gathered together in the class Frogs. A document about teaching using audiovisual aids will be analysed as 'teaching – audiovisual aids', or 'operation – agent'. 'Maintaining motor vehicles in the tropics' will be analysed as 'motor vehicles – maintenance – tropics', or 'thing – operation – place'. Of course the classifier or indexer does not have to decide this; the creator of the scheme must structure the system and provide rules for combination that make sure this happens correctly.

Why is this order, the standard citation order, chosen? There are three main reasons behind it:

- the order progresses from concrete to abstract
- each facet is to some extent dependent on preceding facets
- it gives the most useful grouping of compounds.

The order of decreasing concreteness puts the concepts in an order of relative importance for most subjects. As we discussed earlier, the 'personality' facets, the things, their kinds and parts, are usually the central focus of the subject; putting them first in the citation order means that they form the primary division of the subject. At the other end of the sequence, space and time are more general, less subject-specific, and least important in document description. We shall see how the order of decreasing concreteness is also important for schedule order when we look at that in the next section.

The idea of dependence is a common sense one; it's not possible to imagine the parts of a thing without the thing itself being there. Similarly operations must have a thing to be operated on, and one must conceive of the operation before the means of doing it (or agent) is brought into play.

Useful grouping of compounds is a practical rather than a theoretical consideration, but it must be the most important factor since it affects retrieval. If you've forgotten about the relationship between citation order and how aspects of the subject are grouped, go back to Chapter 3 (page 9) where we talked about sorting out the literature books. The way in which users will expect to find the subject organized is always the most important thing in deciding on what will come first in the citation order.

Variation in citation order

The standard citation order is a good order for the majority of subjects; if one could have only one citation order in a whole system, this order would serve best. In practice a general scheme of classification is a series of special classifications for the individual main classes or disciplines, and the citation order can vary from one subject to another.

Standard citation order is very suitable for scientific and technical subjects, and most schemes will follow this order, whether they are faceted schemes with rules for building classmarks, or enumerative schemes where compound classes are listed but adhere to some general principles of combination.

In the social sciences and humanities it can be more difficult to match the primary facet with a 'thing' and its associated parts and properties. In organizing a history collection most people would want to make place the primary facet, so that the history of individual countries is the first division of the collection. In standard citation order place is very well down the list and would not achieve the best order for most libraries.

In the fine arts, place and time are also important facets (as they are in literature), more important than their position in standard citation order would allow. However, the operations facet of the creative arts (which includes painting, drawing, sculpture and so on) will probably be best as the primary facet in that class.

There is nothing fixed or absolutely true about citation order. The standard citation order is the most generally helpful, but the optimum order should be decided on for each individual subject. What really matters is that the citation order chosen is systematically applied, so that the order of classes and the location of compound subjects are both predictable. Then retrieval will be much easier.

Summary
- Relations within a facet are hierarchical or semantic relations
- Relations between facets are determined by the order of combination of terms, or citation order.
- All systems where terms are combined have a citation order, even where this is implicit, as in enumerative schemes.
- Standard citation order is suitable for most subjects.
- Where it is not very helpful (as in some humanities subjects) an alternative citation order can be used instead.
- Citation order should always be chosen to give the most helpful arrangement of the material.
- Once decided on, citation order should be applied consistently, so that the location of items is predictable.

Schedule order

Let's look again at our BC2 example of medicine. The citation order for the class will be:

(Thing)	Human beings
(Kind)	Women, children, old people, etc.
(Part)	Head, legs, muscles, bones, heart, brain, lungs, etc.
(Process)	Respiration, digestion, reproduction, disease, etc.
(Operation)	Surgery, drug therapy, physiotherapy, etc.
(Agent)	Doctors, nurses, equipment, buildings, etc.

If we have a document about the use of physiotherapy in bone disease in the elderly, the citation order will be 'elderly – bone – disease – physiotherapy'. The use of lasers in surgery for gallstones will be cited as 'gall bladder – calculi – surgery – lasers'.

Unfortunately this order won't serve us very well in terms of arranging books on shelves or documents in a file or screen display. If we use this order for physical arrangement it will look very odd, because the most specific things will come at the beginning, together with all of the complicated compound subjects. Most users will expect to find more general, less specific subjects at the beginning of the sequence, and very particular things at the end. Think of the order of sections in a practical book about some activity – a sport for instance, or dressmaking, or do-it-yourself. The book may start off with some general background, perhaps about the history of the sport or the craft. It will then usually consider the equipment needed, and any materials, go on to discuss general skills and techniques, and finish with some specific projects or areas of activity. A book that I have about gardening has the following chapters:

1 History of gardening
2 Tools and equipment
3 Garden buildings, fences and pathways
4 Garden soil
5 Gardening techniques: digging, mulching, planting
6 The flower garden
7 The vegetable garden
8 The herb garden

This seems a very logical order. It would be odd to have these chapters the other way round. In a collection of books about gardening the same general order of subjects would be natural and intuitive for most users.

Compare this with the standard citation order. The categories are much the same; 1 = time, 2 and 3 = agents, 4 = materials, 5 = operations, 6, 7 and 8 = things or entities. The order however is the *reverse* of standard citation order. Because this order, with the general things first and the specific things at the end of the sequence, is more natural to users, we turn the citation order upside down when we come to list the facets in the schedule. (Remember that the order in the schedule will be the same as the order of the books on the shelves when they are classified.)

We start the schedule with the time and place facets, and work backwards through the citation order to finish with the primary facet as the last thing in the classification schedule. Such a schedule is called an **inverted schedule**, and the theory behind it is known as the **principle of inversion**. We can see the principle of inversion in BC2 Class J, Education (Figure 20.9).

J	Education	
J7	History of education	(Time)
J8	Education by place	(Place)
JE	Psychology of education	(Process)
JF	Educational performance	(Process)
JG	Students, pupils	(Patients)
JH	Teachers	(Agent)
JI	Teaching methods	(Operation)
JK	Curriculum	
JL/JV	Educands and educational institutions	(Thing/kind)

Figure 20.9 Inverted schedule in BC2 Class J

Although the citation order here is not standard citation order (the agents of the operation 'teaching' are collocated with it, and the 'curriculum' facet has no equivalent category), you can clearly see the inversion of the citation order in the schedule order.

The principle of inversion clearly gives us a good general order of subjects on the shelf, but it also allows for logical building of compound classes. Figure 20.10 shows how this is achieved in a simplified (hypothetical) classification for gardening.

Let's try to make a proper inverted schedule for our gardening classification. In order to make things clearer we'll simplify it a bit, and only use four facets: time, agents, operations and entities. In each facet we'll put just a few terms to show how things work. In this example we can see the

```
(Time). History of gardening
    Mediaeval
    Sixteenth century
    Nineteenth century
    Twenty-first century
(Agents). Tools and equipment
    Hand tools
        Spades
        Rakes
        Sprays
    Power tools
        Trimmers
        Mowers
        Cultivators
(Operations). Practical gardening
    Designing
    Digging
    Planting
    Pruning
    Pest control
(Entities). Plants
    Flowers. Flower gardens
        Roses
        Bulbs
    Vegetables. Vegetable gardens
        Carrots
        Potatoes
    Herbs. Herb gardens
```

Figure 20.10 Faceted structure for gardening

terms organized into facets and the facets inverted into the order we agreed was best for intuitive arrangement and browsing. Now let's look at what happens when we try to put in some compound subjects.

Suppose our first topic is 'pruning roses'. The citation order for this will be 'entities – operations', or 'roses – pruning', and the document will be placed with the entity 'roses'. Similarly 'planting bulbs' will be analysed as 'bulbs – planting' and placed with bulbs, and 'mediaeval herb gardens' will become 'herb gardens – mediaeval' located with herb gardens.

We can add some more complicated topics, such as 'hand digging in the vegetable garden' (vegetables – digging – hand tools), 'designing a modern flower garden' (flowers – designing – twenty-first century), 'sprays for pest control on potatoes' (potatoes – pest control – sprays) or '19th-century hand tools for pruning herbs' (herbs – pruning – hand tools – 19th century).

Each time the compound will file with the first facet in the citation order, followed by subsequent facets (Figure 20.11). I hope you can see how the filing order runs from 'time → entities', while the citation order, the order of combination of terms, runs the other way, from 'entity → time'. Apart from conforming to the general intuitive order of the gardening book example, this meets other classification theory requirements.

It complies with Ranganathan's rule of increasing concreteness: abstract notions such as time precede more concrete classes such as 'roses' and 'carrots'. It also meets the very important requirement always to have general before special. The rule of general before special means that we shouldn't put the compound 'roses – pruning' under pruning in the middle of the schedule, because that would *precede* its broader class, roses, further down the schedule. Pruning of roses can only be entered into the schedule when both of its broader classes, pruning and roses, have been listed, so it must necessarily file under the most specific, i.e. later scheduled, element. This means that the order of combination of terms (citation order) is always 'later term – earlier term' so that the compound files in the correct place.

In a general classification, this **principle of inversion** operates only within a given main class or discipline, since most schemes have limited facilities for building across main classes. Interestingly, the first published faceted classification, the Colon Classification, doesn't demonstrate the principle of inversion; if you look at the scheme you'll see that the order of classes follows the facet formula exactly.

If you find the principle of inversion difficult to understand don't worry. It is one of the trickiest ideas in classification theory and many

Filing order	Classes
T I M E	(Time). History of gardening Mediaeval 16th century 19th century 21st century
A G E N T S	(Agents). Tools and equipment Hand tools Spades Rakes Sprays Power tools Trimmers Mowers Cultivators
O P E R A T I O N S	(Operations). Practical gardening Designing Digging Planting Pruning Pest control
E N T I T I E S	(Entities). Plants Flowers. Flower gardens Flower gardens – designing Flower gardens – designing – 21st century Roses Roses – pruning Bulbs Bulbs – planting Vegetables. Vegetable gardens Vegetables – digging Vegetables – digging – hand tools Carrots Potatoes Potatoes – pest control Potatoes – pest control – sprays Herbs. Herb gardens Herb gardens – mediaeval Herbs – pruning – hand tools – 19th century

CITATION ORDER

ENTITY OPERATION AGENT TIME

Figure 20.11 Inverted schedule for gardening

students never really master it. It won't stop you doing good practical classification.

Summary

- Citation order is the order of *combination* of concepts in compound classes, but it doesn't give a good order for shelving or filing.
- The reverse of the standard citation order is a more natural and intuitive order.
- A schedule in which the order is turned upside down in this way is known as an inverted schedule.
- In an inverted schedule rules of increasing concreteness and general before special are preserved.

Now that we've applied all these processes of sorting, and ordering to facets and arrays we have something very close to a faceted classification structure. The final stage is to attach the notation.

Notation in the faceted scheme

Notation is very important in the faceted scheme because it's the notation that controls the order of the schedule and the business of building the compound classmarks.

Notation falls into two main types: notation using facet indicators and retroactive notation.

Notation using facet indicators

Faceted classifications commonly use symbols of some sort to introduce a new facet, whether these are characters from the main notational base or special symbols used only as facet indicators.

DDC uses the zero to precede a notation from the table for standard subdivisions, and –09 is recognized to indicate place or time. For example in the classmarks:

Cultivated plants of Southern Africa 635.0968
Greek insects 595.709495

the 09 notation introduces the notation for Southern Africa, –68, and for Greece, –495. You can be sure that 09 in DDC precedes a notation for place of some sort. DDC isn't consistent in its use of the facet indicator, however, since a zero in a DDC number may not be a facet indicator at all. In the numbers:

664.902	Preservation techniques, slaughtering, meat cutting
664.805	Specific vegetables and groups of vegetables

the zeros are just part of an enumerated number and don't indicate any new facet or synthesized number.

CC uses a facet formula for each main class, in which the various facets are clearly introduced by a facet indicator using punctuation symbols. For example, in library science the facet formula is 2 [P] ; [M] : [E] where 2 is the main class number. Each facet consists of a numbered list of 'foci' (Ranganathan's name for concepts), so that university is 34 in the P facet, 43 stands for periodicals in the M facet, and cataloguing is 55 in the E facet. The classmark for the subject 'Cataloguing periodicals in the university library' hence becomes 234;43:55, the punctuation showing which is the P, M and E component of the classmark.

You are already familiar with the facet indicators for the auxiliary tables in UDC, and these are some of the clearest examples of facet indicators to be found in the general schemes (Figure 20.12). Where "…" indicates the time facet, and –03 is from the materials facet, and so on, there's no doubt where the notation for a new facet begins.

Lacemaking in the nineteenth century	746.2"18"
Public sector borrowing in Germany	336.27(430)
Women in the theatre	792–055.2

Figure 20.12 Facet indicators in UDC

The price paid for this clarity in the structure of the classmark is the length and cumbersome nature of the notations, and the fact that the awkward symbols confuse the filing order and make shelving more difficult. The symbols do allow the notation to be used over again in different facets, so the notation does not have to be spread over the whole classification. For example, in library science in CC, 55 is used for both government publications and cataloguing, the difference being denoted by the two facet indicators, ;55 and :55 respectively. In the UDC main tables 376 is the class for special schools, but in the auxiliary tables it can also stand for ancient Rome (376), or for study periods "376", since the facet indicators make it clear that these aren't main table numbers.

Retroactive notation

Retroactive notation is a cleverly devised notation used in BC2, and in some of the special schemes that preceded it, where facet indictors aren't needed because the notational codes can be added directly together.

Retroactive simply means that the codes for individual concepts are being added together in the reverse of the schedule order, as you would expect in an inverted schedule. As we saw in the gardening example, an earlier class is always added to a later class. Because BC2 constructs the compound classmark in this way, the editor can allow notational 'space' to add on all of the earlier part of the schedule directly. For example, consider the abbreviated schedule for Social Welfare, Class Q, shown in Figure 20.13.

QAG	Social welfare administration
QD	Social work
QE	Social services
QG	Persons in need
QGP	Deprivation, poverty, unemployment
QH	Housing, accommodation
QJD	Victims of cruelty, violence
QJS	Immigrants
QK	The family
QKK	Family planning
	(Members of the family)
QKL Y	Single, unmarried people
QKQ	Mothers
QKQ T	Fathers

Figure 20.13 Retroactive notation in BC2 Class Q

Here, the first enumerated sub-class of QK is QKK. The classes QKA to QKJ will be synthesized classes, arrived at by adding classes QA to QJ directly to QK (the first letter of the main class being dropped in synthesis). We can build these classes as shown in Figure 20.14. Each time the notation from earlier classes can be added directly without the need for a facet indicator

QK A G	Family social welfare administration
QK D	Family social work
QK G	Families in need
QK JD	Domestic violence
QK JS	Immigrant families
QKQ	Mothers
QKQ E	Social services for mothers
QKQ JD	Mothers as victims of domestic violence
QKT	Fathers
QKT LY	Single fathers
QKT LY H	Housing for single fathers

Figure 20.14 Retroactive number building in BC2 Class Q

because the space has been left for the earlier classes to slot into.

This makes classmarks very easy to construct in BC2 because there are no additional symbols to insert, and the classifier doesn't even have to think about the facet 'status' of individual concepts. The classmarks are simpler, and there are no awkward characters to confuse the filing order.

On the other hand, although the retroactive synthesis in BC2 is a very elegant device for achieving brief classmarks, it does not help retrieval in an automated environment, because it compromises the integrity of the notation. The facet structure of the classmarks isn't apparent, and it's impossible to search for a concept by its notation (as you can in UDC) because this can change when the concept is part of a built classmark. In this respect the notation is rather like that of DDC, where things are generally less consistent and more unpredictable than in UDC.

Summary
- Notation in faceted schemes can use facet indicators or be retroactive.
- Facet indicators can use the scheme's own characters (as in DDC) or special symbols (as in UDC and CC).
- Facet indicators can make the classmarks longer, but their facet structure is evident.
- Retroactive notation in BC2 builds classmarks without facet indicators.
- This is elegant and the method is easy for the classifier, but it can disguise the facet structure of the classmark and hinder machine retrieval.

Facet analysis is important because it provides a scientific basis for building classification schemes, and because it formalizes a great deal of earlier classification theory. Features that were previously regarded as of practical value, such as the rule of general before special, now have a proper philosophical basis. It's possible to see in all the general schemes of classification a tighter and more rigorous approach to the organization of classes. Inverted schedules and carefully organized arrays are now normal, as are increased facilities for classmark building in a logical and structured manner. Even when you're working with an enumerative scheme you can look out for these signs and think of the work of Ranganathan, the student who was so puzzled by his classification lectures.

21 Managing classification

So far we have looked at a number of aspects of the theory of classification, at the central activity of applying particular schemes, and, of course, at how the two are related. Another important factor is the management of the scheme, both at the editorial level and in the local situation.

The management and maintenance of schemes

It's important for the institutional user to be aware of the arrangements in place for the upkeep of the classification system. The classification is a major tool in the organization of the library (more important than is generally acknowledged) and you need to be assured that it will be maintained and kept current, and that its editors will respond to the changing needs of collections and to changes in technology. We'll consider the different publication formats in some detail below, but the broader concerns of the currency and stability of the classification are independent of any particular version.

The general management of classifications

Most schemes are managed by an institution or organization that ensures its continued existence. The larger and more stable this organization, the more likely it is to support the classification well. The biggest classifications, such as DDC and LCC, have a considerable machine behind them that can accommodate the general running of the classification, its publication, the dissemination of information to users, the promotion of the scheme, the creation of training materials, the provision of bibliographic services, and research into the theory and applications of classification. The availability of all these secondary features can make the classification more attractive to the end-user and greatly enhance its usefulness. All of them additionally serve to create a sense of community among users and to promote loyalty to the system – they're all good public relations exercises.

Revision and maintenance

The most important of these operations, as far as the classification itself is concerned, is the ongoing upkeep of the scheme, particularly the revision of the scheme to accommodate new subjects. It's absolutely essential to have robust mechanisms for identifying and incorporating new topics in the literature, and for informing users about such additions and amendments. The reverse process, the pruning of obsolete terms, and, in some cases, removing biased or politically incorrect terminology and structures, needs also to be in place.

On occasion the changes won't be restricted to the addition or removal of concepts, but will affect the functionality of the scheme. The increased facility for synthesis in DDC is a good example of this 'syntactical' expansion.

A regular bulletin or service keeping users in touch with changes is a vital part of good classification management, as is the publication of complete new editions either of the whole scheme or constituent classes, when minor changes have become very numerous. The regularity with which this is done must be judged carefully, since alongside the need for currency is a reciprocal need for stability, and there is no doubt that the managers of large collections dislike major changes in their systems, and will usually resist reclassification. There are, of course, financial considerations here since reclassification, other than on a small scale, is hugely consumptive of resources. In these days of electronically maintained classifications the whole new edition may be a thing of the past, but the constantly shifting structure of the electronic classification can itself be problematic for the librarian trying to work to a standard.

Despite these caveats, currency of the classification is normally a concern for users. The need for currency does vary across subjects: scientific and technical subjects with a rapid rate of discovery of new knowledge and constant inventions create a particular demand for the vocabulary to keep pace, whereas 'traditional' humanities disciplines may have a much slower rate of change, and classificatory structures there can remain stable and usable for longer periods of time. Nevertheless, new topics constantly arise and a well-managed scheme must deal with this fact.

Nowadays the authority files of most classifications are held in database formats which greatly eases the task of management, particularly in respect of making changes and of auditing change.

Local management of the classification

Most libraries won't use a scheme exactly in line with the editorial instructions. We've already looked on several occasions at how we often need to make local decisions about how the classification is operated. We could recap these:

- decisions about the broadness or closeness of classification
- decisions about alternative locations
- decisions about alternative citation orders
- decisions about the treatment of particular subjects, such as biography.

It's very important that careful records, or authorities, are kept concerning these decisions, and that everyone is aware of the local policy. When classifying you should use your authority files and not make independent decisions. Nowadays of course you'll use the library management system to generate authority files as items are catalogued, but classifiers should remember to refer to these authorities, and not go their own way.

The cost of classification

The cost of in-house cataloguing has been a concern for a number of years, and there are few libraries now that undertake all of their cataloguing in-house. Various other approaches include downloading of records, copy cataloguing of external records and outsourcing of the entire job, the last option being common in the case of retrospective conversion of catalogues. Classification presents some different problems, and may be considered independently of cataloguing as a whole.

It's unarguably the case that classification is generally more difficult than most cataloguing, and in many libraries the classification or other subject assessment is carried out by subject specialists rather than cataloguing staff. If that happens then the costs may be regarded as irrelevant since they won't affect the cataloguing department directly.

The central issue is usually whether the classification data available from external sources is acceptable to the home library. Two factors come into the equation here: the limitation on choice of the classification scheme, and the appropriateness of default classification within a scheme.

As regards the choice of scheme, a library that wishes to import records must resign itself to either LCC or DDC as the system of choice, unless it is a specialist collection with some appropriate national collection providing bibliographic services. The National Library of Medicine is the obvious example here, but others are difficult to find. The availability of records from the Library of Congress and OCLC has undoubtedly caused many libraries to adopt those schemes, and for a general collection this may be a sensible choice with some considerable savings effected in time and money.

Other libraries will find that, though the scheme may be acceptable at a general level, the particular decisions made don't match local requirements very well, and the classification part of the bibliographic record has to be amended. If this is likely to happen to any great extent, then the library should consider whether there is any useful purpose to be served in adopting the cataloguing service's classification. The service could still be used to provide catalogue records, but the classification of choice could be employed for subject access.

Print or electronic format

A major decision that needs to be taken by the user is the format of the classification. Most classifications are available to the user in print and electronic format, and there are advantages and disadvantages attached to each.

I often feel that the print version of a scheme is much easier for novice classifiers to cope with. You have a much better sense of the structure of the scheme and the context of individual classes; it's easier to browse the schedule, and it's easier to compare one part of the scheme with another. On the other hand, locating the correct class can be slower and more frustrating.

It's also much easier to annotate a hard copy of the scheme – an important factor if the material to be classified is complex, lots of local decisions have been made, or local modifications have been inserted. New terms can be added as they occur, without waiting for editorial decisions. If a scheme has lots of alternatives those not chosen can be struck through. In other words, a hard copy can be customized in a way that a electronic version cannot.

This advantage is diminished if a lot of people do the classifying, since a single working copy can't be very widely shared, and if amendments have to be reproduced in several copies the chances of mistakes become more likely. Nevertheless, the advantages of having a fully customized version are considerable in a small organization.

One advantage of a hard copy that seems not to have been much discussed in the literature is the question of stability. Large libraries don't very often reclassify when a scheme is revised, except perhaps to address particular thorny problems in restricted areas. You'll often hear it said 'we use 19th (or 20th or whatever) Dewey', by which is meant that specific edition of the scheme, which remains in operation even when a newer version is available. In an online classification this function is lost, since the classification is constantly amended and is potentially not the same from one day to the next. In theory libraries can't continue to use an 'old number' since the 'old number' will have been removed. It's not very clear how this difficulty will ultimately be solved, but it seems to me to be of considerable significance, particularly for libraries with very large collections.

From a narrower management point of view, a hard copy incurs a one-off cost (until the library decides to update) and it is usually cheaper than an online subscription – at least if only a small number of copies are needed.

On the minus side the print version is obviously bulkier, can't be easily moved around, and is more prone to damage and physical deterioration. It's not updated so frequently, and this may be problematic in a rapidly changing subject.

In the matter of currency the online subscription has everything to commend it. The user gets the benefit of additions to the scheme, and this can be a real advantage in a fast-moving subject. Of course, not every online classification is updated very frequently, but some are, and in any event it will usually be much more frequent than the revision of the print version. One also has to consider whether publishers will continue to maintain paper copy in a digital world.

The online classification can also be shared by a large number of classifiers, and it can be accessed from any terminal, making working practices more flexible.

Choosing a classification

It's not very likely that you will ever be in a position to select a classification scheme for a large library, but the question of classification for smaller collections arises more frequently than you might imagine. This usually happens because a collection has never been classified, because a local, in-house classification has been used or, less often, because collections using different schemes are being merged.

As we've seen in our investigation of the general schemes, there is no perfect scheme. Nevertheless, the different schemes do all have distinctive characteristics which make them better suited to particular types of collections, materials and users.

Important questions to ask in this context include:

- what is the subject of the collection
- what is the intellectual level and complexity of the content
- what sorts of materials and formats are represented
- who is available to do the classifying
- what sort of subject tools and services are required
- who will use the collection.

The subject of the collection

One might imagine that general classifications will treat all subjects equally, but this isn't necessarily the case. Most are stronger in some areas than others. Remember too that it isn't just the level of detail that is at issue; the provision for fringe topics and the general collocation of subjects need also to be taken into account. In an academic library whether there is a match between the structure of the classification and the structure of courses will also be an important factor. You can only really decide this one by looking at the schedules of the different schemes and seeing how they correspond to your needs.

In general terms UDC has the best provision for scientific subjects, whereas LCC contains very considerable detail in the arts and humanities, particularly in respect of naming individual writers, artists, persons in history, events and primary texts of all kinds and in all subjects. DDC probably has the best balance between subjects, with less detail but fewer obvious shortcomings.

For a very large subject specialist collection it may be better to choose a special scheme if there is a well-established one available; the reasons for doing so are discussed in more detail below.

The level of the material

Two factors come into play here. The first is related to the previous section, and concerns the amount of detail in the scheme; the second concerns the capacity of the scheme to express complex subject content.

The detail in the scheme is usually perfectly evident to the eye, but remember that the extent of the vocabulary and the number of the classes are only part of the equation. A scheme with a modest vocabulary but with auxiliary schedules and facilities for combining classes has a very much greater number of potential classes. An enumerative scheme can achieve the same thing in a different way, by pre-coordinating compounds and listing them in the schedule.

The real issue lies in whether the subject requires great specificity in the hierarchy, i.e. whether the vocabulary itself is very technical and detailed, or whether the subjects of documents are complicated in terms of their content analysis. In the latter case, capacity for combining terms is really essential, particularly if most of the terms are likely to be sought terms in retrieval. An analytico-synthetic scheme has much to offer if this is the case, and you should look for the capacity to combine notations, either through a faceted structure or by means of auxiliary tables.

The format

The same considerations tend to apply if the material is in unusual formats, report literature, for example, or ephemeral material or non-text material of various kinds. The subjects of documents such as these are likely to be more complex, and in any event there probably needs to be some way of expressing these different forms. If the classification or indexing language is required to provide metadata for digital resources, this will also create a need for considerable precision and flexibility in the scheme.

The classifiers

The experience and level of professional education of the staff also affect the choice of system, since it is undoubtedly the case that some schemes are easier to apply than others. A scheme such as LCC requires little more than copying from the schedules, whereas UDC will need some understanding of issues such as complex content analysis and citation order; such a scheme also often assumes an advanced understanding of the subject in order to get to grips with the detailed vocabulary. DDC with its extensive instructions and class definitions can aid the inexperienced, although it's generally a more complicated scheme to apply.

Where there is help on hand, and more experienced classifiers to train and advise, this will be overcome, but in a small organization with inexperienced staff, this can be a pressing problem. In such a situation copy cataloguing or the downloading of records is a sensible solution, and may anyway be considered for reasons of cost.

Nowadays, the use of other institutions' records is the norm in a great number of libraries. There are so many online catalogues with free access to bibliographic data, as well as subscription bibliographic services, that it can represent a considerable saving in time and effort to outsource cataloguing. Classification is slightly different and more complicated in terms of using external data, and certain factors will affect your decision:

- In a general library this will almost certainly restrict you to using DDC or LCC since these are the only widely available schemes.
- In a special collection you may be able to copy classification data from the online catalogue of another special collection, but you will have to accept their choice of classification and all the decisions they make about the treatment of particular items.

This second factor is a significant one, since there is little point in choosing a detailed and flexible scheme only to find that you can't take advantage of its detail and flexibility. A related matter is the coverage of any special or unusual materials that you hold, and this can also affect the usability of the general schemes. If you have lots of ephemeral resources or other unusual formats that won't appear in other libraries' catalogues, much of the advantage of copy cataloguing is lost.

For these reasons many libraries that choose to take records from external sources do so only in respect of their author/title cataloguing and leave classification as an in-house activity.

Subject access tools

This is perhaps a minor consideration for many libraries, but an important one for those libraries that do use their classification for reasons other than shelf arrangement. It's probably more significant for special libraries or those operating at the research level than it is for the general collection.

A flexible and detailed classification will be invaluable in a situation where it's required to manage bibliographies, printed lists or search results, or anywhere where a detailed breakdown of resources is required. We've already mentioned the use of the classification for metadata, and here again detail and flexibility are important. The notation can also be of concern where retrieval rather than browsing is the purpose of the classification. An expressive notation aids retrieval, as does a notation whose integrity is preserved in number building, enabling search and retrieval on elements in a built classmark. This can be particularly important in a special or technical library with large amounts of complicated subject matter.

The users

In the previous section we considered the needs of those at the most demanding level of information storage and retrieval. Users such as these will probably take trouble to learn and manipulate any classification or indexing system, but the same can't be assumed of students or of the general library user. Here simplicity and usability of the scheme take much greater priority. Supporters of DDC often make much of the familiarity of the scheme as being in its favour, but I'm not convinced that even the broad structure of the scheme is evident to the general user. Certainly, when I worked in a college library, few of the academic staff had registered the fact that our classification was the same as that in the public library and that they could advise students to seek out the same numbers for their subjects in the two places. Most expressed surprise and delight when this useful phenomenon was pointed out to them.

What does seem important is that the filing order of the system is relatively simple, so that users can find things easily. The use of odd symbols will undoubtedly confuse all but the most determined user. Brevity of notation is also important in remembering classmarks between the catalogue and the shelf. For some reason numbers appear to be more memorable than letters, although of course numerical classmarks will be longer than alphabetical classmarks for the same level of detail.

Much of this depends on how sophisticated is the use made of the catalogue by the readers; those who search in a complex way will appreciate the advantages offered by a more complicated system. The more casual user will simply be perplexed by it.

Of course, the major purpose of the classification in a print-based collection will be the physical arrangement of the items, and for many users the browsability function of the classification is paramount. They will probably never use the catalogue and rely on the collocation of items to find what they need. For these users the general structure of the scheme, although they may be quite oblivious to it, is what aids their use of the collection. In such cases the broad structure of the classification and its approximation to the way users will look for things will be an important factor in its adoption.

The general versus the special scheme

In this book we've looked in detail at only the general schemes of classification. The managers of a special collection may find some advantage in using a classification specifically designed for their subject.

You will be able to find a special classification for the majority of subjects, but most of them aren't very well known, and there may be as many disadvantages as benefits in adopting one. There are some very well established special classifications in major 'special collection' subjects: the National Library of Medicine scheme and the Moys classification for law books are two that immediately spring to mind. Points in favour can be summarized as follows:

- The special scheme will offer a much more detailed vocabulary.
- The general order of subjects and arrangement of fringe disciplines will be tailored to the needs of the specialist users.
- The scheme will make provision for special forms of publication.
- It may be possible to find an online catalogue for a comparable specialist collection which can be used as a source of classification data.

But on the other hand:

- The arrangements for maintenance and revision of the scheme may not be comparable with those of the general schemes.
- The scheme may not be updated as regularly.
- There may be no formal arrangements to support copy cataloguing or provide bibliographic services.
- There may be very limited opportunities for training in the scheme, or for other sorts of advice and support.

For the library that has a lot of material not covered by the big publicly available catalogues or that isn't in national bibliographic services, the advantages of better structure and detail can be very attractive. Certainly in major areas such as medicine or law the greater number of user institutions can provide reassurance about the stability of special schemes.

Glossary

accession number a running number allocated to items as they are processed by the library, serving as a unique identifier for the item within the collection.

alphabetical subject catalogue: a catalogue or index in which entries are arranged by the names of the subjects stated in the form of **subject headings**. Subject headings may be taken from an authority such as the **Library of Congress Subject Headings,** or can be derived from the subject strings used for classification.

alternatives optional treatments or locations for particular subjects. Where an alternative is available, an initial decision must be made as to which is used, and the other alternative abandoned; in the library situation non-preferred alternatives should be deleted from the schedules.

analytico-synthetic classification an analytico-synthetic scheme in which classmarks not represented in the **schedules** may be created by the classifier; the content is *analysed* and classmarks for the different elements are linked together to *synthesize* the new classmark. See also **faceted classification.**

approximation to the whole the matching in DDC of the subject of a document to the class to which it is assigned. If the main subject of the document is equivalent, or nearly equivalent, to the class, it is said to approximate to the whole. For example, 'horsemanship' would approximate to the whole of the class 'riding'.

array a group of sub-classes all derived by applying the same principle of division to the containing class: e.g., if the class of 'human beings' is divided by the principle of 'age', the sub-classes 'babies', 'children', 'adolescents' and 'adults' form an array.

aspect classification a classification in which the first division of the classification is into disciplines or fields of study, such as history, science, technology, art. These divisions are known as **main classes.** An entity or phenomenon (rabbits, castles, water, administration) may appear in several places in the classification according to the aspect from which it is considered. **Bibliographic classifications** are normally aspect classifications.

authority file   a file in which previous decisions are recorded, and used to ensure that subsequent decisions conform. In electronic catalogues authority files are usually the sum of all data in a specific field.

auxiliary schedules   schedules or tables which deal with commonly occurring concepts such as place, time or form, and which can be added to any classmark from the main schedules. In some schemes special auxiliaries exist for use in a particular class.

auxiliary table   see **auxiliary schedules**.

bibliographic classification   a classification for indexing and organizing documents; a conventional library classification.

bibliographic details   attributes of a document (such as the author, title, publisher, date and place of publication) which are conventionally used to describe it in catalogues and bibliographies.

BC1, BC2   see **Bliss's Bibliographic Classification**

Bliss's Bibliographic Classification   a scheme often regarded as the most scholarly of the general schemes. It was never used in Bliss's native America, but was favoured by a number of UK and Commonwealth academic and special libraries. Because of its unique main class for social welfare, the first edition, BC1, was widely adopted by many charity and social welfare libraries in the UK. The second edition, BC2, is the only general scheme built on faceted principles published in the Western world.

book number   a number constructed for each item in a collection that uniquely identifies it. A book number (on the model of the Library of Congress) consists of a **classmark** plus a code for the author's name, and may also include other elements such as a date of publication or edition number. In other libraries the **accession number** of the book may serve the same purpose.

bottom-up classification   a classification which is built up from the vocabulary of a subject, by analysing and then grouping individual terms into arrays and facets.

broad classification   classification in which the items are classed more generally than their subjects might warrant. Broad classification is sometimes used for arranging books on the shelf (for **browsing**), while a more precise classmark is provided on the catalogue record (for **retrieval**).

broader term (BT) term which is more general in meaning than the term to which it is related: e.g., 'citrus fruit' is a broader term related to 'oranges'.

browsing the process whereby users physically scan the collection, gaining an overview of its content. In an automated catalogue or database users may also browse the indexes for the same purpose. Browsing is often contrasted with catalogue searching (or retrieval) where the object is to locate one or more specific items.

call-mark the shelf-mark of a book which comprises the classmark and any other notation representing the author name, date of publication, edition information, size, form, etc..

caption the class description or heading in a classification scheme. See also **scope note**.

categories the groups into which terms are sorted in **facet analysis**. In modern classification theory the generally recognized categories are 'thing', 'kind', 'part', 'material', 'property', 'process', 'operation', 'agent', 'space' and 'time', although others are found in particular disciplines.

categorization (1) the allocation of terms to **categories** in facet analysis.

categorization (2) a system of very broad classification used by some public libraries in preference to a traditional bibliographic classification. See also **reader interest classification**.

CC see **Colon Classification**.

characteristic of division see **principle of division**.

citation order the order in which the parts of a **compound subject** are combined when creating a classmark or subject heading. The citation order determines which aspects of a subject are brought together and which are scattered. See also **distributed relatives, filing order, schedule order**.

class a set whose members share some common feature; sometimes used as a synonym for **main class**.

classification (1) the process of assigning objects to classes.

classification (2) the process of identifying classes and organizing them into a **classification scheme**.

classification (3) the process of assigning a **classmark** or **subject heading** from a particular scheme to a given document.

classification scheme a set of classes organized in a systematic fashion to show the relationships between them; the classification consists of a **vocabulary** (the terms used to represent the classes) and **syntax** (the rules for combining classes). A classification scheme is an example of a **controlled indexing language**.

classificationist a person who designs or builds classification schemes.

classified catalogue a catalogue in which the entries are arranged using the classmarks of the items. In broad terms it replicates the shelf order of a collection. It will integrate into a single sequence material shelved or filed separately, such as journals or non-book items.

classifier a person engaged in the operation of classifying documents.

classmark a notational code representing the subject of a document, and used to place it in a sequence on the shelves or in a classified file. The classmark may be part of a **book number**.

close classification the assignment of classmarks that exactly match the subjects of documents; precise or specific classification.

closed access a system where the items making up the collection are stored separately from the areas used by readers, and must be fetched by staff.

collocation the association or bringing together in the classification sequence of related classes or items.

Colon Classification the only complete example of a fully faceted classification. A complex scheme, and one never popular outside its native India, it serves to illustrate the classification theory developed by its creator S. R. Ranganathan, one of the great theorists and innovators of librarianship.

common subdivisions commonly occurring concepts in a classification scheme (such as place, time and form) which are usually provided for by generally applicable **auxiliary schedules** or tables.

compound subject a subject in which two or more constituent simple concepts are combined, e.g. 'economic history' or 'brain surgery'.

concept analysis the process of identifying the constituent parts in the subject of a document as a preliminary to assigning a classmark or subject heading.

consensus the generally held view about the content of, and relationships between, classes. Consensus is important in determining the order and arrangement of classifications. See also **educational consensus**.

content analysis the process of determining the subject of a document. See also **document description**.

controlled indexing language   a system used for classifying or indexing documents which uses a more limited set of terms than are found in **natural language**. A controlled indexing language consists of a **vocabulary** (the terms used for indexing) and **syntax** (the rules for combination of terms). **Classifications, thesauri,** and **subject heading lists** are all examples of controlled indexing languages.

co-ordinate classes: classes of equal status in a hierarchy, so that neither is subordinate or superordinate to the other. See **subordination, superordination.**

cross-classification   a situation that arises where, because of lack of logical structure in the classification, or failure to provide clear rules for combination, it is not obvious where to place a document with compound subject content. As a result documents with the same subject content may be cross-classified, or located in different places in the classification. Where this is likely to occur, cataloguers must decide on their preferred location, and/or establish their own local rules for citation order.

cross-disciplinary   refers to a field of study where the primary focus is on a phenomenon or entity, rather than a traditional **discipline,** and where the phenomenon or entity is studied from the point of view of a variety of disciplines. Typical examples are women's studies, mediaeval studies and regional studies.

DDC   see **Dewey Decimal Classification.**

decimal notation   a numerical notation which files as if the classmarks are decimal subdivisions, i.e. following a real or imagined decimal point, as in the sequence 21, 212, 223, 26, 35, 354, 37. See also **ordinal notation.**

decreasing concreteness   the principle which Ranganathan used to determine the **citation order** of his **fundamental categories.**

Dewey Decimal Classification   the first of the well-known library classification schemes, originally published in the USA in 1876. In the UK it is used in almost all public libraries, and is increasingly favoured in academic libraries because of its familiarity to users and its excellent support services. Originally an enumerative classification, DDC has incorporated many analytico-synthetic features over the years.

dictionary catalogue   a catalogue in which authors, titles and subjects are all inter-filed in a single sequence.

discipline   a field of study or subject domain. See also **fundamental disciplines.**

distributed relatives   when a citation order is applied to compound sub-jects, the aspects of the subject that are not cited first and thus become scattered throughout the sequence. For example, if a collection of lit-erature is organized first by language, literary forms such as poetry or drama will be separated from each other within the different language groups. These are known as distributed relatives.

document description   the process of deciding on the subject content of a document and creating a concise statement of that subject.

domain   a field or area of study.

educational consensus   a principle used in constructing classification schemes which aims to reflect the way in which subjects are grouped for study and teaching; its application should produce arrangements that are logical and intuitive for end-users.

entity classification   a classification of objects or phenomena based on their attributes. In an entity classification each entity has a unique place in the classification. Entity classifications are common in the natural sciences. See also **aspect classification**.

enumeration   the listing of classes in a classification scheme.

enumerative classification   a classification scheme in which all the pos-sible classes are listed in the schedule, and where classifiers are not able to create classmarks by synthesis. Enumerative classifications contain many pre-coordinated compound classes.

exhaustivity   the property of indexing whereby all the different facets of a compound subject are identified in the index description.

Expansive Classification   a scheme created by Charles Ammi Cutter in 1891. It was contemporaneous with DDC and was seriously considered for use in the Library of Congress; early LCC schedules were modelled on it.

expressive notation   a system of **notation** in which the symbols reflect the structure of the classification. Commonly, notational codes may increase in length with the position of the class in the **hierarchy** of the classification, as in UDC, where 3 = Social science, 34 = Law, 343 = Criminal law. Additionally, symbols may be used as **facet indicators** to show the composition of the classmark, as in DDC's use of 09 to intro-duce period or place.

facet   a group of terms within a subject field produced by one broad prin-ciple of division; e.g., in medicine, the facets include 'parts of the body', 'types of disease' and 'methods of treatment'.

facet analysis   the assigning of terms in a subject to their appropriate facets, either when building a classification scheme or when determining the content of a single document in practical classification.

facet indicator   a notational symbol used to indicate a particular element of a compound subject: e.g. in DDC, 09 is used to introduce place, and in UDC = indicates the language of the document.

faceted classification   a classification scheme in which only simple classes are listed, and where the classifier must create classmarks for compound subjects.

filing order   the order in which classified documents are arranged on the shelves or in a classified list. Filing order corresponds to **schedule order**, or the order of classes in the classification scheme. See also **citation order**.

fixed location   a system of organizing books in libraries in which the shelves or bookcases are numbered (or lettered) and the books coded to correspond with these. Fixed location systems normally have broad subject groupings. The disadvantage is that if the collection grows the shelves have to be renumbered and major upheaval occurs. Fixed location is only encountered nowadays as an inheritance of old established collections. See also **relative location**.

flexibility   the provision of alternative methods of dealing with subjects; these may include alternative locations for a subject, or the potential to vary citation order according to local needs.

form of a document   the physical nature of the item (**outer form**), or the way in which the information is organized (**inner form**); although it is quite separate from the subject of the document, most classifications allow for some forms to be represented in the classmark or description.

fringe disciplines: for a particular discipline, additional disciplines which impinge on the discipline or are necessary to its understanding. For example, mathematics is a fringe discipline of physics. In the overall structure of a classification the collocation of a discipline with its fringe disciplines is desirable.

fundamental categories   the categories identified by S. R. Ranganathan in his theory of facet analysis; they are personality, matter, energy, space and time.

fundamental disciplines   very broad approaches to phenomena which employ different methods of dealing with them; for example, science, history and philosophy use different criteria for the examination and evaluation of knowledge. Fundamental disciplines may be subdivided into the more traditional academic disciplines such as physics or chemistry.

general before special   the idea that a sequence of classes, or of classified items, should begin with the most general and proceed to the most specific. This order seems to be intuitive to most users browsing a collection or file.

general classification   a classification scheme that deals with all subjects, intended to be used for a general collection. DDC, UDC and LCC are examples of general classifications.

generalia   a term for a class of documents that deal with knowledge generally, or are very wide-ranging in their subject content. Generalia classes usually have provision for 'form' classes, such as encyclopedias, dictionaries and bibliographies, and often include subjects such as library science, publishing and computer science.

generic relationship   sometimes called genus–species relationship, the relationship between an entity and its types or kinds, e.g. between 'trees' and 'oaks', or between 'chairs' and 'armchairs'.

gradation in speciality   a principle for ordering in which classes filing later in the sequence are more complex and sophisticated in nature than earlier ones, e.g. an order of living things that places micro-organisms at the beginning and man at the end of a sequence.

hierarchical   having the structure of a **hierarchy**.

hierarchy   a set of classes showing the subordinate and superordinate relationships between them. Strictly, a hierarchy should only display **semantic** or **generic relationships**, but many classifications include other relationships in the hierarchical display. See **subordination**, **superordination**.

hospitality   the capacity of a scheme to accommodate new subjects, or combinations of subjects.

increasing concreteness   one of Ranganathan's principles of classification, the principle of increasing concreteness requires that a sequence of classes begin with the more abstract concepts and move towards more concrete concepts. For example, the theory of a subject should precede its application.

index (1)   an ordered list used as a means of locating information in a collection; often used interchangeably with catalogue, e.g. subject index, classified index.

index (2): that part of a classification scheme in which the classes are arranged alphabetically to provide a quick means of access to the systematic arrangement.

indexing the process of deciding upon the content of a document and assigning an index description to it.

indexing language a set of terms or classes, with rules for ordering and combination, used in creating formal subject descriptions of document content, such as subject headings, classmarks or index entries.

inner form the way in which the information in a document is presented or organized, e.g. report, statistical table, periodical.

interdisciplinary refers to the interaction of two disciplines. The most common situation is where the methods of one discipline are applied to the subject matter of another, as in the case of biomathematics or computational linguistics. The phenomenon is referred to as interdisciplinarity.

inverted schedule a classification schedule in which the schedule order (or **filing order**) of facets is the reverse of the **citation order**. Inversion maintains the order of general-before-special.

known item retrieval the process of locating individual documents whose **bibliographic details** are already known.

LCC see **Library of Congress Classification**.

LCSH see **Library of Congress Subject Headings**.

Library of Congress Classification created by the Library of Congress for its own collections in the early twentieth century, LCC is the classic example of an **enumerative classification**. Although it was never intended for wider use, it is increasingly favoured as a scheme for academic libraries.

Library of Congress Subject Headings designed to be used in conjunction with LCC, LCSH provides more precise subject description than the fairly broadly based classification, and is therefore the principal means of subject retrieval in LCC libraries. LCSH is now very widely used in academic libraries even where a classification other than LCC is employed.

linear order the order of items on a shelf or in a list. Many of the features of traditional library classifications are concerned with solving the problem of representing compound (or multi-dimensional) subjects in a linear (or one-dimensional) order.

literal mnemonics see **mnemonics**.

literary warrant   the principle which requires that the classes in a classification are based on the subjects of published literature, rather than being derived from a philosophical view of knowledge. This is taken to its logical conclusion in the LCC where, traditionally, classes are created only to accommodate items in the Library of Congress collection.

main class   one of the primary divisions of a classification scheme; main classes usually correspond to traditional academic disciplines (such as literature, chemistry or philosophy) or other important areas of interest or activity (naval science, bibliography).

main class order   the sequence of **main class**es in a classification. It is impossible to allow for every useful collocation of main classes, and most schemes can be criticized for separating related subjects.

main tables   an expression used (mainly in connection with UDC) to denote the classification schedules proper, and to distinguish them from the **auxiliary schedules** or **tables**.

mnemonics   features of notation that act as an aid to memory. Mnemonics are of two main types: **literal mnemonics**, where a notation using letters corresponds with terms in the classification (e.g. in Bliss's classification, C is the main class for chemistry, and CE is the class for electrochemistry), and systematic mnemonics, where the notation used for commonly occurring concepts is consistent. The latter is very common in schemes which build classmarks synthetically.

multi-disciplinary   refers to a situation where a subject is regarded from more than one disciplinary point of view. Some traditional academic fields are multi-disciplinary, for example classics, which combines language, literature and history, or theology, where philosophy, history and textual criticism form part of the traditional curriculum. The term is sometimes used interchangeably with **cross-disciplinary**, but they are not synonymous.

mutually exclusive classes: classes in the same array; the correct application of the principle of division should mean that a document cannot be assigned to more than one class in an array.

narrower term (NT)   a term which is more specific in meaning than the term to which it is related; e.g. 'spaghetti' is a narrower term related to 'pasta'.

natural language   the language used in everyday speech and communication, as contrasted with the artificial **controlled language** of indexing. The term natural languages is also used to represent the languages used by different nations and cultures: e.g., French, Russian and Arabic are all natural languages.

notation symbols used to represent classes in a classification scheme; the notation is used to maintain the order of classes in the scheme, and, when applied to documents, to maintain the order of items on the shelf or in a list. The notation may (but need not) express the structural relations between classes within the scheme. See also **expressive notation**.

open access a system where items in the collection are housed in the 'public' areas, and users may browse the collection and help themselves to materials.

ordinal notation a numerical notation in which classmarks file in order of their numerical value, as in the sequence 21, 26, 35, 37, 212, 223, 354. See also **decimal notation**. The term ordinal notation is also used to describe a notation which simply serves to maintain the order of classes, and is not expressive of **hierarchy**.

outer form the 'physical' nature of a document, e.g. film, three-dimensional object, PDF file.

parallel subdivision a device in number building where extra detail is provided in one class by adding to a base number the notation from another class. For example a class for 'Fruit growing' in horticulture might take the notation for specific fruit from classmarks in the Botany class.

partonomic relationship a relationship between a whole and its parts e.g. the relationship between 'house' and 'roof', or between 'foot' and 'toe'.

phase relations relations between two subjects that are of a dynamic nature, as contrasted with the normal semantic or syntactic relations within a classification scheme, which are essentially static. Phase relations involve a process of some sort between the two elements, such as comparison (phase) or influence (phase), or the use of one subject to the ends of the other, as in exposition phase (where one subject is used to explain another) or bias phase (where the content of one subject is presented for the practitioners of another). See also **semantic relationships, syntactic relationships**.

phenomenon classification a classification of entities and activities themselves rather than subjects and fields of study. See also **aspect classification, entity classification**.

post-coordinate strictly, referring to a system in which the index terms (for a compound subject) are brought together only at the point of search. The index description is not used to organize the items in the collection (as in the case of descriptors or keywords in a database or an online catalogue). Compare **pre-coordination**.

pre-coordination strictly, a system in which index terms (for a compound subject) are combined by the classifier at the time of indexing because they are used to organize the material in the collection (as in the case of a classification used for shelf order, or subject headings in a file). Pre-coordination is also used to describe a situation when the terms used to describe **compound subjects** are already combined in a published classification schedule or headings list. Compare **post-coordinate**.

predictability the potential for knowing where a compound subject will be located. Predictability is related to the soundness of the classification's structure, and is essential to efficient retrieval.

preference order the order of priority used in DDC where the compound subject of a document contains two aspects that cannot both be expressed notationally; the preference order indicates which aspect is to be chosen.

principle of division the defining factor in an array or group of terms, e.g. in the array 'babies, children, adolescents, adults', '(persons by age), is the principle of divison. Also known as **characteristic of division**.

principle of inversion See **inverted schedule**.

qualifier a term used to distinguish words with more than one meaning, or two identically spelled words represent different concepts: e.g. bed (furniture) and bed (horticulture); lead (metal) and lead (principal role).

reader interest classification broad systems of classification adopted by some UK public libraries in the 1980s; they usually consisted of about 25 'main classes' based on social and recreational themes (such as hobbies, travel, sport) without any further subdivision, and used colour coding of books rather than notation. This type of classification is sometimes called **categorization**.

recall when searching, recall refers to the completeness of the search results. It is related to **relevance** in inverse proportion: i.e., the more results are obtained the likelier it is that many will be irrelevant. **Broad classification** or indexing improves the degree of recall but does not help **relevance**.

related term (RT): a relationship in an indexing system: (1) between two terms that are co-ordinate or at an equivalent level in a hierarchy; (2) that is not of a hierarchical nature, e.g. between terms from different facets.

relative location a system of organizing books in which the books themselves are labelled with the classmarks. As the collection expands the relative order of books remains unchanged and they can be moved along the shelves without any disruption. Relative location is the norm in libraries today. See also **fixed location**.

relevance when searching, relevance is the extent to which the results match the search criteria. Relevance is aided by accurate, specific and exhaustive indexing. See also **recall**.

retrieval the process of locating indexed items by means of a search; the effectiveness of retrieval is closely related to the quality of the initial indexing.

rule of ten a classification practice which requires that no more than ten books in a collection should have the same classmark. If this occurs some further means of subdivision must be applied. Figures other than ten may be the criterion, the general intention being to achieve **close classification** and consequent easy location of items.

schedule that part of a classification scheme which lists the classes in systematic order. The schedule consists of the class headings, or **captions**, the **notation**, and explanations and instructions for use; it is complemented by the **index**, which lists the terms alphabetically.

schedule order the order of classes in a classification schedule, corresponding to the **filing order** of classified documents.

scope note a note explaining or amplifying the **caption** or heading for a class.

semantic related to semantics, that is the study of meaning. Often used in classification terminology as quasi-synonymous with 'subject' (e.g. **semantic relationships, semantic content**).

semantic content the significant content of a document, its subject content..

semantic relationships relationships which are regarded as permanent within the structure of a **discipline** or subject field; they are usually either thing–kind (genus–species) or whole–part relationships. See also **syntactic relationships**.

shelf-mark see **call-mark**.

sought terms words that a user is likely to select when searching.

special auxiliary table   an **auxiliary table** which is applicable to only certain specified parts of a classification scheme. See also **systematic auxiliary table**.

special classification   a classification designed for use in a specialized subject collection; it normally has a more extensive vocabulary and detailed structure than a general scheme. A special classification often includes subjects related to its principal subject, and arranges classes in a way that may be more appropriate to study of the subject than does a general scheme. Widely used special classifications include the National Library of Medicine classification and Moys classification for law..

specificity   the precision with which a document is classified with respect to the level of hierarchy used. For example, a book about rabbits which is classed as 'animals' lacks specificity. See also **close classification**.

standard citation order   the default order of combination of facets in a faceted classification; established by the UK Classification Research Group in the middle part of the 20th century.

sub-facet   see **array**.

subject   a field of interest or activity; also, the content of an individual document.

subject access   the means by which users are enabled to find material on the basis of its intellectual content.

subject cataloguing   that part of cataloguing which deals with the content of the document.

Subject Classification   a classification scheme developed by James Duff Brown in the early 20th-century; quite widely used in British public libraries before World War 2, it has been replaced by DDC.

subject heading   a description of a document's content, using words rather than a **notation**. Headings consist of the principal concepts arranged in a predetermined order. See also **pre-coordination**.

subject heading list   a **controlled indexing language** used to provide alphabetical access to the subject of documents. It consists of 'ready-made' and mainly pre-coordinated headings; these are selected as needed by the cataloguer and attached to the catalogue record of each item, and together they form a searchable alphabetical subject index to the collection.

subject retrieval   the process of locating items dealing with a particular topic. Also known as **subject searching**.

subject string   an ordered list of concepts representing the subject of a document used as the basis for classification or subject indexing.

subordination   in a **hierarchy** the relationship of a class to the class which contains it, e.g. the class 'hounds' is subordinate to 'dogs'; the relation of a **narrower term** to a **broader term**.

superordination   in a hierarchy the relationship of a class to another class which it wholly contains, e.g. the class 'cats' is superordinate to the class 'Siamese cats'; the relation of a **broader term** to a **narrower term**.

synonym   a word whose meaning is the same, or substantially the same, as another word. A feature of **vocabulary control** in a **controlled indexing language** is the removal of synonyms as index terms.

syntactic relationships   the relationships between classes in a classification, or terms in an index description, that are not of the thing–kind or whole–part variety, i.e. the relationship between terms from different **facets**. For example, the relationship between 'blood' and 'circulation' where 'blood' is a *part* of the body and 'circulation' is a *process* is a syntactic relationship.

syntax   in a controlled indexing language, the instructions for practical application, particularly the rules for combination of terms or classes.

synthesis   the process of building up a classmark or heading from the constituent parts of a compound subject.

systematic auxiliary table   an **auxiliary table** which is applicable throughout a classification scheme. See also **special auxiliary table**.

systematic mnemonics   see **mnemonics**.

taxonomic relationship   a genus–species relationship, or the relationship between an entity and its kinds or types; also known as a 'thing–kind' relationship. Examples would include the relationship between 'hat' and 'beret', or between 'cake' and 'doughnut'..

taxonomy   conventionally, a classification where all the classes are related hierarchically, such as a classification for living organisms. Taxonomy is often used more loosely to mean any sort of a classificatory structure.

term   a keyword, descriptor or other word used in indexing, as opposed to a **class** which is conceptual in nature. Terms are often derived from the titles or text of the document to be indexed, but a controlled indexing language such as a thesaurus may be considered to consist of terms rather than classes.

thesaurus   a controlled indexing language commonly used to index documents where physical arrangement is not necessary. Thesauri consist of single terms or concepts, which are combined by the indexer to create the document description. The thesaurus relates each term to other terms in the vocabulary by indicating broader, narrower, and otherwise related terms, enabling the indexer to navigate the vocabulary.

top-down classification a classification which starts with the whole of knowledge and divides and sub-divides it into smaller and smaller classes.

tree a visual representation of a classification in which the successive stages of division are shown as the branches of a tree, rather in the manner of genealogical, or family, trees. Tree structures are commonly used to depict biological taxonomies and also feature in philosophical classifications, such as the tree of Porphyry.

UDC: see **Universal Decimal Classification**.

uniform heading principle the requirement that all the materials on a subject should be brought together in the same place in the subject catalogue. Each subject should be represented by only one heading (the uniform heading) and there should be no possibility of alternative headings.

unique definition, place of the place in a classification which primarily defines a subject. For example, the place of unique definition of the horse is in the zoology class; although the horse may appear again in equine sports, or within the military or police service, or as a means of transport, its most fundamental classification is as an animal. The place of unique definition is useful for placing cross-disciplinary studies.

universal classification another term for a **general classification** scheme; a scheme which deals with the whole of knowledge.

Universal Decimal Classification an adaptation of Dewey's scheme with many additional synthetic features and auxiliary tables, first published by the Brussels Bibliographic Institute in 1905. It is the commonest classification encountered in Eastern Europe, and is favoured elsewhere by many technical and special libraries because of its flexibility and huge technical vocabulary.

vocabulary the terms used in a classification or other indexing language; also, the terms used in classification or indexing of documents.

vocabulary control the process of limiting the number of terms available to the classifier or indexer for describing documents. See also **controlled indexing language, synonym**.

Bibliography and further reading

The following is not intended to be in any sense an exhaustive list of titles in the subject. It includes bibliographic details of the classification schemes covered in the text, and of the standard textbooks for those schemes. The addresses of official websites are also given. Some further reading at a basic or intermediate level is included. Classification hasn't been a fashionable subject in recent years and there are relatively few good modern books, but it is well represented in the journal literature, and a search of LIS databases should prove fruitful. The leading journals include *Knowledge Organization* (for theoretical aspects) and *Cataloging and Classification Quarterly* (generally more concerned with applications).

General and background reading
General textbooks on classification

Foskett, A. C. *The subject approach to information*, 5th edn, London, Library Association Publishing, 1996.

Marcella, Rita and Newton, Robert *A new manual of classification*, Aldershot, Gower, 1994.
Both the above are general, comprehensive textbooks mainly about classification, but touching on some other aspects of subject work.

Mills, J. *A modern outline of library classification*, London, Chapman & Hall, 1960.
Although it is now very out of date in terms of the general schemes, and obviously has no account of recent developments, this is nevertheless one of the most lucid statements of the theory underlying classification and its application.

Surveys of current trends and practice

Maltby, Arthur and Marcella, Rita (eds) *The future of classification*, Aldershot, Gower, 2000.
A collection of papers about classification theory and practice at the beginning of the 21st century; it includes material on the general clas-

sification schemes.

Williamson, Nancy and Beghtol, Clare (eds) *Knowledge organization and classification in international information retrieval*, Binghamton, NY, Haworth, 2003.
A rather more advanced collection, with the emphasis on technical applications of classification.

History and theory of classification
Important older works on classification theory

Chan, Lois Mai, Richmond, Phyllis A. and Svenonius, Elaine (eds) *Theory of subject analysis: a sourcebook*, Littleton, CO, Libraries Unlimited, 1985.
A collection of seminal papers and articles on systems of subject access from throughout the 20th century.

Bliss, Henry Evelyn *The organization of knowledge and the system of the sciences*, New York, Holt, 1929.

Bliss, Henry Evelyn *The organization of knowledge in libraries and the subject approach to books*, 2nd edn, New York, H. W. Wilson, 1939.

Ranganathan, S. R. *The elements of library classification*, 3rd edn, Bombay, Asia Publishing House, 1962.

Ranganathan, S. R. assisted by Gopinath, M. A. *Prolegomena to library classification*, 3rd edn, London, Asia Publishing House, 1967.

For material on the history of classification

Sayers, W. C. Berwick *Manual of classification*, 4th edn rev. by Arthur Maltby, London, Deutsch, 1967.
An older textbook, valuable for its chapters on the history of library classification, and for the treatment of general schemes no longer current. The material on the current general schemes is very out of date, but the historic aspects haven't been reproduced in more recent textbooks.

Alphabetical approach to subject access

Coates, E. J. *Subject catalogues: headings and structure*, London, Library Association Publishing, 1988.
Now rather old (this is a reissue of the original published in 1960) but a valuable statement of subject heading theory.

Lopes, Maria Inês and Beall, Julianne (eds) *Principles underlying subject headings*, Working Group on the Principles Underlying Subject Heading Languages; approved by the Standing Committee of the IFLA Section

on Classification and Indexing, München, Saur, 1999.
A survey of practice and principles in various national systems of subject headings.

Library of Congress Subject Headings

Library of Congress Subject Headings 27th edn, 5 vols, Washington, DC, The
Library of Congress, 2004.
Classweb: http://classweb.loc.gov
Chan, Lois Mai *Library of Congress Subject Headings: principles and application*, 3rd edn, Englewood, CO, Libraries Unlimited, 1995.
The standard work on LCSH.

Library of Congress Classification

Library of Congress Classification (various dates), 43 vols, Washington, DC,
The Library of Congress.
Classweb: http://classweb.loc.gov
Chan, Lois Mai *A guide to the Library of Congress Classification*, 5th edn,
Englewood, CO, Libraries Unlimited, 1999.
The standard work on the Library of Congress Classification.

Dewey Decimal Classification

Mitchell, Joan S. et al. (eds) *Dewey Decimal Classification and Relative
Index, Devised by Melvil Dewey*, 22nd edn, Dublin, OH, OCLC, 2003.
DDC website: www.oclc.org/dewey/
Chan, Lois Mai et al. *Dewey Decimal Classification: a practical guide*, 2nd
rev. edn, Albany, NY, Forest Press, 1996.
A very useful guide to DDC 21, with a number of exercises for practical work.
Chan, Lois Mai and Mitchell, Joan S. *Dewey Decimal Classification: principles and application*, 3rd edn, Dublin, OH, OCLC, 2003.

Universal Decimal Classification

Universal Decimal Classification – International Medium Edition (1993) English text, 2nd edn, BS 1000M:1993, London, British Standards Institution.
Universal Decimal Classification: Pocket Edition PD 1000:1999, London,
British Standards Institution, 1999.
UDC website: www.udcc.org
McIlwaine, I. C. *The Universal Decimal Classification: a guide to its use*. The

Hague, UDC Consortium, 2000.
The official guide to the use of the UDC, and the standard work on the scheme; it is available in translation in several other languages.

Faceted classifications
Published faceted general schemes of classification
Mills, J. and Broughton, Vanda *Bliss Bibliographic Classification*, 2nd edn, London, Butterworth, then Bowker-Saur, 1997–.
The introductory volume of the scheme contains a full statement of modern faceted classification principles.
Bliss Classification Association website: www.sid.cam.ac.uk/bca/bcahome.htm
Ranganathan, S. R. *Colon Classification*, 7th edn, rev. M. A. Gopinath, Bangalore, Sarada Ranganathan Endowment for Library Science, 1987–.

Foundation works on faceted classification
Dating mainly from the 1960s and 1970s these titles reflect the work of the UK Classification Research Group. Very little has been published on faceted classification since that period.
Foskett, D. J. *Classification and indexing in the social sciences*, London, Butterworth, 1963.
Langridge, D. W. *Classification and indexing in the humanities*, London, Butterworth, 1976.
Vickery, B. C. *Classification and indexing in science and technology*, 2nd edn, London, Butterworth. 1959.
Vickery, B. C. *Faceted classification: a guide to the construction and use of special schemes*, London, Aslib, 1968.

Other schemes of general and special classification
Bliss, Henry Evelyn *A bibliographic classification*, 4 vols, New York, Wilson, 1952–3.
Brown, James Duff *Subject classification*, 3rd edn, rev. James D. Stewart, London, Grafton, 1939.
Cutter, Charles A. *Expansive classification*, 2nd edn, Northampton, MA., 1902.
Moys, Elizabeth M. *Classification and thesaurus for legal materials*, 3rd edn, rev. Elizabeth Moys, London, Bowker-Saur, 1992.
National Library of Medicine Classification 5th rev. edn, Bethesda, MD, National Library of Medicine, 1999.

Index